RED HILLS
AND COTTON

SOUTHERN CLASSICS SERIES
John G. Sproat, General Editor

King Cotton and His Retainers:
Financing and Marketing the Cotton
Crop of the South, 1800–1925
By Harold D. Woodman

The South as a Conscious Minority, 1789–1861:
A Study in Political Thought
By Jesse T. Carpenter

Red Hills and Cotton:
An Upcountry Memory
By Ben Robertson

John C. Calhoun:
American Portrait
By Margaret L. Coit

The Southern Country Editor
By Thomas D. Clark

Red Hills and Cotton

an upcountry memory

by Ben Robertson
with a new introduction by Lacy K. Ford, Jr.

University of South Carolina Press

CONTENTS

GENERAL EDITOR'S PREFACE

The Southern Classics Series returns to general circulation books of importance dealing with the history and culture of the American South. Under the sponsorship of the Institute for Southern Studies and the South Caroliniana Society of the University of South Carolina, the series is advised by a board of distinguished scholars, whose members suggest titles and editors of individual volumes to the general editor and help to establish priorities in publication.

Chronological age alone does not determine a title's designation as a Southern Classic. The criteria include, as well, significance in contributing to a broad understanding of the region, timeliness in relation to events and moments of peculiar interest to the American South, usefulness in the classroom, and suitability for inclusion in personal and institutional collections on the region.

*　　　　*　　　　*

Long viewed as a classic in the literature of nostalgia, *Red Hills and Cotton* is an evocative tribute to the South of Ben Robertson's youth. But it is more than a mere memoir of a faded era. As Lacy Ford observes in

General Editor's Preface

his introduction to the volume, Robertson's elegiac tone conveys to discerning readers a penetrating critique as well as an appreciation of the region. In a welcome examination of the author's life and career, Ford also presents Robertson as a roving journalist and brilliant war correspondent, the farthest thing from a provincial dreamer, yet also as a southerner whose worldly awareness of paradox never diminished his love for his native South. For old friends of *Red Hills and Cotton*, as well as for a later generation of readers, the book now takes on new and even more poignant meaning.

> John G. Sproat
> General Editor, Southern Classics Series

INTRODUCTION TO THE
SOUTHERN CLASSICS
EDITION

"What we need in the South is a new leader," Ben Robertson told an audience at the College of Charleston in late June 1939, "what we need is a man with the heart and mind of Jefferson and the tactics of Huey Long."[1] Robertson's warm endorsement of the Sage of Monticello surely surprised few, if any, of his listeners. The twentieth-century South, and especially its intellectuals and literati, commonly embraced the region's presumed Jeffersonian heritage enthusiastically. Many Southerners viewed the Age of Jefferson as the republic's golden age of decentralized power and rural egalitarianism. By the 1930s, almost any Southerner could place Jefferson in his or her pantheon of personal heroes with little fear of evoking a hostile reaction from a Southern audience. But Robertson's favorable mention of Huey Long doubtless stunned most of his Charleston audience. Before falling to an assassin's bullet in September 1935, the controversial Louisiana Kingfish had won a significant national following with his flamboyant style, bare-knuckled tac-

Lacy K. Ford, Jr.

tics, and homespun "share-the-wealth" radicalism. But Long's rhetorical assaults on privilege and wealth and his credible populist record as governor of Louisiana had also made him an anathema to bankers and businessmen long before his talk of mounting a radical challenge to President Franklin Roosevelt alienated him from the many rank-and-file Democrats who saw FDR as the nation's political savior. The conservative Charleston patricians who comprised most of Robertson's audience in 1939 had viewed Long with a combination of alarm and disdain when the Kingfish was alive and had little use for his memory. In fact, by 1939, many of these same Charlestonians had even grown disenchanted with Roosevelt and certainly had no sympathy for anyone who postured consistently to FDR's left, as Huey Long had done.

If Ben Robertson had politely shocked his conservative audience, he had doubtless intended to. It was one of the young journalist's standard tactics. Two years earlier, Robertson had left his friends among Upcountry newspaper publishers and textile executives incredulous with his enthusiastic praise of United Mine Workers' president John L. Lewis, the chief architect of both the Congress of Industrial Organizations (CIO) and its primary tactical innovation, the sit-down strike. Ben Robertson liked to keep his listeners off-balance, to make them feel at least a touch uneasy. Yet Robertson had not mentioned Long in his speech solely for shock value, nor had he chosen the onetime Louisiana senator randomly. Instead, Robertson had selected the components of his model new-style Southern political leader with considerable care, seeking to balance his respect for the region's best traditions (Jefferson) with what he saw

Introduction

as the region's desperate need for new energy and determination, and for a revived populist vision (Long).[2]

Robertson's improbable blend of cavalier egalitarian and swashbuckling populist revealed his own profound ambivalence about the condition of the South in the late 1930s and something about his personal vision of the region's future. As loyal a son as South Carolina and the South ever produced, Ben Robertson found much to admire in his native region. He cherished what he judged its best traditions: a strong sense of personal independence and responsibility, the rejection of crass materialism, a deep piety that was both revealed and mocked by Bible-belt religiosity, and, most of all, a love of freedom and corresponding willingness to make the sacrifices required to sustain freedom. Yet Robertson also knew that the South of the 1930s needed changing. He repeatedly lamented what he perceived as the region's many shortcomings: its poverty, its racial hierarchy, its political impotence, its collective lack of intellectual curiosity, and, above all, its tendency to blame all of its twentieth-century problems on the defeat of the Confederacy and "Northern occupation" during Reconstruction.[3] This tendency irritated Robertson to the point of distraction. More than twenty years before Robert Penn Warren, in *The Legacy of the Civil War*, described the South's penchant for using Confederate defeat as a "Great Alibi" for all the region's postbellum failures, Ben Robertson declaimed repeatedly against the tendency of Southerners to use defeat, or their "beaten idea" as he called it, as an excuse for failure and inaction. To Robertson, the Lost Cause seemed not so much a comforting myth as an ideology of paralysis and irresponsibility. If nothing else, he found in Huey Long a

Lacy K. Ford, Jr.

man of action, a "doer," a man who had broken free of the region's paralysis. In his Charleston speech, Robertson urged his audience to go out and plant a tree every time they thought of Gettysburg. At least then, he maintained, some small good would come out of the South's obsession with losing the Civil War. The region's landscape, if not its mindset, would be changed for the better.

It was this Ben Robertson, a Southerner good and true but not an uncritical booster of his native region, who wrote *Red Hills and Cotton: An Upcountry Memory* in the fall and winter of 1941. Robertson's prose in the book exudes a grandfatherly affection for the South Carolina Piedmont that was his boyhood home. But he was only thirty-eight when he wrote *Red Hills and Cotton,* and although the book was, in some sense, the labor of a lifetime, he spent less than six weeks in the fall of 1941 gathering material for it and completed the actual writing in two-and-one-half weeks. Using only lower case letters, Robertson hammered out the manuscript on a manual typewriter while staying at his father's house in Clemson. A friend then retyped his drafts and returned them to him for quick proofreading.[4] Robertson's editor, Bernard Smith of Alfred A. Knopf and Company, finished reading the entire manuscript by late January 1942, and immediately congratulated Robertson on "a wonderful job." The editor's only complaint—that the "last few pages . . . sort of trail off"—was not unexpected.[5] After the Japanese attacked Pearl Harbor on December 7, 1941, Ben Robertson did not have time to tarry over the concluding section of *Red Hills and Cotton.* His considerable talents as a journalist, always in

Introduction

demand, were valued at a premium once the United States became an active participant in World War II.

At the time he sat down to write *Red Hills and Cotton* in 1941, Ben Robertson was already an internationally known and respected journalist. He had served as White House correspondent for the Associated Press during Franklin Roosevelt's first term, covered the war in Europe for the innovative national daily *PM* during 1940–41, and published a moving account of the Battle of Britain, *I Saw England,* in 1941. In the spring of 1942, Robertson rejoined *PM* to cover the war on the Eastern front. He returned to the United States in December 1942 and saw the published version of *Red Hills and Cotton* for the first in the Atlanta home of his friend and fellow Clemson alumnus Wright Bryan of the *Atlanta Journal.* He inscribed Bryan's copy: "Nine days out of India and on Peachtree Street." In January 1943, he accepted an offer from the *New York Herald-Tribune* to become chief of that paper's important London Bureau. He was on his way to London via the Iberian peninsula when he was killed on February 22, 1943, when the plane in which he was flying crashed near Lisbon during a fierce storm. Robertson was four months shy of his fortieth birthday.

Born June 22, 1903, at Clemson, South Carolina, Benjamin Franklin Robertson, Jr., was the son of Benjamin Franklin and Mary Bowen Robertson. Through the Robertson and Bowen lines young Ben enjoyed kinship ties to Claytons, O'Dells, Craigs, Allgoods, and other large families that figured prominently among the hundreds of sprawling cousinages which still constituted the bulk of the South Carolina Upcountry's rural white population in the early decades of the twentieth century. Ben's great-grandmother, Hattie Boone McKinney, was a great-niece of pioneer adventurer Daniel Boone, giving Ben an ancestral claim on the American frontier spirit which served as a source of personal pride throughout his lifetime. Ben's father, a member of Clemson College's first graduating class in 1896, worked for most of his adult life as a chemist on the Agricultural Extension Service staff at Clemson. The elder Robertson won national scientific recognition for his experimental work leading to the development of new fertilizers, and from 1912 until his retirement in 1942, Robertson, Sr., also served as the state toxicologist, a job whose duties included providing expert testimony at several well-publicized murder trials. A devout Baptist and an ardent Democrat, the elder Ben Robertson was, by the standards of his era, an unusually well educated man and a respected professional who tried to teach his son and namesake the virtues of education, knowledge, and curiosity, as well as the rewards and obligations of close family and kinship ties and deep religious faith. The son later honored the father in the dedication to *Red Hills and Cotton* as "the salt of the Southern earth."

Mary Bowen Robertson was a graduate of Winthrop, the women's college and teacher preparatory school founded by Ben Tillman and his followers in the 1890s as the female counterpart to Clemson. Many Upcountry wags noted the Robertson-Bowen marriage as among the first of many such Clemson-Winthrop unions. Like the Robertsons, the Bowen family had deep Upcountry roots. Mary's father, William Thomas Bowen, was a Confederate veteran and a locally prominent politician. An active member of the Farmers' Alliance,

Introduction

William T. Bowen served two terms as state senator from Pickens county and represented that county in the South Carolina Constitutional Convention of 1895. A strong supporter of Ben Tillman, Bowen generally, but not uniformly, voted with the Tillmanite majority on issues before the convention, but as a good Baptist, he displayed considerably more interest than Tillman in securing a constitutional prohibition on divorce (which was already illegal) in South Carolina. After Mary Bowen Robertson died in 1910, when young Ben was only seven, her parents played an extremely important role in his upbringing. In 1913 Ben Robertson, Sr., remarried (Hattie Boggs of Liberty, S.C., the daughter of a nearby cotton farmer), but young Ben continued to visit his Bowen grandparents often throughout his childhood and adolescence. Later he remembered these visits in *Red Hills and Cotton* as formative influences on his character and described the Bowen household as a place where "there was certainty about everything, about heaven and hell, about the South, about us and the purpose of our civilization." As an adult, Robertson concluded that his upbringing had taught him "more about character than about culture." Culture, Robertson's family insisted, "could be acquired" but "character had to be formed." The aim of his parents and allied relatives, Robertson recalled, "was to set me in the mold—to make me a Carolinian, a Democrat and a Baptist. Once they had accomplished that—well, hell and high water could try as they liked."

Always a good student, Ben Robertson won an essay contest sponsored by the Daughters of the American Revolution before graduating from Clemson-Calhoun High School in 1919. After high school, Ben followed in

Lacy K. Ford, Jr.

his father's footsteps to Clemson College where he majored in botany (horticulture) while taking as many English and literature classes as his major curriculum would permit. Having grown up on the Clemson campus, he was accustomed to using the college library even before he enrolled as a student, and while he was matriculated he became an even more frequent library user. Though its holdings were modest by national standards, Robertson told Wright Bryan that "anyone who could learn a small part of the knowledge" housed in the Clemson library "could set the world on fire."[6] As an undergraduate, Robertson wrote for the student newspaper, *The Tiger*, edited the college yearbook, *Taps*, during his senior year, and even tried his hand at writing a fight song for the popular Clemson football program. He took his bachelor of science degree in 1923 as a classmate and "devoted friend" of future governor and United States senator J. Strom Thurmond.[7]

As Thurmond left Clemson to begin his first career as a teacher and coach in his native Edgefield county, the quietly ambitious Robertson decided to begin formal study of journalism at the University of Missouri, where he worked closely with the school's respected Dean of Journalism, Walter Williams. In 1925, Robertson interrupted his studies with a year at the *Charleston News and Courier,* where he worked out of the city room and covered local sports. Robertson had no intention of spending his career as a sports writer, but he used his brief stint with the *News and Courier* to develop friendships that would prove valuable in the future. The general editor during Robertson's tenure was Herbert Ravenel Sass, who later became an author of local and regional repute; and Tom Lesesne, the city editor, who

Introduction

supervised Robertson, later exerted considerable influence in South Carolina through his *News and Courier* editorials. It was also probably during this year that Robertson first made the acquaintance of a rising prodigy of Charleston politics, Burnet R. Maybank. The friendship between Robertson and Maybank blossomed over the years, giving Robertson access to the South Carolina governor's office once Maybank occupied it in 1939. After a year in Charleston, however, Robertson returned to the University of Missouri, where he completed his bachelor of journalism degree in 1926. Anxious to see the world, he then landed a job with the *Honolulu Star-Bulletin* through the good offices of Walter Williams. He worked for the *Star-Bulletin* for two years before resigning to embark on an odyssey through even more exotic areas of the Pacific. He traveled through Borneo to Java, where he worked for a few months in 1928 as a clerk in the American consulate in Surabaya. Ultimately Robertson arrived in Australia and joined the staff of the Adelaide *News,* where he worked a year before he was enticed back to the United States by an offer from the *New York Herald-Tribune.*

Most of Robertson's work in the Pacific took the form of conventional feature reporting. He searched out interesting, and unusual, people and places and fashioned their stories into straightforward accounts which entertained as well as informed his readers. If any particular characteristic distinguished Robertson's reporting in these early years, it was his knack for finding the interesting and exotic in seemingly humble or ordinary folk. While in the Pacific, he conscientiously gathered material which he would later shape into feature articles for such magazines as *Scribner's, Current History, Asia,*

Lacy K. Ford, Jr.

and *Travel*.[8] Representative of Robertson's writing from this era was his sketch of a small Australian outback town, which appeared in *Asia* in August 1929. Entitled "No Sunday-School Town," it described the isolated, river town of Broome, located between the Indian Ocean and the Great Sandy Desert, or, as Robertson put it, "far from the influence of the Women's Christian Temperance Union and the Anti-Saloon League . . . between the Australian devil and the Australian deep blue sea." Robertson focused sympathetically on the rough life of the down-under fishing and pearling town, turning clever phrases about painted Japanese women who "smile the professional smile known the world over" and the "come-in-hither signs" of saloons looming on "strategic street corners." Though conventional travelogue pieces in many ways, essays of this sort allowed Robertson to refine his natural talents for perceptive description and disarmingly straightforward narrative that were to prove hallmarks of his journalistic career.

His power of description and keen eye for human interest stories served Robertson well during his five years (1929–34) as a reporter for the *New York Herald-Tribune*. When he joined the paper, it was one of the nation's most respected dailies. Robertson spent much of his time pounding the streets of New York looking for stories. For relaxation, the amiable Robertson, despite his Baptist upbringing, joined other reporters at Bleeck's, the famous speakeasy near the *Herald-Tribune* offices, for hours of story swapping and political arguments. In 1934, at age thirty, he left New York and the *Herald-Tribune* for a job as a political reporter with the Associated Press's Washington bureau. Though he re-

mained with the wire service for nearly three years
(1934–36), he later admitted that he had "never
intended staying" with the AP for very long but that he
had been eager "to get to Washington" and the AP offer
had served that purpose.[9] Apparently Robertson enjoyed his Washington years immensely and he certainly
earned a reputation there as an up-and-coming young
journalist. He served alternately as White House and
Supreme Court correspondent for the Associated Press,
and in 1935 he went abroad to cover the London Naval
Conference.

Robertson's tenure with the Associated Press
spanned the last three years of Franklin Roosevelt's
eventful first administration, an era when the nation's
capital was brimming with a new sense of self-impor-
tance as people with ideas from around the country
flocked to Washington to become part of the New Deal.
It was a heady time indeed for the rosy-cheeked young
reporter from the South Carolina hillcountry who covered many of Roosevelt's press conferences. Almost immediately, Robertson recognized the pivotal role the
calm inspiration provided by the patrician sage of Hyde
Park played in the whole New Deal enterprise. The
"greatness of Roosevelt over Hoover," he wrote, "is
merely faith and courage."[10] In shaping Robertson's as-
sessment of the New Deal more generally, the economic
populism of his Upcountry background won out over the
cultural conservatism of the same origin as the young
journalist's broad empathy for common people translated
into strong sympathy for FDR's rhetorical assaults on
"economic royalists" and New Deal programs designed
to promote economic recovery and reform. Robertson's
neo-populist, pro-New Deal leanings were clearly re-

Lacy K. Ford, Jr.

vealed in the private journal he kept during his Washington years. "Business must be kept on the run, so it would seem, if there is to be any survival of the old American hope for better things in this country," he observed in March 1936; "Business has its own way of not starving." Adapting his personal creed in the face of modern industrial realities, Ben Robertson joined those convinced by the Great Depression that new, forceful Hamiltonian means would be needed to achieve long-cherished Jeffersonian ends. "The people are now employees," he reasoned, "and their only chance is the government and not in a government that acts merely as a police power but in one that has for its purpose the protection of the poor." No longer was that government best which governed least; instead an activist government was needed to aggressively protect the interests of the common people. In the age of corporate capitalism, Robertson noted, "the people are organized only as voters."[11]

Despite the excitement of working in FDR's Washington, Ben Robertson quit his job with the Associated Press in September 1936 and returned home to Clemson. He left Washington partially out of frustration. "I was at the White House," he told a friend in January 1937, "but I couldn't stand the . . . gutless way of fence riding between the few Democrat publishers and the thousands of Republican publishers." Robertson admitted that he had known "what it would be like when I went to work for a press service" but added that he had "wanted to get to Washington and it seemed the only way." But primarily Robertson quit the AP in order to fulfill his ambition of writing a novel. Back in Clemson, he followed what he called "a kind of vague, confused

Introduction

plan." Between September 1936 and January 1937, Robertson completed the writing of a novel based on ideas that he had been tossing around in his mind for a number of years, ideas about the innate restlessness of the American people and their struggle to settle the West. Though the idea was originally conceived while he was reading a tattered copy of Whitman's *Leaves of Grass* in "faraway Java," he maintained that his story was based on his "own background," on "a family that is old in an old state" and on a South Carolina "old in spirit" and thus "a center from which people have always gone in each generation to settle the West—lonely, searching people, never at rest. . . ." Robertson tried to write his story "with all the pure passion" he could muster, but he confessed that he did not "know whether I have succeeded."[12]

In fact, despite repeated efforts, Robertson failed to find an established publishing house willing to take his novel. Finally a couple of friends helped Robertson scrape up money "equal to the price of four mules or nineteen bales of 8-cent cotton" (about six hundred dollars) and published the novel themselves under the imprint of The Cottonfield Publishers at Clemson, South Carolina. While he waited for *Travelers' Rest*, as he had titled the novel, to appear, he resumed work on another book "about this restlessness which I think is a national characteristic." For years he had been gathering "reams of notes" on the subject, and in 1937 he planned to travel around the world on a freighter in order to complete his research on the "lonely restless searching" of Americans by studying "the simplest of the American professional wanderers—the sailors."[13] Robertson left on his voyage in May 1937, and did not return until December. Once

Lacy K. Ford, Jr.

back home in Clemson, he set out to finish the manuscript he had gathered material for during his travel. He completed a rough draft, titled "The Pilgrim," in 1938, but the manuscript remained unpublished when Robertson died in 1943.

By 1938, whether by happenstance or by choice, Ben Robertson had become what he would remain for the rest of his life, a striving author and a successful freelance journalist. He told friends in early 1938 that he excepted to return to New York to look for work as soon as he finished his second book manuscript. But a couple of unexpected developments kept him in the South Carolina Upcountry longer than he had intended. In late February 1938, Theo Vaughn, a close friend of Robertson's, told Ben privately that he intended to challenge the state's senior United States senator, Ellison D. "Cotton Ed" Smith, in the Democratic primary that August, and Robertson vowed to stay in South Carolina and help Vaughn with publicity through the election. Vaughn, a Southern progressive, had emerged from a cotton mill background to graduate from Clemson College and do graduate work in rural sociology at Columbia University. Robertson recognized that the young Vaughn faced an uphill struggle against the entrenched incumbent, but he hoped that Cotton Ed's age and his criticism of the broadly popular New Deal might give a capable young challenger an outside chance. Robertson considered Smith "a strange anomaly" even for South Carolina. As the young journalist explained to a friend in New York, Smith "never has been too highly regarded; . . . he has usually been elected because the majority had rather have him than have the man opposing him. There is a saying," Robertson continued, "that

Introduction

it is better to have Cotton Ed's luck than [to] have a license to steal." He conceded that Smith was "a brilliant story teller on the stump," perhaps ranking "above even Pitchfork Ben Tillman and [Cole] Blease as stumpers" and that he "always makes capital of 'nigger lovers.' . . . " Still, Robertson observed hopefully, "Times are changing."[14] By June 1938, however, when the full field of senatorial candidates came into plain view, Vaughn decided to bow out of the Senate contest in favor of a race for an Upcountry seat in the Congress. Disappointed, Robertson nevertheless decided to remain in South Carolina and cover the hotly contested Senate race between the conservative Smith, the avidly pro-New Deal governor Olin D. Johnston, and the influential and pro-New Deal state legislator Edgar A. Brown, as well as to report on the fortunes of his friend Burnet R. Maybank in the eight-man gubernatorial free-for-all, for the nearby *Anderson Independent*.

In early June, Robertson's attention was momentarily diverted from politics by the controversy aroused by the appearance of his novel, *Travelers' Rest*. The privately published work received, at best, tepid reception from respected reviewers. *Time* called it an "honest, spotty book" which traced "an old Southern family through their fights with nature, neighbors, and each other" and showed "old pioneers" involved in "wenching, gambling, stealing, murdering." Another review judged the book "a pretty sketchy performance" that read "like a county history interspersed with inspired and poetic passages."[15] And it was precisely the "county history" nature of the candid novel that provided fodder for controversy in South Carolina. In June, Mrs. John Logan Marshall, state regent of the Daughters

Lacy K. Ford, Jr.

of the American Revolution, ignited the controversy
when she criticized Robertson for portraying the ancestors of modern South Carolinians as a drinking,
swearing, whoring, and murdering lot and pronounced
the book unfit for decent South Carolinians to read.
Robertson had, in fact, based at least a portion of the
book on an old set of family papers, and a number of
Robertson family neighbors could hardly have failed to
identify characters in the novel who closely resembled
some of their forbears. By Robertson's account, one
Clemson woman claimed that she "blushed for three
days after reading the book," while another complained,
"I try to be broadminded but I agree with Mrs.
Marshall, . . . really he's slung mud over us all."[16] The
press, and especially the *Greenville Piedmont*, even succeeded in drawing Governor Olin D. Johnston's wife
into the fray. The press queried Mrs. Johnston about
whether or not *Travelers' Rest* was a book she would
recommend for South Carolina children. Mrs. Johnston
prudently declined comment until after she had read the
book. Sometime later, she went public with a list of
books she would urge South Carolina school children to
read, but explained that she had not thought it appropriate to include *Travelers' Rest*. Finally, in August 1938,
Ben's kinfolk, gathered at a family reunion in Pickens
county, had nearly the last word on the subject when
they came out four-square in defense of their kinsman,
the author. Though the controversy over *Travelers' Rest*
certainly ruffled some feathers around South Carolina,
Robertson apparently enjoyed the flap immensely. Indeed, he and a few of his friends in the newspaper business probably orchestrated the entire controversy in an
effort to publicize the novel and help them recoup the

Introduction

small sums they had invested in the publication. Robertson thanked George Chaplin, a friend and city editor of the *Greenville Piedmont,* for the way his paper had "handled things." All "has been wonderful," he wrote, and "we certainly have enjoyed it over here [at Clemson]."[17] After the controversy died out, some of Robertson's newspaper friends tried unsuccessfully to generate yet another war of words with the state chapter of the United Daughters of the Confederacy.

Robertson next turned his attention to the political stump meetings which traditionally dominated the month of August during even-numbered years in South Carolina. His articles on the 1938 stump meetings, published mainly in the *Anderson Independent,* rank among the most colorful and thorough accounts of these important political gatherings ever written. Though his published accounts were almost entirely free of bias, Robertson was clearly disappointed when Cotton Ed Smith won re-election decisively over Governor Olin Johnston (though he was no great admirer of Johnston), but his hopes for his state were buoyed when his friend Maybank overcame strong anti-Charleston sentiment and emerged from a crowded pack to win the gubernatorial race.[18]

Since winning the Democratic primary was tantamount to winning election in South Carolina in 1938, the political season was over after the run-off primary in early September. For the rest of the year and throughout 1939 Robertson free-lanced. He traveled widely and wrote a few travel pieces for the *Saturday Evening Post.*[19] His most frustrating effort, however, was undertaken closer to home. In the summer of 1939, he decided to write a feature on Atlanta writer Margaret

Mitchell, whose 1936 novel, *Gone With The Wind,* won lasting fame when the epic movie version appeared in 1939. After spending some time on the story, Robertson confessed, "I stepped in where the angels don't tread." Mitchell "won't talk," Robertson told an editor, "but her friends will talk their heads off." Mitchell objected to some of the information Robertson garnered from those who knew her and wrote Robertson "a letter as long as *Gone With The Wind*" calling him "no gentleman and a betrayer of great authors in the homes of their intimate friends." Even worse, from Robertson's point of view, were Mitchell's threats to sue him for slander.[20]

Early in 1940, Robertson accepted a job with *PM,* the newly founded New York daily published by former *Time* executive Ralph Ingersoll with strong financial backing from Marshall Field III and Marian Rosenwald Stern, heir to the Sears-Roebuck fortune. Avowedly liberal in its editorial policy, *PM* claimed it was "against people who push other people around" and that it preferred "democracy to any other principle of government." From its first issue, *PM* criticized isolationism and argued in favor of American intervention in World War II. In June 1940, Robertson went to Great Britain to cover the British war effort. Though he had earlier written critically of British hauteur, Robertson was now quickly impressed with the intense patriotism of the British and their bravery under the daily air assaults launched by the Germans between June and December of 1940. Robertson's moving dispatches to *PM* from London were unquestionably his best journalistic work. From his reports on strategy sessions at No. 10 Downing Street to his interviews with charwomen in London's underground bomb shelters, Robertson captured not

Introduction

only the drama of war but also its enormous emotional impact on ordinary British subjects. He also displayed considerable personal courage, remaining above ground during bombing raids on London and watching spectacular air battles between the *Luftwaffe* and the Royal Air Force from the white cliffs of Dover.[21]

It was while covering the Battle of Britain that Robertson forged friendships with other war correspondents of the first rank. His associates in London included Whitelaw Reid, Eric Sevareid, Helen Kirkpatrick, and Edward R. Murrow. Sevareid later remembered Robertson for his "sheer likability" and remarked on Robertson's gift for making people feel "comfortable" around him.[22] But it was Murrow who became Robertson's closest friend and companion. Murrow, who was fast making a name for himself as the best of the extraordinarily capable correspondents covering the war for CBS, anonymously substituted for Robertson as columnist for *PM* when the latter traveled to the United states on furlough, and Robertson, despite his slow Southern drawl, was heard as guest commentator on Murrow's "This is London" nightly radio broadcast.[23]

In January 1941, Robertson returned to the United States on furlough, and during January and February he drew on his notes and diaries to write *I Saw England*, a moving account of the war in general and the Battle of Britain in particular. When the book appeared that summer, it met with widespread critical approval. The *Times Literary Supplement* said that of the "number of books written about the Battle of Britain" none was "so vivid and sincere" as Robertson's. *I Saw England* was "a book British people should read."[24] The *New York Times* called it "a stimulating, and, in some ways, inspiring

Lacy K. Ford, Jr.

book, one not to be missed," while Robertson's old paper, the *Herald-Tribune,* lauded it as "an enthralling account" marked by "a passion for detail and a talent for anecdote."[25] Robertson's own hope for the book was that it would rally Americans behind the British cause and prepare them for the direct American intervention that he already believed both desirable and inevitable.

Robertson openly admitted that his experience covering the war had given him not only a new appreciation for freedom and the responsibility it entailed, but also a new and stronger sense of his own mortality and immortality. In *I Saw England,* Robertson explained that sitting on Shakespeare Cliff near Dover and watching air battles "changed me as an individual. I lost my sense of personal fear," he continued, "because I saw that what happened to me did not matter. We counted as individuals only as we took our place in the procession of history. It was not we who counted, it was what we stood for. And I knew now for what I was standing—I was for freedom. It was as simple as that. . . . We were where we were and we had what we had because a whole line of people had been willing to die."

What Robertson discovered at Dover was what he believed his American forbears had discovered in crucial battles at other times and places. "I understood Valley Forge and Gettysburg at Dover," the young Upcountryman wrote, "and I found it lifted a tremendous weight off your spirit to find yourself willing to give up your life if you have to—I discovered Saint Matthew's meaning about losing a life to find it. I don't see now why I ever again should be afraid."

Only ten days after he sent *I Saw England* to the publisher, Robertson returned to London to resume his

Introduction

duties with *PM*. He remained abroad from March until
August, when he returned to the States to write a series
of articles and make public appearances designed to encourage American entry into the war. By early fall, still
on furlough, he was home again at his father's house in
Clemson, seriously contemplating running for a seat in
Congress and working furiously on what most of his
friends thought was another book about the war.
Robertson had toyed with the notion of running for Congress in 1940. One of Robertson's South Carolina newspaper friends had told him then that he would "either
win by a big margin, or get hell beat out" of him. In
1940, the general consensus of observers in South Carolina's Third Congressional district was that Robertson's
"knowledge of publicity" and his "liberalism" would give
him the decided advantage over one of his likely oppo-
nents, the conservative John Taylor, in the Upcountry
district dominated numerically by small farmers and textile workers, but that Robertson might find the political
going tough against pro-labor incumbent, Butler Hare.[26]
Whatever his chances in 1940, Robertson had dropped
his political plans when *PM* offered to send him to London. By 1941, however, he was even more determined to
consider a political career and began putting out serious
feelers.[27] Among those Robertson asked for advice was
the powerhouse of South Carolina politics during the
1930s and 1940s, Senator James F. Byrnes, whom Roosevelt had named to the United States Supreme Court in
the spring of 1941. "The reporting side of newspaper
work keeps a man sitting on the fence, seeing both
sides," Robertson told Byrnes, "and I have now reached
the point where I want to get down off the fence and
pitch in and do what I actually can to get things done."

Lacy K. Ford, Jr.

Byrnes's response to Robertson was polite but hardly encouraging, and Robertson again decided to postpone his turn at politics for a while longer.[28]

Instead, he used his fall at Clemson to work on his next book. From September through December of 1941, Robertson quietly, almost furtively, gathered material for the volume. When Wright Bryan visited him in Clemson on December 5, he found the journalist "sitting in a back room with his typewriter and masses of notes on a table, with maps, pictures, and diagrams tacked to all the walls." Robertson was working feverishly on a book, but, following an old author's superstition, chose not to tell Bryan what the book was about. He did tell Bryan, two days before Pearl Harbor, "I must work fast. We'll be in this war soon and my paper will want me to go abroad again."[29] The book Robertson was writing at such a furious pace was not another war book but the manuscript of *Red Hills and Cotton*, which he shipped off to the publisher in January 1942. Robertson revised the concluding passages a little in early February, but by spring he was headed overseas again for *PM* to cover the war in northern Africa, the Soviet Union, and India.

Red Hills and Cotton: An Upcountry Memory, Ben Robertson's hastily composed, precocious memoir, appeared in the summer of 1942. Because it was not a war book, *Red Hills and Cotton* attracted less attention initially than *I Saw England*, but the bulk of the attention it received was favorable. The critic for the *New York Times Book Review* said the book "casts a witching spell" that would "linger long and happily in the reader's mind."[30] James Kirk Paulding in *Commonweal* agreed, observing that "Mr. Robertson writes with almost Old Testament eloquence of his own people."[31] Writing for

Introduction

the *New Republic,* noted Southern novelist Stark Young deemed *Red Hills and Cotton* "a good book" about the "other country" of the South, the "antithesis" of Charleston, the Carolina Piedmont. Young, one of the Twelve Southerners who issued the "Agrarian Manifesto," *I'll Take My Stand,* in 1930, acknowledged that the Piedmont of Robertson's *Red Hills and Cotton* was "not the South I grew up with, which was plantation, cavalier, and cotton; but the whole . . . is so truly and deeply viewed, so proudly and deeply felt . . . that I recognize without any reservations its validity as a Southern record." Moreover, Young, unlike many future readers who focused primarily on the author's obvious affection for his home region, also recognized, as Robertson hoped his readers would, that "in the very soundest sense" *Red Hills and Cotton* was "a commentary on our American democracy, not in the thumping Times Square variety of song and radio, but drawing from the ancient life of our country."[32]

Privately, kudos for Robertson flowed in to his family, friends, and publisher. Historian H.C. Brearley told Robertson that *Red Hills and Cotton* was "a charming piece of writing" and the "best plea for agrarianism" that he had ever seen. The arguments of Donald Davidson, Allen Tate, John Crowe Ransom, and others in *I'll Take My Stand,* Brearley allowed, were "sentimental" but Robertson's were "realistic."[33] Chapel Hill-based sociologist Howard W. Odum, founder of the Regionalist school of sociology and vocal critic of the Agrarians, also had high praise for *Red Hills and Cotton.* "Nowhere have I found a more realistic, vivid, and sympathetic portraiture of The Way of the South," he told publisher Alfred A. Knopf. Odum commended Robertson for "de-

Lacy K. Ford, Jr.

scribing a regional culture" in such detail that his book would help "social anthropologists to understand the culture of the South."[34] Ironically, one of the few negative commentaries on *Red Hills and Cotton* was written by another native Upcountryman and journalist, Harry Ashmore. Robertson had met Ashmore at a panel discussion among journalists held at Clemson in early 1941 and had found young Ashmore a stimulating conversationalist. Ashmore later described his relationship with the older Robertson as one between "an admiring young reporter and a very senior journalist."[35] But for all they had in common, Ashmore had serious reservations about *Red Hills and Cotton*. A young Southern liberal nurtured in the same hillcountry valleys as Robertson, Ashmore found the book entirely too favorable an account of Upcountry life. "We refused to yield to progress," Ashmore lamented; "we made a virtue out of poverty, out of doing without. We transmitted our dogma from one generation to another . . . and we ruthlessly discouraged any signs of budding intellectual curiosity." Further, he insisted that Robertson's hope for a future guided by the "Yankee mind and Southern heart" was "fatuous." The "only future we have any right to hope for," Ashmore maintained, "is the one we'll make for ourselves with our own hands and minds when we . . . accept the fact that the only certainty is change." Ashmore found it ironic that most Upcountry folk "scorned the Charlestonians because they couldn't stand defeat, because they retired into a dream world to embroider the memories they cherish" without realizing "that there is no real difference between a mouldy old mansion on The Battery and [a] few red acres in the Keowee Valley" as long as both serve "as a refuge for a people who ran and hid

Introduction

because their grandfathers once took a terrible lick-
ing. . . ." Ashmore thought the chief problem with *Red
Hills and Cotton* was suggested by its subtitle, *An Upcountry Memory*. Robertson remembered the Upcountry "the way any man remembers his childhood; the
good things stand out, the bad things fade." A more
appropriate title, in Ashmore's view, was: "Epitaph for
the Upcountry—In Loving Memory Of a World That
Existed Only in The Minds of a Few of Us."[36]

Unquestionably *Red Hills and Cotton* is suffused
with Robertson's deep affection for his native Upcountry,
and, at times, the book's prose reveals the nostalgia that
the restless, globe-trotting, cosmopolitan journalist felt
for his provincial childhood of deep roots and settled
habits. But Harry Ashmore and others who have read
Red Hills and Cotton as little more than an emotional,
rose-colored memoir have fundamentally misunderstood
the book. *Red Hills and Cotton* is an appreciation of
Upcountry life and culture, to be sure, but Ben
Robertson, no hidebound traditionalist, hardly admired
all that he described. The tone he sought in *Red Hills*
was not so much sentimental as elegiac, one that would
recall a proud but flawed rural society which was quickly
and quietly giving way to the gradual but steady en-
croachment of industrialization. In a sense, Robertson's
elegy, despite what Ashmore conceded was a "lyric, almost Biblical style" and despite Robertson's "fine ear for
the speech of upcountry South Carolina," was pre-
mature, eulogizing the passing of a society still alive
but headed for rapid destruction in the decades which
followed World War II.[37] Even if he foresaw the dramatic postwar changes imperfectly, the well-traveled
Robertson clearly had a good feel for their general

Lacy K. Ford, Jr.

shape, direction, and scope. In *Red Hills and Cotton*, Robertson tried to leave a record of that disappearing rural society's best traditions and characteristics in the hope that this record would instruct those who shaped the coming order, but he did not turn his back on the fading society's many failings.[38]

Red Hills and Cotton is marked by Robertson's recognition of the paradox and complexity of his Upcountry heritage. Upcountry folk, he wrote, were "a strange people, complicated and simple and proud and religious and family-loving, a divorceless, Bible-reading murdersome lot of folks, all of us rich in ancestry and steeped in tradition and emotionally quick on the trigger." There is fondness, even sentimentality, in his peroration, but there is also puckish humor, tongue-in-cheek jibes at those who would take the region's claim of unblemished piety too seriously. For Robertson, Southern virtues were clearly Jeffersonian, a devotion among plain folk to the idea of a republic of independent producers, freeholders all. "Like Jefferson," he continued, "we believe in a country of small farms, with every family independent, in a country that is tempted neither by poverty nor by great wealth but is hedged about by goodness and truth." Yet in the same breath Robertson admits that even Upcountry plain folk too often strayed from these ideals. "We own more land than Democrats and Baptists ought to," he conceded; "for when men own more than a thousand acres, Satan is apt to come among them when they present themselves before the Lord." Even as "believers in an economy of small units," he admitted, there was also a quality about Upcountry folk "that makes us dissatisfied until we have bought all the land that joins our land. We cannot resist buying land." Praising the

Introduction

common people, "the hickory-nut homespun Southerners" of the "inland and upland South," Robertson claimed he and his kinfolk believed "in self-reliance, in self-improvement, . . . in loyalty, in total abstinence, in total immersion, in faithfulness, righteousness, justice, in honoring our parents, in living without disgrace." As Southerners, it was "essential to my kinfolks that they live by an ethical code, that they live their lives with dignity to themselves, that they live them with honor." A "Southerner who loses his honor loses all, and he would rather die than live in disgrace," Robertson wrote. "Honor is at the base of our personal attitude toward life. It is not defeat that we fear, it is the loss of our intimate honor." Yet Robinson knew that for all their professions of piety Southerners were sinners who failed in their efforts to lead pious lives, no matter how hard they tried. "In the end we stake our immortal souls on the ultimate deathbed repentance," he acknowledged; "we put our faith in the promise of Paul the Apostle that in a moment, in the twinkling of an eye, we shall be changed." And no matter how firm an allegiance Southerners pledged to their code of honor, Ben Robertson knew that "in a great house there are not only vessels of gold and silver but also of wood and of earth" and "trifling low-down kinfolks." Robertson insisted that "we are not abandoning the South to wild palms." The South, he knew, "must progress."

It is true that, at times, Robertson seemed sympathetic with his Grandfather Bowen's indictment of industrialization, that "new factory system of the North." The "factory system smothered the individuality of life, it killed a man's inner glow," he remembered his grandfather saying. But if Ben Robertson feared the "power of the great factory" and "the wealth it accumulated in the hands of a few," his fears may have been traditional, even Jeffersonian in some overarching sense, but they were hardly pastoral or romantic, coming as they did from a man who had seen firsthand the misery of working people in the great American industrial cities during the depths of the Great Depression. And Robertson did not spare the Upcountry's traditional agricultural system from his folksy criticism. "Our wagon was hitched to cotton's star, where it had been hitched for a hundred years and where it is still hitched," he lamented. "Sometimes I think a Southerner's idea of heaven is a fine cotton-growing country with the price pegged at ten cents a pound," he wrote, but then quickly amended "heaven is a fine cotton-growing country with the price of cotton pegged at twenty cents a pound."

Robertson's indictment of Southern agricultural stagnation went beyond his critique of the region's excessive dependence on cotton as a cash crop. In *Red Hills and Cotton,* he also criticized the growing evils of tenant-farming as an economic and a social system. In the late nineteenth century, tenancy "was natural" for the region. "We lived in a country that had almost no money, that had no chance of raising cash to pay for wages, so we made an arrangement that did not involve money," Robertson wrote. "We owned more land than we could tend, so we provided families who had no land at all with a house and livestock and with plows and fertilizer, and they and we shared the crop." The tenants "were either white families who had lost or sold their original property or black families that until lately had been slaves." The landowners, he recalled, "lived in our big plain houses about as the tenants lived in their plain three-room ca-

Introduction

bins, and as the colored people lived in their houses."
The South's well-defined racial hierarchy kept white
landowners and tenants socially distinct from their black
neighbors, but Robertson argued that there was little or
no "social difference between us and our white tenants
in those days." Whether landowner or tenant, Robertson
claimed, whites attended the same schools and churches, "came from the same stock," and "had nothing to
explain to one another, no pretenses nor appearances to
keep up." This system, which made the best of a bad
situation, worked "reasonably well," Robertson believed, until it began to lose its temporary, *ad hoc* character and harden into a permanent social and agricultural system. By the 1930s, a scholarly study of
tenants in Robertson's native Pickens county revealed
that no tenant family had ever sent a son or daughter
through college. Landowners, he reported, "were horrified by this information, and immediately . . . tried to
deny it." But the study was accurate. "We were appalled
by this discovery," Robertson insisted, "for we knew
what it implied. The tenants were becoming a caste, a
class was being formed in our midst." The old Southern
idea that white supremacy protected white equality, that
the region's racial stratification fostered a society which
permitted no class distinctions among whites, was being
challenged by a new social reality, not just in cotton mill
villages but also throughout the countryside. "These
were our own people, and in our own country,"
Robertson wrote angrily in *Red Hills and Cotton*, "[and]
this had become their fate."

If the neo-populist Robertson lamented the hardening of class lines among whites, he was cautiously op-
timistic regarding the future of race relations in the

Lacy K. Ford, Jr.

South. Among Southerners of his generation, Robertson's views on racial matters were considered moderate. The evidence suggests that he did not believe in white supremacy, and he was certainly not a hard-line segregationist. Moreover, he supported strong federal anti-lynching legislation at a time when such a position remained extremely unpopular among white Southerners. In 1936, Robertson confided to his private journal that "negroes should be accorded the same right enjoyed by every other taxpayer and voter."[39] Yet he was reluctant to indict his fellow white Southerners for their racial intolerance, and his public statements on racial matters were decidedly more circumspect than his private denunciations of bigotry and inequality. In *Red Hills and Cotton,* Robertson explained segregation in a manner that largely exonerated whites of responsibility for the system. "The facts in the South were the facts," he wrote, "and they had caused us all trouble and suffering." Despite "lynchings and riots," he contended that race relations had gotten better and "will continue to get better." Robertson recognized that "the South was the colored man's home just as it was the white man's home" and believed whites and blacks intended to live "side by side, in the South until the end of time." But improved race relations would come only gradually rather than through a dramatic civil rights revolution. "Suddenness was not the way," Robertson concluded as he surveyed postbellum race relations. "There was too much poverty and too much ignorance for suddenness." Racial justice in the South would come "step by step, generation by generation—from position to position." These views hardly qualify Robertson as a crusader for racial equality, but they represent racial moderation when measured

Introduction

against the normative views of the white South of the 1940s.

Thus, for all his manifest affection for his native South and his unmistakable nostalgia for his years as a youth in the South Carolina hillcountry, Robertson was often a critic, though hardly an unyielding one, of the society in which he had such deep roots. To be sure, Robertson wrote *Red Hills and Cotton* as a fond appreciation of his native Upcountry as well as a constructive critique, but he would surely have been disappointed, if not surprised, to see the extent to which most readers of the volume embraced the appreciation and ignored the critique.

After finishing the manuscript for *Red Hills and Cotton* early in 1942, Robertson quickly resumed his duty as war correspondent with *PM*. In May he went to the Soviet Union to cover the war on the "Russian" front. While there, he repeatedly urged the Americans and British to open a "western" front in order to divide German energies and bolster Soviet morale. Ultimately, however, Robertson found his eastern-front assignment frustrating because the Soviets kept the press away from the fighting and released information sparingly. When he asked *PM* for a transfer, the newspaper sent him to India. There, his dispatches implicitly criticized British colonial officials for their arrogance and intolerance and also revealed how repugnant the instinctively egalitarian American found the Indian caste system. Robertson's pieces from India were among his most hard-hitting and trenchant.[40] Moreover, his close contact with the caste system seemed to nudge Robertson toward sharper and more outspoken criticism of racial segregation in the American South.

Lacy K. Ford, Jr.

Robertson spent his last Thanksgiving in New Delhi, eating peacock rather than turkey. On the first anniversary of Pearl Harbor, he headed back to the United States by way of North Africa and spent the Christmas holidays of 1942 at home in Clemson. In January, he resigned from *PM* to accept the most prestigious job of his career as chief of the *New York Herald-Tribune*'s London bureau. Robertson looked forward to a reunion with old friends, especially Ed Murrow. In February, he notified his family that he had top priority for a flight to the United Kingdom. On February 22, 1943, his plane, the *Yankee Clipper,* approaching Portugal by way of the Azores, crashed into the Tagus River near Lisbon. The plane, a Pan American "flying boat," apparently got caught in a major storm and crashed while attempting an emergency landing. Initially Robertson was officially listed as "missing," but days later his body was recovered from the Tagus River and eventually his remains were returned to South Carolina for burial at the family plot near Liberty.

Condolences to the Robertson family and words of affection and praise for Ben came from his worldwide network of friends and acquaintances. John P. Lewis of *PM* remembered Robertson as a "sensitive, understanding" newspaperman.[41] A writer for the *New York Herald-Tribune* recalled him as "a sunny person by nature with a fondness for the trivial and whimsical in human behavior,"[42] and, as Wright Bryan recalled it, Mrs. Ogden Reid, the *Herald-Tribune*'s "guiding force," eulogized Robertson as a man who possessed "a rare spiritual quality, a discernment of the heart in addition to that of the mind."[43] Closer to home, the *Anderson Independent* obituary noted that Robertson "could count

Introduction

thousands of Andersonians as his friends"[44] and his Clemson classmate Strom Thurmond wrote Ben's father that Robertson was "able and profound, yet kind and affable," a man "held in high esteem" by virtually everyone who knew him.[45] Robertson's considerable talent as a journalist was perhaps best summarized by his friend Tom Waring of the *Charleston News and Courier,* who claimed that "Ben's chief charm was his handling of irrelevancies which finally added up to an aggregate of importance."[46] But probably the most fitting tribute to Robertson the man as well as Robertson the journalist came from Edward R. Murrow. Years after Robertson's death, Murrow continued to tell associates that the South Carolinian "was my best friend" and Murrow's leading biographer claims that of all the losses Murrow suffered during the war Robertson's death "was the one to which Murrow could least reconcile himself."[47] The eulogy Murrow delivered on his CBS radio broadcast of February 28, 1943 was both moving and heartfelt. "This was his war from the moment he reached London," Murrow reported, "for he understood the people who were fighting it." Murrow judged Robertson "the least hardboiled newspaperman I've ever known," explaining that he rejected cynicism because "his roots were deep in the red soil of Carolina" and he "had a faith that is denied to many of us." Thus, the CBS reporter recalled, "there was never a night so black Ben couldn't see the stars." Murrow concluded his eulogy with one of Robertson's favorite anecdotes, a war story about the difficulty newspaper people had getting the needed "priority" to travel. If you had priority, Robertson had often joked, authorities demanded "double priority." Recalling Robertson's meditation on the suddenness with which

Lacy K. Ford, Jr.

Christ had beckoned the thief on Calvary to Paradise, Murrow declared "If any man I know ever had double priority for the long trip into the unknown, it was Ben Robertson."

Ben Robertson's early and tragic death did more than deprive Edward R. Murrow of his best friend. It also deprived South Carolina and the South of a loyal native son whose courage, wisdom, and humor, together with his skill at conveying them through both spoken and printed words, would doubtless have enriched both region and nation during the decades of dramatic change which followed World War II. Of Robertson's many talents, his greatest gifts lay not in the realm of social criticism, though his social commentary merits attention, or in the field of descriptive journalism, though his best narratives are indeed good, but rather in his ability to capture in soaring prose life's brief but precious moments of reverie. There is no better or more moving passage in *Red Hills and Cotton*, and none which quite so accurately reveals the spiritual essence of its author, than the paragraph which explains how Robertson "learned contemplation" while growing up: "In the solitude of the long Southern afternoons I found how to retire within and retreat and how to hear in the great orchestra of the wind the high note. I learned to lie fallow, like the fields in winter, and to live beyond the world and some of its loneliness." Thus, *Red Hills and Cotton* has rightly proven Robertson's richest legacy. Through its pages, generations of readers have shared such moments of reverie with Robertson. Perhaps this Southern Classics edition will allow ever more readers, across new generations, to enjoy moments when they too

Introduction

can listen to "the great orchestra of the wind" and perhaps hear for themselves that elusive "high note."

Lacy K. Ford, Jr.

Notes

1. *Charleston News and Courier,* July 1, 1939, p. 12.

2. Entries of March 28, 29, 30, 1937, Ben Robertson Journal, Ben Robertson Papers, Special Collections, Robert Muldrow Cooper Library, Clemson University, Clemson, S.C. (hereinafter CU).

3. Ben Robertson to B.O. Williams, December 6, 1937, Ben Robertson Papers, CU.

4. Jeanne Gadsden to Tom Waring, February 26, 1943, Ben Robertson Papers, CU.

5. Bernard Smith to Ben Robertson, January 29, 1942, Ben Robertson Papers, CU.

6. Wright Bryan, "About Ben Robertson," in Ben Robertson, *Red Hills and Cotton: An Upcountry Memory* (Columbia: University of South Carolina Press, 1960).

7. J. Strom Thurmond to Ben Robertson, Sr., March 9, 1943, Ben Robertson Papers, CU.

8. For examples, see Ben Robertson, "A Follower of the Prophet in Australia," *Asia* 33 (May, 1933): 60–61; Ben Robertson, "Our Sailors Sleep in the Palace of the Czar," *Scribner's Magazine* 91 (May, 1932): 298–299; Ben Robertson and McCoy Hill, "At the Heart of Desolation," *Travel* 52 (February, 1929): 38; Ben Robertson, "The Hawaiian Melting Pot," *Current History* 36 (June, 1932): 312–315.

9. Ben Robertson to John Whitaker, January 3, 1937, Ben Robertson Papers, CU.

10. Entry of February 5, 1935, Ben Robertson Journal, Ben Robertson Papers, CU.

11. Entry of March 31, 1936, Ben Robertson Journal, Ben Robertson Papers, CU.

12. Ben Robertson to Edgar Snow, January 3, 1937, Ben Robertson Papers, CU.

13. Ben Robertson to Edgar Snow, January 3, 1937, Ben Robertson Papers, CU.

14. Ben Robertson to Turner [Catledge], March 1, 1938, Ben Robertson Papers, CU.

Lacy K. Ford, Jr.

15. *Time*, July 4, 1938, p. 45; F.T. Marsh, "Review of *Travelers' Rest*," *Books*, June 19, 1938, p. 7.

16. Ben Robertson to George Chaplin, June [?], 1938, Ben Robertson Papers, CU.

17. Ben Robertson to George Chaplin, June [?], 1938, Ben Robertson Papers, CU.

18. See Robertson's articles in the *Anderson Independent*, beginning on August 3, 1938, and appearing almost daily through the rest of the month.

19. Ben Robertson, "King George Strives to Please," *Saturday Evening Post*, February 4, 1939, pp. 5–7; "The Lucky Girls of Aruba," July 8, 1939, pp. 8–9.

20. Ben Robertson to Bob Neville (?), July 30, 1939, Ben Robertson Papers, CU.

21. For examples, see articles under Robertson's by-line in *PM* from August until December 1940.

22. Sevareid quoted in William S. Walker, Jr., "Ben Robertson, War Correspondent" (M.A. thesis, University of South Carolina, 1971), p. 64.

23. Ben Robertson to Bob [Neville?], August 5, 1940, Ben Robertson Papers, CU; see *PM*, December 29, 1940, p. 6.

24. *Times Literary Supplement*, August 23, 1941.

25. *New York Times*, April 6, 1941, p. 5; *New York Herald-Tribune Books*, April 6, 1941, p. 3.

26. Earl Mazo to Ben Robertson, May 11, 1940, Ben Robertson Papers, CU.

27. Roger C. Peace to Ben Robertson, July 23, 1941, Ben Robertson Papers, CU.

28. Ben Robertson to James F. Byrnes, July 5, 1941; James F. Byrnes to Ben Robertson, July 23, 1941, Ben Robertson Papers, CU.

29. Wright Bryan, "About Ben Robertson."

30. Katherine Woods, "In South Carolina's Upcountry," *New York Times Book Review*, August 23, 1942, pp. 5–7, 21.

31. James Kirk Paulding, "Review of *Red Hills and Cotton: An Upcountry Memory*," *Commonweal*, October 2, 1942, pp. 569–570.

32. Stark Young, "More Souths," *New Republic*, October 5, 1942, p. 421.

33. H.C. Brearley to Ben Robertson, October 7, 1942, Ben Robertson Papers, CU.

34. Howard W. Odum to Alfred A. Knopf, February 1, 1943, Ben Robertson Papers, CU.

35. Harry Ashmore to T. Stanley Cook, March 4, 1986, John Dewey Lane Papers, CU.

36. Quotations taken from Harry Ashmore to John D. Lane, October 15, 1942, John Dewey Lane Papers, CU; see also Harry Ashmore,

Introduction

"Robertson Kept Mind Clear in the Midst of Furies of War," *Greenville News*, February 25, 1943, p. 1; for an introduction to the work and values of Harry S. Ashmore, see his *An Epitaph for Dixie* (New York: W.W. Norton, 1957).

37. Harry Ashmore to John D. Lane, October 15, 1942, John Dewey Lane Papers, CU.

38. The most thorough recent analysis of *Red Hills and Cotton* is Tony Stanley Cook, "Remembering the South Carolina Upcountry: Ben Robertson's *Red Hills and Cotton*," *Southern Studies* 26 (Fall, 1987): 217–238.

39. Entry of March 17, 1936, Ben Robertson Journal, Ben Robertson Papers, CU.

40. See *PM*, June 25, June 28, July 5, July 15, July 20, August 14, 1942, and February 22 and 23, 1943.

41. *PM*, February 24, 1943.

42. *New York Herald-Tribune*, February 24, 1943.

43. Bryan, "About Ben Robertson."

44. *Anderson Independent*, February 24, 1943.

45. J. Strom Thurmond to Ben Robertson, Sr., March 9, 1943, Ben Robertson Papers, CU.

46. Tom Waring to Jeanne Gadsden, March 1, 1943, Ben Robertson Papers, CU.

47. A.M. Sperber, *Murrow: His Life and Times* (New York: Freudlich Books, 1986), pp. 165–167, 231, 381.

I   To my cousin, Lieutenant William Porter, the second Sergeant York: he has the courage and the bravery, and furthermore he practiced for years, firing at targets.

II   To my cousin, Professor B. O. Williams of the University of Georgia: he has the knowledge and the vision and the power to inspire.

III   To my father: he is the salt of the Southern earth.

RED HILLS
AND COTTON

CHAPTER   I

By the grace of God, my kinfolks and I are Carolinians. Our Grandmother Bowen always told us we had the honor to be born in Carolina. She said we and all of our kissing kin were Carolinians, and that after we were Carolinians we were Southerners, and after we were Southerners, we were citizens of the United States. We were older than the Union in Carolina, and our grandmother told us never to forget that fact. Our kinfolks had given their personal consent to the forming of the Union, we had voted for it at the polls, and what we had voted to form we had had the right to vote to unform. We knew of course what our grandmother was talking about, for our grandmother was an old Confederate lady — she was reconstructed but she was reconstructed in her own way, so whenever she got to talking about us and the grace of God, we said "Yes, ma'am" to our grandmother.

My grandmother believed the finest country in the world was America and the most precious part of America was Carolina. The sun rose and set in our valley; it hovered between Glassy Mountain in the east and Six Mile in the west, then it dropped into darkness, into the dark night of despair; it sank off to shine for a few odd hours on the heathen down in China. I think my grandmother believed God had chosen us for our country, that he had said to us as He had to Joshua: "Arise and go over this Jordan, thou and all this people, unto the land that has been promised." A hundred and ninety years ago God had brought us into Canaan from eastern Pennsylvania.

Once we were sitting in the summertime on the back piazza, talking about heaven. Jim, old and crippled, a colored man who had lived with us always, said he believed the golden shore was like the Book said it was — a city, clothed in fine linen, and purple, and scarlet, and lighted by the glory of God. Mary, who too was colored, said heaven was a small place, for Jesus said no more sin would enter the kingdom of God than could push through the eye of a needle. Mary said it would be obliged to be

And Cotton

a close place — only a few of the strictest brothers and sisters would ever slide through such a crack. My grandmother, speaking in a calm and confident tone, said heaven would be like Carolina in the month of May in the early morning. The sun would never rise more than an hour high, and there would be peace and rest forever.

By Carolina my grandmother of course meant South Carolina. North Carolina to her, and to all the rest of my kinfolks, was hardly more than West Virginia — just nothing but new and rich. North Carolina had not joined us in the revolution of 1719, nor had it nullified in 1832. North Carolina had not even come into being until 1689, and to my grandmother it practically did not exist.

I and all the families of my kinfolks lived for nearly two centuries in two old and fertile valleys at the foot of the Blue Ridge Mountains in the northwest part of our paradise — in the foothills, and in the valleys, and in the plains, and in the wilderness, and in the south country. It was a land of smokehouses and sweet-potato patches, of fried pies and dried fruit and of lazy big bumblebees buzzing in the sun — a country of deep dark pools, of the soaring spirit, of little rooms stored with apples, and of old Confederates and tenant farmers and colored people and swarms of politicians and preachers. An ideal country for cotton farmers and dreamers; a brooding great country that had caught the sight of God. You can see a wedge of sheldrakes, a cloud drifting in southern space, and there before you are the old, contemplative mountains, a long range sifted with a powder that was blue. Sometimes the valleys are filled with showers, melting into yellow light, and in the evening in the depths the woodthrushes sing. It was a disturbing country that rested us and somehow never let us rest. There seemed to be a divine discontent, a searching for its soul.

Most of my kinfolks, when I was growing up, were located on Pea Ridge between Glassy and Six Mile Mountains, on a long rise of fine cotton country between two lonely spurs of pine-grown granite — we lived and some of us still live in the winding open valley of a river called the Twelve Mile. The rest of our kinfolks live to the west of us, they have their houses along both banks of the river Keowee. Twelve Mile in our valley is a narrow muddy stream, red with eroded clay, but Keowee is wide and clear and crystal-pure, a swift river of the spirit flowing out of pine and oak and poplar forests. One time, many years ago, my Great-Aunt Narcissa took us to a high cliff to look down on our two streams just where they come together. She wished us to see for ourselves how quickly the water of a little muddy stream could foul all the clean pure water of a big one. Our Great-Aunt Nar-

And Cotton

cissa said to us: " A wonderful example of sin."

We always grew cotton for our living in our valleys — cotton that in spite of droughts and freshets and boll weevils still yields for us a bale to an acre. A heaven-given crop. We are farmers, all Democrats and Baptists — a strange people, complicated and simple and proud and religious and family-loving, a divorceless, Bible-reading murdersome lot of folks, all of us rich in ancestry and steeped in tradition and emotionally quick on the trigger. In many peculiar and particular ways my kinfolks and I are quite remarkable people. Anyhow, we think we are. As one instance, we are poor, yet we live like Job of old in our country, with cooks to do our cooking and washwomen to do our washing, with Jim to cut stovewood and Windy Bill to feed the mules. Our kinfolks' substance is a thousand bales of cotton and ten thousand bushels of corn and five hundred dairy cows and thirty or forty thousand acres of land, and a very great household. We have all of the simple things that money can buy except we have little money. We raise the things that money can buy, we grow them on the place.

For miles and miles up and down the Twelve Mile and Keowee the land is our land, and the houses are our houses, the white Baptist chapels are our chapels, even the burying grounds are our burying grounds. We own so

much land in our foothills that one time when my cousin
Enid and I were driving toward Pickens, our county seat,
to attend a rural electrification meeting, my cousin Enid
said to me: "I think I'd better address Uncle Tom as
Mister Chairman — if I call him Uncle Tom then I'll have
to say: 'Uncle Tom, Mamma says if you will stretch a
power line from Uncle Wight's to Uncle Ross's and by
Grandfather O'Dell's to Cousin Cody's and to our house,
we all will guarantee two customers a mile.'"

We own more land than Democrats and Baptists ought
to. Often we have wished we owned less — land gets
Southerners into trouble, especially cotton land, for when
men own more than a thousand acres, Satan is apt to
come among them when they present themselves before
the Lord. Both spiritually and economically we are opposed to great holdings and great estates. Like Jefferson,
we believe in a country of small farms, with every family
independent, in a country that is tempted neither by poverty nor by great wealth but is hedged about by goodness
and truth. The reason we ourselves own big farms is that
the Sabeans have fallen upon us. We are Puritan American as well as Southern, and we are of a paradox — we are
believers in an economy of small units, but we are slain by
the edge of swords; there is also a quality within our character that makes us dissatisfied until we have bought all

And Cotton

the land that joins our land. We cannot resist buying land.
The wind from the wilderness smites us. With us, buying
land is a fever.

I and my kinfolks are Southerners of the inland and upland South. We and the ten million like us call ourselves
the backbone of the Southern regions, the hickory-nut
homespun Southerners, who while doing a lot of talking have also done a world of work. We are of Scotch-
Irish stock, improved Scots of Ulster extraction, and it has
never been said of any of us that we have held back from
sounding our horn. We are forthright and outspoken. We
are plain people and our houses are plain — you will not
find on our front piazzas tall white columns holding up
the roof. We are the Southern Stoics. We believe in self-
reliance, in self-improvement, in progress as the theory of
history, in loyalty, in total abstinence, in total immersion,
in faithfulness, righteousness, justice, in honoring our parents, in living without disgrace. We have chosen asceticism because all of our lives we have had to fight an in-
clination to license — we know how narrow and shallow
is the gulf between asceticism and complete indulgence;
we have always known much concerning the far outer
realms, the extremes. We have tried throughout our lives
to keep the Commandments, we have set for ourselves
one of the strictest, sternest codes in existence, but our

9

country is Southern and we are Southern, and frequently we fail. In the end we stake our immortal souls on the ultimate deathbed repentance. We put our faith in the promise of Paul the Apostle that in a moment, in the twinkling of an eye, we shall be changed.

We believe in hard day labor, and in spite of all our cooks and bottle-washers we hold that every farmer should take his turn in the field — he should plow and pick cotton and thin corn. All that eat should sweat. Some of us, of course, have never sweated, but always we have thought we ought to. We are formal — we address God in prayer as " Thou " and " Thee." We are intimate — we like to call old married ladies by their lost maiden names, " Miss May Belle," " Miss Minnie Green." We flatter — we call men " Colonel " and " Judge " and " Major." Of all the colonels among my kinfolks, only one ever really held that rank. My Great-Uncle Bob was a real colonel. Once he had commanded a regiment of infantry in the army of General Jackson. The rest of our colonels were like my cousin Colonel Tom, of whom my father said: " He is just a Southern colonel." He looked like a colonel, so we called him one. We honored the distinction of his stately appearance. Many of my kinfolks have charm — if I do say it myself. Like almost all Southerners, white and black, we were born with manners — with the genuine grace that

And Cotton

floods outward from the heart. I must add also that many of us, far from home, have learned that we can trade on our Southern manners. We do not hesitate to do so, either — we flatter and charm when we can without a flicker of regret.

As Southerners, it is essential to my kinfolks that they live by an ethical code, that they live their lives with dignity to themselves, that they live them with honor. A Southerner who loses his honor loses all, and he had rather die than live in disgrace. Honor is at the base of our personal attitude toward life. It is not defeat that we fear, it is the loss of our intimate honor. We do not only disgrace ourselves, we disgrace all the others, and we cover our heads, for each of us was born in the image and glory of God.

But in a great house there are not only vessels of gold and of silver, but also of wood and of earth; and some to honor and some to dishonor. We have had trifling low-down kinfolks who whittled and fiddled and fished, a great-uncle who was shot in a brawl, a cousin who wounded his son, and a relative closer than a cousin who had to be bailed from jail by our Great-Aunt Narcissa. We have been hit in our pride, for we have known that all of us have carried weaknesses within. Our Great-Aunt Narcissa said even the shame of Aaron Burr was on us.

Red Hills

He was kin to us through the Allstons of Charleston. She said it would not have been wicked necessarily if Burr had killed Alexander Hamilton at the right time and for the right reason; Burr's evil was that he did neither. Our great-aunt said it was Burr really who died that day at Weehawken. The mischief that Hamilton had done to the Federal Union was a seed already sown — Hamilton lived on in the Republican Party.

We do not boast about our honor. About it we are humble and contrite.

We understand the wobbly warped Southerners in *Tobacco Road*, their decay, curdled like a cheese; they have slipped into the quicksand, their eyes are the eyes of flesh, their souls are tired of living. We understand the futile people in *Look Back to Glory*. All are a part of the whole, but a part only, and upon either or upon both anyone can dwell; we all come together in judgment. But the South that I and my kinfolks seek in books is in *Vein of Iron* and *Look Homeward, Angel*. There is fire among those pages and it is for strength that we look, as we are not the kind to stand by and merely watch; we are not abandoning the South to wild palms. The South is our South and it must progress. My kinfolks and I are not worn-out, tired Southerners. We are strong men and women, who have worked hard for a living all of our

And Cotton

lives. We still are working. In our long and difficult time we have done many things which we should not have done, and we have not done many things which we should have done, but we have never forgiven ourselves in our hearts for a single breach of the gospel. Emotionally, morally, we have paid personally for every sin. We have been like Windy Bill. He came back to our house from the penitentiary, and on the first Sunday night after his return he went over to Big Abel Baptist Church, stood up, and in a humble maner confessed that he had raped, stolen, and killed but never once had he lost faith. " I'm sorry for the bad things I have done," Bill said. The congregation sang: " Lord, he's sorry."

The South we belong to is a good country, a valiant country; it always has had valor, and it has had industry and thrift. Our house is painted, our grass is green. For those of us who bend our backs and put our shoulders to the wheel, the South is still Canaan land; it is milk and honey.

My own kinfolks have never written much about themselves. They have been talking people, and people who talk the entire time seldom have the art to write. Talking and writing are mutually consuming gifts — one must win over the other, for there cannot be action and at the same time contemplation. We have poured out our creative en-

Red Hills

ergy in words spoken on front porches on summer nights,
and about log fires in the kitchen fireplaces in winter. We
have had wonderful conversation at the houses of my
kinfolks, great story-telling and discussion and argument,
but it has been like the chimney smoke — it has drifted
away. What has remained is what we have remembered.
The library of early American knowledge was the principal theme of my kinfolks' conversation — the passing on
from one generation to the next of histories, codes of
laws, prophecies, some memorized songs and proverbs,
and letters. Biblical, Puritan, Southern, it was a variation
on a single driving constant theme, rich and homely and
timeless, of backwoods people trying in the backwoods to
set up a certain sort of life. The tale moved through the
middle of one of the main currents of the United States —
trailing down the Appalachian Mountains to Carolina,
swerving westward and on across the continent. Always it
had travel in it, the effort to escape.

My kinfolks have had a trying, complicated experience
during their two hundred years in South Carolina. Within
the great granite frame of American philosophy they have
carved with their own tears a thing from stone. From the
start these Southerners have known what sort of people
they wanted to make of themselves and what sort of
country they wanted to create from our holy earth. They

14

And Cotton

have believed in high exalted qualities even in lowest places; they have believed in the rainbow; in the rising sun.

My kinfolks have always been a kind of restless people, like other Americans, but there is a timelessness about our cotton fields and the worn ridge of hills about Twelve Mile Valley that has enabled us in our lifetimes to feel periods of still. Time has accumulated about us like deep water in a pool, and there is no beginning and no end — our house is a real pool, a place of quietness and rest among many rocks in a swift river, a momentary sanctuary shaded by rhododendron and a stopping place for a night. Sometimes for days and weeks we can plow cotton and hoe and sit on the front piazza and rock, and sleep on hot afternoons after we have eaten a watermelon. We can forget time in our country and be contented, and then the old restlessness will stir again, like a wind rising, and we have to travel. We are all like that. High winds and lonesome sounds disturb us, something within makes us go. We must ride to town or visit among the kinfolks or strike out for Texas. We must see what is going on, see what other folks' crops look like, cross into new country. Motion inspires us. My Uncle Wade says my Aunt Bettie will go anywhere with anybody at any time. He says that if someone comes along and says: " Let's go to Green-ville," my Aunt Bettie will say: " All right " even if she must get up from her deathbed. My Uncle Wade says if someone should drive by in a buggy with a mule and say to my Aunt Bettie: " Come on, Bettie, let's start out for Europe," that my Aunt Bettie would reply: " Wait till I get my hat." My Uncle Wade declares that for all of our kinfolks and especially for those like my Aunt Bettie there is no doctor like " old Doctor Go." We have always en-joyed hard travel — it rests us.

We have rambled long distances in our time, for the road that passes our house leads all the way to California, and we have never been able to resist it — traveling on that road has been a vice with us and a virtue. Once one of my cousins came in and said: " Let's go to the Pacific Ocean." I said I had no business at the Pacific Ocean. " I haven't either," said my cousin, " but let's go — let's see what it's like." Before I could say anything more, my Grandmother Bowen, who was sitting in a chimney corner, said to me: " Go ahead — go while you have the chance." So I did go. My cousin and I started out the next day for California in the opposite direction. We decided that on our way to the Pacific Ocean we might as well take in Petersburg, Richmond, and Jamestown in Virginia. Once another of my cousins was hitch-hiking to South Carolina

And Cotton

from the University of Wisconsin, and somewhere on the broad prairie of Illinois he met some people who were going to Los Angeles and, in an instant, he changed his plans and went with them. In Los Angeles he went to a company that arranges automobile trips and asked what cheap tours had they scheduled. They told him he could go to El Paso for five dollars and a half. " I've been to El Paso," said my cousin. "What do you have in some other direction? " They had a car leaving, they said, for Pocatello, Idaho, so my cousin went to Pocatello. He had never traveled in that direction. My kinfolks, I think, were born to ramble. It is a troubling quality in a people who are religious and serious and who have been drilled from their youth to accept duty, to work hard, to settle down. It is our temptation, and we reveal ourselves when as our most desperate criticism of a person we say he can never be found twice in the same place.

Not so long ago in our valley, one of my young cousins came to me in a deep attitude of remorse. " I'm weak," he said, " I have no will."

"What have you done? " I asked him.

" Well, I'll tell you," said my cousin. " The other Sunday I took a drink and went to church. I heard a fine sermon and listened to beautiful singing, and it did something to me I couldn't stand. Suddenly I had to do something I had never done before, I had to go somewhere I had never been to."

"What happened?" I said.

"I went to the crossroads and hitch-hiked," said my cousin, "I hitch-hiked clear to Macon, Georgia. I left all my obligations, all my duties."

"What did you do in Macon?" I asked.

"I went to cafés and picture shows," said my young cousin. My cousin then bowed his handsome head. Sorrowfully, he concluded: "I like that sort of life."

Daniel Boone belonged among our kinfolks, and Aunt Mollie Boone, who is buried in our burying ground, told a sister-in-law of hers who told her granddaughter who told my Great-Aunt Narcissa that Mrs. Daniel Boone said Daniel was a mighty poor provider — he would leave her and the children with a crop to make. Mrs. Daniel Boone said Daniel traveled for nothing so much as the trip. James Robertson, the founder of Nashville, was another of our traveling kinfolks, and so was Horseshoe Robertson, the Revolutionary scout. Horseshoe said: "A man picks up some good everywhere, if he's a mind to — that's my observation," and "When a man's conscience begins to harden, it does it faster than anything in nature." One of our boys is buried at Cumberland Gap, where Boone fought the Indians; one is buried on the battlefield at

And Cotton

Kings Mountain, another lies in Mexico at Churubusco; we lost boys in the Civil War all the way from Gettysburg to the Brazos River. There is a town named for us in north Georgia, a county in Texas, a hotel in Tennessee, and we have statues in state capitols and one bust in the Hall of Fame — all because we have wandered. We have traveled but we also have resisted ourselves — we have stayed at home. We and the people like us, during our time, have been great because the country we have lived in was great, and we have been at our best in crises; we have been at our greatest on occasions that have demanded most. We have been a hard-fighting wilderness people. Our home is in our valley, but we have walked across a continent with angels holding our hands.

Our folks are old and settled in our country; we have a sense of continuity, of the infinite age of time — the history of the United States has been told to us in our valley by kinfolks who have been told it by their kinfolks, and it is a personal epic, a personal saga, and in it from the beginning we have been taking our part. We know why we were fearful of adopting the Federal Constitution — it took from us a part of our power; and we know why we opposed the Civil War in the hill country but fought it anyhow because we were Carolinians and Carolina was Carolina. Time and again the old folks and relations have told us during the talk of the night to stand together, to remember what we are, to remember that blood flows thicker than water, that blood will tell, that we are obligated to our kinfolks, that we must amount to something, we must be somebody, we must never bring disgrace upon the kinfolks. Time and again they have told us we are obligated, we have our duty, we must be willing to fight against whatever it is that threatens. We have been told to ask about everything: Will it leave us free?

We are like kites in the hills of Carolina, like ships riding at anchor — we have our red hills and our cotton fields, our big wooden white houses. Someone is always keeping the home place, someone always is there, and no matter how seldom or unexpectedly we may come in, we know someone will rise to give us our welcome. We can stay for a day, for a week, for a month. We can sit in a corner if we like and read a book, or we can milk the cows or feed the chickens, or shoot squirrels in the oaks along the spring branch. It is a great comfort to a rambling people to know that somewhere there is a permanent home — perhaps it is the most final of the comforts they ever really know. Perhaps that is why one of our favorite hymns is that spiritual: "I got a home in that rock, don't you see?"

And Cotton

We have been since the beginning in our valleys — in the same houses, on the same land. We have driven from the same hilltops to vote for all the presidents — we supported Thomas Jefferson the first time he ran, and from that time on we have voted the straight ticket of the Democratic Party. Some of our lands have never even been divided — they have been passed down from oldest son to oldest son, they have never been wrangled over in the courts.

Our original kinfolks, whom God directed southward over the first western trail — a family of twenty-one — took up an English league of land from the King of England at six and a quarter cents an acre, and like a sovereign state our kinfolks made a treaty of their own with the Cherokee Indians on Big Cherokee Creek in the deep heart of the Cherokee country. Later we drew up another treaty for still more land, and neither they nor we broke our treaties. They did not take hogs and cattle bearing our mark; we did not hunt on their land. However, in the end, when the whole country was at war, we did become involved in the general struggle and we had finally to win our territory by conquest, by force. We took our land from the Cherokees who had taken it from the Creeks three hundred years before. Sometimes in Twelve Mile Valley we forget about the Puritans and the Pilgrims,

sometimes we have had a feeling that we have come down
the dusty ages through the red men, that we have lived
in America forever. The Cherokees loved our beautiful
country, they honored the worn mountains with epic leg-
ends, they told stories about Keowee and Twelve Mile.
God to them was God. They sang a hymn to our evening
star.

In a foreign country, once, a customs official said to
me: " What is your racial ancestry? "

" American," I said.

" There is no such racial ancestry as American," the
man said, insolent and arrogant. " Americans are hybrid.
What is your racial nationality? "

I answered: " I am Cherokee Indian."

In addition to our Cherokee land, we were given
bounty land by Congress when the Revolutionary War
was over. It was a payment to our soldiers for service in
the Continental Army. We have lived since 1750 on our
territory, so in our foothills we do not understand what
foreigners mean when they say America is a young country. To us it is ancient, it is wild and worn and lovely like
the Blue Ridge Mountains, the center of everything and
the oldest part of the earth. In Carolina we have little
cross-shaped stones that were dropped by the angels who
brought to America the news of the Crucifixion. Mary, the

And Cotton

colored woman in our kitchen, is of the belief that the
Ark on the fortieth day stopped on the top of Six Mile.
We know what Madame Chiang Kai-shek means when
she says it is difficult to pour old wine into new bottles.

It is lost wars that age a people in their country, and we
have lost more than one struggle in South Carolina. We
were beaten by Spaniards in 1702 and by Indians in 1761;
we have lost costly campaigns to the English and have
been overwhelmed by the Yankees. Of course we have
won some wars; we have whipped Frenchmen in our
state, we have whipped Spaniards, Indians, and English-
men, but successful wars are forgotten — they are like
other kinds of fulfillment. You have accomplished something you have started to accomplish, it is finished. It is
defeat that lives on and takes the years to smother. Of all
people in the world, we in the South should have been
forewarned about the Germans — we should have known
what defeat would do to the German nation. We should
not have forgotten our successful war of 1918 with its
half-defeated peace. We of all people should have known
we should either have demolished the German Empire or
have restored it to glory.

We should have been forewarned in 1918 because twice
within one century our own state was pillaged and burned
by enemy armies. Our state is pocked with battlefields —

Red Hills

Cowpens, Kings Mountain, Eutaw Springs. Old Charleston, fragile and chilled with beauty, was until 1914 one of the most bombarded and besieged cities in existence. The mellow·bells in St. Michael's white tower have been back and back again over the ocean. And then there is Columbia on the high hills of the Congaree — the city that Sherman burned. There are still scars on our State-house in Columbia from the cannons of Sherman — damaged stone that for eighty years we have refused to repair. We are too proud to repair those battlemarks, so we have just left them as Sherman left them, and have placed bright bronze stars beside each one of them to fix the attention of the stranger. Trouble and defeat have been with us so much in our state that we have turned trouble into a glowing virtue. Trouble is made to shine in our sky. One of the sayings my Grandmother Bowen used to quote us was: " Shrink not from facing sorrow — she is the messenger of God to thee."

Hard times either embitter you or leave you mellowed like crabapples and turnips after the iciness of frost. Troubles have given us perspective in our country, a kind of sorrowful sympathy and understanding — a view of all life as alternate capture and release. We know in Carolina that nothing lasts forever — neither victory nor de-

And Cotton

feat, nor spring nor summer — and no matter what comes up, we can usually find within our rich experience some precedent to steer us. We know if the cotton fails that the corn will probably prosper. If there is drought and the young begin to worry about all the crops, the old will tell us not to give up hope — it can't be worse than 1845, when the rivers dried to a trickle and even our cows died. If the summer is cold — there was the year it frosted on the 6th of June; if the winter is mild — well, the roses once bloomed at Christmas. We have been at the top and at the bottom in South Carolina. We almost alone in our small Southern state directed the history of the American Union from 1830 up to 1860 — one brilliant Carolinian after another was produced as we needed new leaders. We have been down now for the last eighty years. We have tried radicalism and have failed, we have tried impatience. Now, whenever we come to any new crossroads, both our white people and our black people are apt to advise caution. We are conservative because of our troubles and because of our age. We are old, but at the same time we are tough; we are a branch of Americans, beaten so many times that we are not appalled any more in the slightest by any kind of dire prospect — not by five-cent cotton nor by forty-cent meat, nor even by another gigantic foreign war. We have hung on in spite of everything for so long now that I cannot think of any sort of threat to America that would ever make us quit.

When we were growing up, our Southern country and all of our older people were still grieving. We had lost the Southern cause — the kind of country we had wanted, the sort of life we had created out of the earlier Revolution. We had lost everything that to us and Thomas Jefferson had been so high and holy, we had been nailed by a Northern economic system to a sort of Northern cross; almost we were strangers stranded in our own country. Always and everywhere as I was growing up, there was the lament: we had lost, we had lost. Among our own kinfolks our Confederate soldiers could not bear to think that so many of our fine and promising and dear relations had died on the battlefields for nothing more than failure. They could not bear to let the lives of so many of our kinfolks sink into such futility and little use. They could not bear that — so they resurrected all the dead. The Confederates who came home from the war spent the rest of their lifetime telling a generation of Southern children and a generation of Southern grandchildren about the men who had died for the South in the Civil War. They gave those dead young soldiers a new life in a glowing

And Cotton

personal legend. I don't suppose there ever was an army that lived on individually as the Confederate army has lived for these last eighty years throughout the South. Today I know a great deal more about my Great-Uncle Joel, who was killed at Fredericksburg, than I know about his namesake, my Uncle Joel — and I knew my Uncle Joel well. My Grandfather Bowen and my Great-Uncle Bob, the one who was shot in the hip at Missionary Ridge — these two veterans sat for years on our wide piazza and told us about the men who had been killed in the battles. We would sit in the warm Southern darkness and the katydids would cry in the oak trees, and the tale would grow and grow. They told us so vividly and in such detail that sometimes I feel I have taken part myself in half the campaigns of the Confederate army.

Like most Southerners, I visit battlefields. Southerners will visit almost any battlefield anywhere, but we are especially fond of the Civil War scenes because we know who fought where and how they did their fighting. Once at Fredericksburg, I heard my Uncle Wade correct a professional guide — a man hired by the government to show visitors about the field. The guide said so and so had happened, my Uncle Wade said he was mistaken. Uncle Wade said: "Uncle Alf said this was the way."

I enjoy walking across battlefields, thinking of other

men in other times, facing their trouble. I cannot keep back the tears even now at Chickamauga and at Manassas. I am overwhelmed at Appomattox — I remember how my grandfather said he had felt there, hungry and tired and beaten. How sorry he said he had felt for General Lee. How broken-hearted for the South. To me one of the holiest of the world's holy places is the field at Gettysburg across which the army of Pickett charged — their gesture was like so many of the world's great gestures, a defeat for the spirit. It is the devotion of the Confederate army that stirs me at Gettysburg and all those places, the bravery, the courage, the manner of the dying.

The past that Southerners are forever talking about is not a dead past — it is a chapter from the legend that our kinfolks have told us, it is a living past, living for a reason. The past is a part of the present, it is a comfort, a guide, a lesson. My Grandfather Robertson was captured in 1865 and walked after the war was over from a prison camp on the Hudson River all the way to South Carolina, a hard long journey in those days. He was ragged when he got there. Sixty-two years later, during the depression of 1932, I was working in New York, and I said to myself I need not worry too much if I lost my job — what my grandfather could do in 1865, I could do in 1932. I had the same valley to return to that he had. Both of us had the hills and the fields and home. And when I had to be bombed in England in 1940, I said to myself that I had come to my Gettysburg, and what my grandfather had gone through, I could go through. I feel now about London as my grandfather felt about that town in Pennsylvania — I have fought over every inch of the ground. The past encourages us Southerners at all times of crisis.

Often I am a sort of Confederate — often I try to be my grandfather's grandson. I even find that I have a queer way of translating the Confederacy straight into the present United States. I in my generation am Southern, but it is the army of the United States that is my army, and I find that it has always been my army. It seems to me it was the North and not the South that seceded, it seems to me that we were the Union, and that the Union went with us — the uninterrupted strain of the United States moved along to Richmond and then back again to the north bank of the Potomac. I cannot imagine any United States that we were not always a part of. Lee and Jackson were our generals and Lincoln was President of our United States. It was Sherman whom we fought, and Sherman was not of America at all; Sherman was like Santa Ana and Cornwallis — he was foreign. Once my Great-Aunt Narcissa told us she hoped William Tecumseh Sherman burned forever in the hottest stove in hell.

Red Hills

I am so unconsciously Southern that even today it surprises me to hear officers of the present United States Army describe movements that Federal troops made during the battles of the Civil War. It startles me to realize that there are Americans who study what Grant and Sherman did. It is just like reading Tolstoy and learning what the Russians did when Napoleon was marching toward Moscow. It is like hearing a Filipino discussing the Philippine insurrection from the viewpoint of General Aguinaldo. I am born so Southern that even in 1941 at a parade in San Francisco, I was astonished when all of a sudden I heard the superb band of the Thirtieth United States Infantry burst into *Marching through Georgia*. My army playing that tune! I could not have been more surprised had it struck up *The Watch on the Rhine*. In my subconscious Southern mind I have rationalized everything. It was not the Confederate army that lost, the Southern cause was never the lost cause — my grandfathers have assured me of that. Out of the grace of God, they have assured me.

CHAPTER II

Our kinfolks on Pea Ridge are intermarried, webbed and woven like a rug, and in the old days the old folks could recite them all — who begat whom and where, who married the ten boys of Cousin Caline, what happened to the eleven girls of Uncle Forrest. We are interested in our ancestors — they were us in another age, they kept the vineyard, plowed the field, dug the well, and they gave everything to us. For them, the winter is past, the rain is over and gone, but we feel gratitude to them — the teachers of our race. Our divination is theirs and whatever of enchantment is about us came from James Robertson and Aunt Mollie Boone and our Great-great-great-Aunt Narcissa.

Red Hills

It is from our ancestors that we have our faith. They have taught us our responsibility, and obligation and duty. We must amount to something, we must be somebody, we must put something by for our old age, we must spend less than we take in. We must stand for complete freedom of the conscience, for absolute liberty of the soul. We alone must be responsible to God for salvation, and the Holy Scriptures form the only absolute standard of faith; and we deny the controlling authority of catechisms, and reject all union between the church and the state. No magistrate has any power over us in faith. We must stand alone. Our ancestors have taught us that each man, rich or poor — whether he likes it or not — is in some way his brother's keeper. It is our duty to promote, in every possible way within our power, the welfare of tenants and of the colored people about us. We must live on our own land, on the cotton fields, and not attempt to buy cheap or to sell dear, nor to profit by another man's labor. Economically, we must work for ourselves, live in our own houses, stay out of debt. Socially, we must bear ourselves with modesty in the presence of others — we stand humbly in the sight of God, but among the earthly we need show no meekness whatsoever, we need bow our knee to no king nor to any crown, for we have had the honor to be born the equal of any person

in the world. We are neither above nor beneath. Our ancestors have taught us to stand up to our troubles, to fight,
to shoot at whoever shoots at us, and to shoot first if we
can. Politically, the rule for us is always to oppose every
Federal tariff, for we have cotton to sell abroad, and every
artificial protection at home is bound in the end to injure
us in the foreign market. What our ancestors have taught
us is this: we are ourselves, we are to be ourselves, and
except to ourselves we owe no obligation to anyone or
anything except the Almighty, the government, and our
fellow man.

We are interested in our kinfolks as kinfolks — in them
as persons to whom all of us, present and past, are obligated; but we are further interested in them because
being closer to them than to other persons, with less hidden, we had a finer chance to understand them as special
personalities — to realize what particularities and peculiarities they possess which make them individual, to
sense the inner gifts and freaks which separate them
from all the rest of us, and even from their own brothers.
We know their transgressions, the iniquity and secret
goodness hid within their bosoms, of the thistles and the
wheat, and of the cockles in the barley.

In the South, being personal in religion, in our way of
living in the cotton fields, in our general attitude toward

Red Hills

almost everything, we are endlessly fascinated by men's personality. We are interested in a man's difference; it is the variation that attracts us more than the type, for it is the variation that has a separate characteristic. We value the individuality of all life — the chance and the strangeness in everything, the mystery, the wonder, the infinity of life's mutations. People to us are characters in a plot, and each man is the center of greatness and meanness, and we had rather know how a man does something than to know what it is he has done. How has a man lived his life? Has he followed the pattern, has he exalted himself, has he hammered fine gold, has he spread a rainbow about the storm? Both our white people and our black people have this curiosity in common, this mutual interest. Every new day for us is a new page, a new chance for renegades, for castaways to grow in grace.

We like the eccentric, the unusual, the vivid person with the live phrase — a man who tells us he has been squirming in hot ashes, a woman who says her hands look as though she has been digging sweet potatoes, a girl who describes a woman as walking like an old cow on thin ice. We laugh a great deal — perhaps because deep within we are melancholy and brooding and touched with the mystic. We talk — we talk and we talk.

Even this morning some of us talked for an hour. I ate

And Cotton

breakfast in the kitchen and Jim, the colored man, sat on the woodbox, sipping coffee from an old chipped cup, and Mary, the cook, sat in a chair by the stove and blew coffee in a saucer. We talked about Lucile, who had fourteen children, marrying the preacher, who had seven, and about their starting in to keep house with a family of twenty-one.

"How many times you been married, Jim?" said Mary, looking over the rim of the saucer.

"Five times," said Jim, twisting himself into a more comfortable position on the stovewood. "Five wives I've had."

"You shot several of them, too, didn't you?" accused Mary.

"Shot two of them," said Jim, calm and unconcerned. "It didn't hurt them much; just winged them in the leg with a little buckshot and it did them both a lot of good." Jim paused and sipped from the cup. "I shot my second wife and my third wife, but all that was 'way back when I was a middle-aged man."

After a time Jim got up and went into the yard to rake leaves. Mary sat on and I sat on, reading the newspaper. There was an item about Negroes going North. "Mary," I said, "why don't you go North?"

"I'm too old and too old-fashioned," she replied, pour-

ing some more coffee into her saucer. " Besides, there's too
many big rivers between here and New York and long
ago I made it a rule not to cross over any water deeper
than ankle-deep." She laughed, then added: " I don't see
anybody coming back rich from up there — white folks
nor black folks."

Mary began to talk about rivers and about drowning.
"Paul drowned in Twelve Mile right there opposite the
Poplar Grove Baptist Church. He was a likker-headed
nigger — he drank a lot of likker, and he came along there
one Sunday morning on the way to church and the river
was 'way up, and he said to the people who were with
him that he was going to swim hell or drown. With
that, he jumped in, and when he got by a big willow
tree, he waved his hands to them and said: ' Fare thee
well, I am gone.' And, bless God, he was gone; he was
drowned."

Mary hummed a line of a hymn; then she began to talk
again. " Uncle John drowned Aunt Millie in that same
place. They were going to cross in a flat-bottom boat and
Uncle John told Aunt Millie to stay on the bank, but she
said she could swim if the boat turned. So she got in and
they started across, and, gracious God Almighty, right in
the middle of the river the boat gave a swerve and
throwed them all in. Uncle John got out, but Aunt Millie

went under. Aunt Millie was drowned with two half-bushels of corn."

Mary began to talk about churches — about Poplar Grove, about Big Abel, about New Olive Grove, and Mount Nebo No. 2. " The last time I was out that way at Mount Nebo No. 2," said she reflectively, "was the time they buried Ella." Mary crossed her legs and sipped mincingly from the saucer. " Ella was a good girl even if she did do the things she did. I liked Ella and I saw her the last morning. I was coming to the kitchen and she came up and shook hands and said hello and I gave her one little kiss on the forehead, for I always did like Ella. Ella went to the Hot Spot that night and Slim came along — that was her main friend — and they started to Seneca in an automobile. Slim throwed the thing wide open and they ran into Cap's stable and Slim was killed and Ella was broken up so she died at the hospital." Mary hesitated a few moments, thinking. Then she added: " I never in my life saw such a crowd as there was that day at Mount Nebo No. 2. The yard was full and the church was so jammed it was leaning to one side. I was scared to go in there, the church was tilting so, but they got to singing such a noble hymn that I decided I'd take a chance anyhow. I pushed in and we all sang ' I'm going to preach my gospel, said the Lord.' It was fine singing — fine singing — but about that time Nina came tipping in and touched me on the sleeve and said: 'Lord, the church is slipping, get out of here.' I looked around and it was wobbling, but there was a lot of white folks in the yard and I didn't want them to see me run, so I stood there very easy. Then the church gave another shake and we all made for the windows and the door. I went straight through a window, and after that the service was continued in the yard."

Mary cleared her throat, reached over for a hunk of cornbread. " That preacher preached the damnedest sermon for Ella I ever heard in my life," said Mary. " He said Ella had everything — a good job and plenty to eat and wear. He said he used to pay a few calls on Ella himself but that it looked like nothing could make her do what was right. He said all the time he was paying her calls he knew she was going with somebody else. He said he went to see her at the Anderson Hospital and that Ella said: 'Sit down, Brother,' but he told her: 'No. It's too late to sit down.'"

" Was that all he said, Mary? " I inquired. " He said that at her funeral? "

" That's what he said."

" Mary," I said, " do you think Ella's soul was saved? " Mary said: " It's between the stirrup and the ground." There was a tap on the door and Lulu came in, looking for work. Lulu sat down on the woodbox. "Lulu," I said, " do you steal? " I had known Lulu all my life, so I could ask her such a question. She knew I was talking to her in fun.

" I'm going to tell you the God's truth," said Lulu; " I don't steal nothing from nobody except liquor."

Aunt Coot was with Lulu. Aunt Coot was a fine, gray-headed elderly colored woman, as close to us as our kin-folks. " Aunt Coot," said Mary, " didn't you sell liquor one time? " Aunt Coot had nothing to hide from any of us, so she gave a simple and candid answer. " I sold liquor for three years," she said. " I kept it under the kitchen floor buried in the ground in a keg and I had a rubber hose that I piped it out of. The police came to my house five times and searched the place and they couldn't find anything and I cussed them all out for coming into a church member's house and carrying on like that." Aunt Coot laughed. " I didn't get into any trouble until a sorry, good-for-nothing boy got mad at me and told on me, and then they got me and I had to put up ten dollars bond. I said to myself then there was going to be real trouble, so I quit selling liquor. I repented and joined the House of Prayer."

Hattie came in, to sell eight eggs. Hattie got to talking about how sorry she felt for Lot's wife in the Bible. She

said she understood how hard it was for Mrs. Lot not to
look back and if she had been walking out of a city like
that she would have looked back too. " I got to look back,"
said Hattie.

" Ain't it the truth? " said Lulu. " And I got to nibble the
fruit."

Cousin Stephen John dropped in, on his way up the
river from the sawmill. He told about seeing a man in the
mountains who had a corn patch in a field between a
mountain and a swift river — a patch from which no road
led. He said to the man: " Friend, how in the world do
you get your corn out of that patch? " And the man answered: " I distil it into liquor and I fight my way out."

A gale of laughter filled our kitchen.

It is about people that we talk; it is not about things.
A thing is worth discussing only when it illustrates the
character of a human being. We are interested in the pure
abstractions of individual character. That is why we will
seldom discuss an issue as such — we consider an issue,
but we prefer to tell about a symbol that stands for the
issue or we will tell you a story about some person involved in such an issue. We are story-tellers in the South.

We are interested in men's tragedies and in their dying
alone and in their getting along with themselves. We are
not gossiping merely when we talk about everyone we

And Cotton

know, and about everyone we have ever seen or heard of. We are absorbed in the loneliness and happiness of men and women, in the degree of their discipline, in their self-control. The reason people live, we think, is to attempt to find happiness and to try to save their souls. We understand Mary when she asks whether it is better to miss heaven by a mile or to miss it by only an inch. We understand Lulu when she announces that were she a man she would head straight for a chaingang — men are not alone on a chaingang; they have companionship, they have fine singers to join them in magnificent hymns about the world and all its trouble, and at night when the men on the gang return to their camp, they do not have to cook their supper, they just sit down to a meal that already has been prepared; all they do is to eat. There is often a plaintive note about the stories we tell in the South, often the theme is sorrow. The world to us is filled with sin, and for our souls there is a struggle that never stops. In the South we had rather save our souls than make a lot of money.

We sit on our piazzas and talk about men fighting and about dusting boll weevils and about trying to grow a crop of cotton. We talk about the pigs getting loose and the cows going dry and about " the goldness of the teeth relieving the plainness of the face " and about the universe as spirit and about eternity and our certainty of

Red Hills

there being no beginning and no end, of our being now in eternity. We talk about the will of God and about trying to be honest and simple and sometimes we try to imagine the non-end of time, to conceive a trillion years and a trillion trillion. Sometimes we talk for hours about ourselves. We will spend whole Sunday afternoons on our front piazzas talking about the kinks of the kinfolks.

There are about a thousand persons in our valley who are counted among our kin. They are of every condition and type and of almost every station, but that does not matter so much — the important fact to us is that they belong to our connection. Some are high and mighty; some go without shoes in the summertime, they follow the plow through the fine clay fields in their bare feet; and a few of our kinfolks cannot read and have no intention of ever learning to read, not wishing to sully their minds with learning. The centering focus of all our interest, however, is that we are blood members of the central families of which my grandfathers were the head.

I myself never knew my father's father, my Grandfather Robertson, the one who was captured and walked home from New York. He died before I was born, but I had two other grandfathers whom I knew personally — really, I had three others. I knew my Grandfather Bowen, my

mother's father, who fought all the way from First Manassas to Appomattox, and I knew my Grandfather O'Dell,
whom I called Grandfather but who technically was not
my grandfather at all — he really was only a cousin. My
Grandfather O'Dell, a drummer boy in Lee's army, was
the grandfather of so many of my first cousins that my sisters and I just called him Grandfather anyhow. The third
grandfather whom I personally knew was the father of
our dear stepmother — he was about a fifth cousin in the
actual blood relationship. Our Grandfather O'Dell was
about our third cousin on our father's side and a fourth
cousin or so on the side of our mother. We felt very close
to our Grandfather O'Dell because one of his daughters
had married our mother's brother, and one of his sons had
married our mother's sister, and one of his sons had married our father's sister, and one of his wife's nephews had
married one of my mother's sisters, and one of my Grandmother Bowen's nephews had married one of his daughters.

Through my father's mother's side, through the Claytons, our Grandfather O'Dell had a great-great-grandfather who also somehow was his great-grandfather
through another line — a generation got lost in that mix-up
by an older man in one family marrying a younger woman
in another. Because of this situation, I had first cousins

whose great-great-great-grandfather was also their great-great-grandfather. I had first cousins who had double first cousins. Even our father was our cousin, and our mother and our stepmother were our cousins, but the cousin relationship in those cases was remote. Our kinships were so interbound that we seldom spoke of our family tree as a tree; we called it a wheel, for no matter in which direction you traced, you always sooner or later came back again to the patriarch from whom you started. We have had strong bodies and strong minds and it has been old age and diseases like fever that have killed us. A number of our kinfolks have been killed by violence, but that was almost a natural way for them to die — the country they lived in was violent and their time was a violent time. Besides, they enjoyed a violent life. They have been shot, scalped, struck by lightning, run over by mules, thrown from horses, killed by automobiles, hanged, hit by falling trees, and they have been drowned in swollen rivers and abandoned wells. One met an ignominious death — he was slashed by a razor. And another one who hid some gold in a coffeepot in the fireplace was bashed on the head with a crowbar.

I never heard of a single person among our kinfolks ever committing suicide. Our lives have been unharried and uninvolved, and we have been economically independent,

and our time has always been our own time — we have
gone fishing when we have chosen to, and if we have lost a
few dollars by closing up the store we have just lost them.
Maybe we have not shot ourselves because we have been
too proud to. Maybe we have been afraid to. We have always been like that colored man in " Old Man River " who
when he was tired of living was also scared of dying — the
Baptist church has always told us we would go straight to
hell for self-murder, there would be no pardon. Suicide
also is considered a disgrace to a person's entire family
connection in the South, and we seldom forget that — we
are too deeply responsible to the kinfolks.

We have been strong-bodied, stern, hill-country Southern people, but none of us would deny that we have been
considered peculiar. Nature, no doubt, has accentuated
the eccentricities in our blood line, and then, being
Southerners, we have accentuated them deliberately ourselves. We have never wished to be like everybody else.
We have tried all our lives to be ourselves, to be different
if the spirit so moved us. We have never been afraid of
becoming set in our ways, nor have we hesitated to form
hidebound opinions, and we have usually been willing to
fight for whatever it was that we wanted — our arbiter has
been the battle. We have believed in having our ideas, in
standing by our character. We have chewed tobacco if we

have wanted to chew it, and we have worn fried-bosom shirts with a collar button and no collar if we have chosen to wear a fried-bosom shirt with a collar button and no collar. We have always been who we were and what we were, and if anybody has wanted to laugh at us — he could laugh, so long as we did not catch him. The one discipline we have demanded of everyone is that he live his life with honor. A man must have a personal standard in a personal state.

My Great-Aunt Narcissa, a wonderful personality in our valley, always wore the same kind of long flowing dresses — season in and season out, she wore them; she said why should she bother about fashion. If she waited long enough fashion would return to her. She said once every twenty years she was dressed in the height of style. My Great-Aunt Unity never sat down to the dinner table at mealtime. She would walk back and forth, a plate in one hand, a fork in the other. She would talk as she ate and make gestures with the fork, and now and then she would lean over and spear a slice of fried ham or a piece of chicken. My Great-Aunt Frances kept her bedroom locked and let no one into it for more than twenty years. She would go down to the spring at sundown, wash her hands, put on a pair of knitted mittens, and after that would touch nothing until it was time to go to bed. My Grand-

And Cotton

mother Robertson, a great lady named Artemissa, smoked a pipe for twenty years — she said she had catarrh. And Windy Bill, the colored man, told everyone who came to our house that he had been in the penitentiary.

We had a ferocious row among the kinfolks when my Great-great-Aunt Tempe decided to marry my Great-great-Uncle Alf. Those two were not only first cousins, they were double first cousins — their mothers and fathers were sisters and brothers, and even our kinfolks thought that was bringing marriage too near. They forbade the wedding, and when my Great-great-Aunt Tempe and my Great-great-Uncle Alf married anyhow, the kinfolks exiled them; they did not visit them nor speak to them for more than twenty years. Aunt Tempe and Uncle Alf lived in one of the calmest of our houses, in a white house among a grove of cedar trees and oaks, and all of their babies died except one beautiful little girl who lived, an invalid, until the age of thirteen. This little girl was born with her heart on her right side, and when she was dying, she asked her mother please not to bury her far away in the cold. Aunt Tempe and Uncle Alf buried this little girl in the front yard, just beside the steps, and on the marble tomb they inscribed: " Our dear darling daughter." Years later Uncle Alf and Aunt Tempe were buried too in the front yard, and they are still there, almost in the parlor.

Red Hills

Once Aunt Tempe shot a man, and we think Uncle Alf did, too — Uncle Alf may have shot two men. It was during the Civil War that Aunt Tempe shot. She was by herself in the exiled house with her small child when one night she heard someone fumbling at the door. A hand came in and pulled at the wooden latch and Aunt Tempe fired away with a pistol. When it was light enough to see, there was the finger of a man on the floor. The man we are pretty sure Uncle Alf shot was a scalawag and thoroughly needed shooting. Both Aunt Tempe and Uncle Alf were Baptists and they took their shooting hard and to heart, for the Baptist church is uncompromising and places on every individual the responsibility for himself. Neither of them ever said anything much about their shooting. They were not the sort of people who felt it necessary to make public confessions; they were tough and, as their faith required of them, they dealt with their consciences alone. What we remember about our Aunt Tempe and our Uncle Alf, besides the sorrow of their life, is that when the time came to shoot they shot. We admire that resolution.

Most of us in our closely spun family have been fortunate in our inheritance. We have had handed down to us the bodies of pioneers, the driving and almost limitless energy of backwoods scouts and Revolutionary soldiers, the rigid strength of Puritan minds. Once, though, there was

And Cotton

one not so fortunate. We never knew who he was — our Great-Aunt Narcissa never chose to tell us, and Windy Bill disremembered. Windy Bill, the colored man, usually told us whatever it was our Great-Aunt Narcissa chose not to. At the old house among the letters of a hundred years we found this — written in indelible purple on strong, fine paper:

" Oliver hadn't been feeling well for some time, suffered from swelling, but we let him alone for a few days. Then we commenced giving him medicine which acted like a charm and the swelling was nearly all gone out of him, but unfortunately, he got to a dish of boiled beef and took a founders. By next morning he was swolled so he could hardly move. Artemissa commenced upon him again but the medicine did not have the same effect, took more for a dose. Swelling though disappeared, got so he could sing, whistle and go about considerable. But again in spite of the utmost vigilance on our part he got to three squirrels which were cooking and took them from the pot and nearly ate them up — this was in the morning and by night he was so badly swelled about the face he could not see his way. And then we put a watch over him all the time.

" Artemissa again commenced giving him medicine, which acted finally, and he again improved fast as you ever saw. One day he was sitting in the yard and Artemissa told him to go into the house and as he started he snatched a biscuit from little Patience's hand and Artemissa did not see him, and but for Patience's crying out she would never have known it at all. Oliver was then so much better he could be about very much and set up all day and said he could go to meeting in a few days, he was singing. But all the time he told little Patience he intended to show Artemissa he would eat — that he had tried eating too often to believe it would kill him. Artemissa was feeding him very little and his appetite was voracious.

" Well, Artemissa was gone to the field a Friday last and Narcissa was watching him closely, as she thought, but there was a good many persons coming in and during the afternoon, her eyes were thrown off him about five minutes and he got to a dish of baked potatoes and eat them all. I then said to Narcissa he is gone sure. After this he went into the back cabin and was caught broiling on the fire some guts of a chicken that I had killed a short time before. These he got in the piazza as he was on the way to the back cabin. I think he eat about half the chicken guts before he was caught.

" Well, sure enough a little after dinner he was taken and died Saturday afternoon at 2 o'clock with a congestion of the brain from overcharge of the stomach. We had him buried in the burying ground. I am sorry it has turned out the way it has, but I think we did the very best we possible could."

We do not know who wrote that faded letter nor to whom it was written. We do not know which Oliver it was, which Artemissa, which Narcissa, which Patience. All we know is that it was a typical letter from one of the more literal-minded among our kinfolks, and that the subject was typical — death. Always we have described death in bitter detail; we have pondered over it. Weddings have not bothered us much, but neither hell nor high water could keep us from a funeral. We seem impelled to stand company at the lonely departure of a soul.

My sisters and I had four grandmothers that we knew. We had our Grandmother Bowen, a lady named Rebecca whom all of her age called Becky; and we had our Grandmother Robertson, who wore silk dresses and smoked a pipe; and our Grandmother O'Dell, who had the wonderful name of Arie and was not our grandmother at all, but we knew no difference. Then there was our stepmother's stepmother. Through this step-step-grandmother we had several half-step-uncles and half-step-aunts. Our stepmother and our step-step-grandmother were sod relations of ours — not grass relations. We do not believe in divorce in South Carolina; it is against the law in South Carolina

to seek divorce, so even until now we have never had a
grass widower among our kinfolks — we have had men
who have been left by their wives, but we do not count
that; there is nothing in the law books nor in the Bible to
keep a woman from leaving a man. Once my Uncle Wade
was telling me that a cousin of ours had left her husband.
My Aunt Bettie said: "You oughtn't to tell that." My
Uncle Wade then remonstrated: "Why not tell it? Dod
blast it, they've separated." My Aunt Bettie replied: "I
know they have, but it makes us feel so ashamed."

We have had one grass widow in our valley. At least one
person among our kinfolks is going to try everything once,
so we had a cousin who became one of the pioneers in
Southern divorce. Years ago this girl went over to Georgia
for a Georgia divorce — it was so long ago that we never
knew why she got it; all that we ever knew was that we
were not to speak to her former husband. We disapproved
our cousin's action, but we took her side and accordingly
for about thirty years we did not speak to the man from
whom she was parted. For nearly thirty years we would
go by his store and he would be sitting outside in a straight
chair propped against the wall, and he would look up into
the leaves of a water oak and we would look toward the
other side of the road. About ten years ago our divorced
cousin married again, and our kinfolks were somewhat

shocked and surprised, but we all forgave her as she went
to live in California, three thousand miles from Carolina.
Distance solved that problem — distance has always been
one of the methods we have used to hush up a trouble.
Often whenever we have been in a predicament, we have
struck out for the West. We would have forgiven our
cousin, though, even if she had stayed on in Carolina. We
sooner or later forgive all of our kinfolks, for we have a
feeling about them that is like the doctrine of the divine
right of kings. Our kinfolks can do no wrong. One time I
remember my Aunt Nora saying to me: " As sorry a man
as old Gee Smith was, your grandmother always said he
was a high-minded man — he had married one of the kinfolks." It has been the blood association that has bound
our family — the troubles which we have not hidden from
one another, the happiness that we have shared. It is a
comfort in your time to have a tremendous family about
you. There is nothing you must tell them, nothing you
need to explain.

From generation to generation we have had favorite
names among our kinfolks. We have had Washingtons and
Lafayettes (we put the accent on the *fay*) and there have
been many with such Southern combinations as Jim Ed
and Stephen John. We have had many with Carter for a

Red Hills

Christian name, for like thousands of Southerners we were related originally to those Carters who settled in early Virginia. Sometimes I have wondered about those Carters — they must have married everyone in sight. We have liked the good sassafras sound of our Southern names — their American sound; names like ours have never been heard of beyond the United States. We have called boys Reece and Forrest and Boone, and girls Narcissa and Clarissa and Temperance and Unity and Jude. Of late we have been naming ourselves after one another, and nowadays only Southerners could understand the maze — such combinations as Willis O'Dell Bowen, Willis Bowen, Willis Chapman, Otis Chapman, Otis Bowen, Otis O'Dell Bowen, William Clayton Bowen, Katie Taylor Clayton, Taylor O'Dell, O'Dell Clayton, Alfred Taylor O'Dell, Wade Taylor O'Dell, Arie Parsons O'Dell, Bowen Parsons, Boone Bowen, Boone Moss, Hattie Boone Robertson, Arretha Robertson Bowen, Genie Moss Bowen, Mary Bowen Robertson, Artemissa Clayton Robertson, Frances Robertson O'Dell. On and on — the wheels in the wheel. We are very fond of one another in our family. We fight among ourselves, we fight naturally because we are so individualistic — sometimes we do not speak for forty and fifty years, but we love one another, and when you deal with one of us, you are apt to deal with us all. My Great-great-Uncle Billie

And Cotton

once at a camp meeting at Cross Roads knocked down a man who had offended my Great-great-Uncle Alf. At that time my Uncle Billie and my Uncle Alf had not spoken to each other for ten years, and after that time they did not speak for another ten. Relationship is irrevocable in our worn and beautiful hills.

CHAPTER III

During the long Southern summers my sisters and I would stay for weeks at our Grandfather Bowen's house on Wolf Creek, one of the little winding streams that ran cross-country in the Twelve Mile valley. My Great-Grandfather Bowen lived at the top of Wolf Creek, then my Great-Uncle Reece, then my grandfather, and beyond my grandfather's place was the place of my Great-Uncle Bob. My Grandfather Bowen's house, like all the rest of our houses, had many rooms, for always there were many people to sleep there; and it stood on a hill because we liked the tops of hills for our houses. You were more open to tornadoes on a hilltop than you were in a valley, and lightning was more liable to strike you, but we took those chances. You felt free on a hilltop, you seemed close to heaven. The long west wind blew across the continent straight to us; and you could see far away into the mountains, and often on our hilltops you could feel the sight of God. A soaring hilltop is the right sort of place to build a dwelling for the spirit.

Our grandfather's house had a high hall that was open at both ends so the west wind could sweep through during the summer, and it had wide piazzas, and the high end chimneys were made of mica-speckled granite and slabs of rocks from our fields, slabs morticed together with red clay and mud. The house had lightning-rods, and there were doorsteps made of solid pieces of granite — it was fine to be a small child in the summertime and to sit on the coolness of those stones. There were conch shells to hold back the hall doors — pink conch shells, the trumpet of the Tritons, and there was a cat-hole in the kitchen door, and in the parlor there was an organ and stereopticon slides and daguerreotypes of dead Confederate soldiers, and furniture upholstered in red and yellow velvet. There was a small cedar-panelled room that always smelt like apples and there were washpans and water buckets on the back piazzas and pegs to hang coats on, and there was a rain barrel — a barrel that my sister and I loved because we could sail paper boats in it without bending

Red Hills

over. The kitchen smelt of fresh wood ashes, the cluttered
cellar smelt of hams and vinegar and melons that were
left there to chill, and the dusty attic was filled with the
serene fragrance of many years — with spinning-wheels
and old Confederate uniforms and worn-out taffeta
dresses and cobwebs and mice. There was a beeswax and
cedar smell about our grandfather's house — a smell too
of leather. My grandfather had a fine secretary, made and
signed by one of our kinfolks — a secretary made from
trees cut near Hunters Mill just after the Revolution.
There were Waterbury clocks and pictures painted by
itinerant Pennsylvanians who wandered through our
country, and in the dining-room there was a cupboard and
a safe that had panels of tin, decorated with holes driven
by a nail. We lived on the piazzas at our grandfather's
house during the summertime; in winter we lived in the
kitchen.

The house was painted a dazzling white, like all of our
houses, and all the high ceilings were blue, the color of the
sky. There was space and depth about that house, an atmosphere of repose. That was always what we tried most
to create about our houses — a presence of stillness and
quiet for we were close to the pioneers in spirit — an outdoor people, farmers who worked all day in the blaze of
the open, and the house to us was a resting place. It was

And Cotton

the secure place, the shelter. We wanted all of our houses to have the feeling within them of peace — we wanted our country to be peaceful, a haven for everyone in the world who felt oppressed.

There were warm log barns and corncribs and cotton houses in our grandfather's yard and smokehouses and a carriage house and there was a gourd tree for the purple martins, and beehives, and there was a well with an oak bucket. One of the happiest experiences of our lives was to see the stars at night reflected in the depths of that well. We lived in a world of stars on our hilltop at night — with honeysuckle to smell and mimosas, with katydids and crickets for a sort of terrestrial chorus. About us for miles were the splendid darkness and silence — sometimes at night we seemed the only people in existence. At our grandfather's house we had time of our own to find ourselves, time of our own to think.

Often during the sunlit day we could hear men and women singing — the colored women at the wash place at the spring branch, the cotton-hoers in the field, the men singing while they plowed. They sang the old familiar Protestant hymns, the hymns about " I think when I read that sweet story of old," about " Must Jesus bear the cross alone? " and " Sweet hour of prayer." We have always liked to sing in the open in the Upcountry — no interces-

Red Hills

sion is needed for you in our cotton fields; your song is sung straight off into the sky.

All of our houses stood in groves of original trees, and all of them had bare sanded yards surrounded by gardens of flowers. We did not care for green grass in our yards, as our country was a Southern country, and white sand to us was more restful and quieter-looking than grass. Besides, there was greenness all about us — the groves were green and so were the cotton fields and the valleys themselves. The white of the sand, shaded by the thick trees, formed an oasis, a solemn thing of contrast. Every Saturday morning, with corn-shuck brooms, we carefully swept the yard.

There was no form at all to our flower gardens. They were never fenced, for somehow there was some quality within us that never went in for a fence. Our gardens were just a mass of myrtles and beautiful roses — the star-of-Holland and the star-of-France, and a yellow rose that bloomed in clusters, and a pink rose that turned pinker and pinker as it opened, one that we called the old-maid's-blush. We had a small blue hollyhock, there were flags and four-o'clocks and bachelor's-buttons and pomegranates and snow-on-the-mountain, and there were high, tossing, silky plumes of pampas grass that gave our gardens a romantic touch. We liked our gardens to look romantic, for we were romantic ourselves — we were a

And Cotton

dreaming people, a romantic people because we were lonely, we spent much of our time alone. We lived in a world of our own creation. We planted morning-glory vines and honeysuckles to climb up the porches; and for yard shade, in addition to the original great red and white oaks, we planted mulberries and pecans and mimosa trees that the hummingbirds liked. We swapped flowers with everyone and nearly every time we went visiting we brought back some kind of plant. I don't think we ever bought a flower.

We cared more for fragrance than for color — there was enough natural color around us in South Carolina, in the rich red soil, in the blueness of the lovely mountains, in the wild Southern flowers, in the high south sky. We liked to smell things. So we planted beds of hoarhound and rosemary and lavender and catnip simply because they had such musty sweetness, such rarity in their scent. We also planted trees — it became a hobby, for we had discovered what a satisfaction it can be to watch a tree grow and develop. Sometimes a tree will turn out better than any of a man's children, and a tree will endure — its life will outlast our life. My Grandfather Bowen liked to plant walnut trees and cedars, and one of his rules was "Never cut a cedar." He would not remove a cedar tree from his cotton fields — not even from the land that grew a

Red Hills

bale of cotton to an acre. My Great-Aunt Narcissa took a pleasure in planting boxwood hedges, and when she was over seventy years old she set out a hedge of the very slowest-growing variety, a hedge that would take a hundred years to develop. One of my great-grandmothers liked to write about her flowers. She once wrote in violet ink in a flower book: "A garden should connect the solemnity of summer with the cheerfulness of spring, and it should be filled with all kinds of fragile flowers, with seats of cammomile and here and there a peach." You could always tell about the character of our people by our trees and boxwood and by the tangled but ordered flowers that we planted in our gardens.

All of that was a secure world that existed when we were children in our valley. It was hard-working and poor but it was safe. No wonder we, with such a background as that, have not succeeded in the industrial age. We have not chosen to succeed in the mechanical era, in the material universe. It has been our choice to wait.

Like most people who live alone and in the greatness of the open, like most simple people, we have been interested, since the beginning of our country, in signs and symbols. We have been dreamers in spite of our violence, lovers of beauty, deeply influenced by the mystic. Like all our traits, these qualities are defects as well as a strength.

And Cotton

We can resist, we can turn our backs, we can remember
for a hundred years, but sometimes when we should be
working we give ourselves up completely to contemplation, to turning within. Magnolias are symbols to us — the
deathlike flowers, and the scentless camellias are symbols,
and so are buzzards that soar like angels in the sky and
feed themselves on decay. Peacocks are symbols. Cape
jasmines. Somehow we have always avoided thinking —
we have felt rather than thought. With unerring intuition
we have followed our emotion. It is a fault, but at the same
time it is a positive quality — intuition has led us in the
South to Andrew Jackson, to Lee and Stonewall Jackson,
to Appomattox too and to Château-Thierry and to Calvary
and the Cross. We have wandered far off the track, but
instinct has never deserted us. We are not lost.

The cape jasmine in our valley is a mystic flower. It is
a kind of gardenia, and it grows easily; almost it is wild
in our gardens. To us in the South, evil is an actual force
in the world and so is good; evil and good exist — the one
must constantly be guarded against, the other perpetually
protected, and in the cape jasmine we have a case in point.
That lovely, frail blossom is perfection — it has beauty of
line, a completeness of composition, a ravishing fragrance,
the purest color in existence — but you touch it and it cor-
rodes; evil in an instant has done its irrevocable injury to

good. A single touch, a breath, and collapse follows. Always, hovering that near, is evil. Sometimes a scent, like the fragment of a song, will bring a flood of recollection, and always when I smell gardenias I think of home, of our houses in the South, and there is a coffin in the parlor and completely shrouding it are those beautiful white flowers. We have tried for a hundred years with cape jasmines to smother death.

At my Grandfather Bowen's house we got up at daylight; we began everything there with the sun. We fed the stock, did the milking, and then we gathered cantaloupes while the chill of the night was still on them. The weeds along the glistening footpaths would be dripping with dewdrops and glittering in the calm sunshine, and we would smell the cleanness and freshness of wild pennyroyal in the pastures — to smell pennyroyal alone was worth all the effort of getting up early. We would see rabbits darting along the cotton patches and we would look at the blue mountains and think of the Hundred and Twenty-first Psalm, and we would hear woodthrushes singing deep in the thickets. We knew all the birds and we had famous ones like the cardinal and the mockingbird, but it was the woodthrush that was our favorite. It sang early in the morning and again in the evening, late,

And Cotton

and its song was a pure melody of glory, lilting and fluid, like the chime of a heavenly clock. It was a fine experience to listen to that shy Southern bird.

All of us liked the early hour of the summer morning, the unviolated feeling it gave you of purity and goodness — of a new chance, of a starting all over again, of the preparation being made on all sides for a great new day. In our country we also liked the heat of noon, a hundred degrees in the shade; we liked a hot day, but there was a spiritual quality about the early morning that vanished before nine o'clock. Nothing seemed impossible at sunup. I believe that always in the South we have unconsciously worshipped the rising sun. Our colored folks understand things by intuition more surely than even we understand them. They have a hymn, "We'll fall down on our knees and face the rising sun; O Lord, have mercy if You please."

At our breakfast table we would sit on benches with our stern grandfather at the head of the long table, and we would bow our heads while in one descending breath he would mutter the grace. We had a set blessing that we used in all of our houses: "Lord, make us thankful for these and all Thy blessings." I never heard this invocation varied except once when one of our cousins, who did not care for cowpeas and fatback, bowed his head and said:

" Good God, look at this." We had quantities of food on our table; no matter how hard the times were, we always had more than we needed to eat, and even when cotton was down to five cents, there was an air of happiness about our boards. We talked, often all of us at once, and we ate, and somebody stood over us with coffeepots and plates of hot biscuits, and somebody with a long-handled paper brush would shoo flies. Sometimes in the middle of a sentence our grandmother would interrupt her talk to say to one of us: " Wipe your mouth " or " There is something on your foot; go clean it "; and then she would continue her conversation without a pause.

At breakfast we had a big bowl of water-ground hominy grits that had simmered for an hour over a slow fire; we never missed having hominy and we never tired of it, we could eat it and we did eat it, every morning of every year, and we were never able to understand why people in the Middle West, in the corn country, did not eat hominy too. Hominy was such a good food, eaten with butter or with sliced tomatoes or with red gravy, and it was so cheap. We do not know what we would do in the South, white folks or black folks, if there were no hominy grits. We had red gravy in bowls and wide platters filled with thick slices of ham, smoked and cured and fried, and we had fried eggs right from the nests. We had pitcherfuls

And Cotton

of rich milk that had been chilled overnight in the spring branch, and we had blackberry jam for the hot biscuits, and preserves made from the little clingstone peaches that grew wild on the terraces in the cotton patches and were sweeter than anything we ever cultivated in the orchards. We liked everything that was wild.

At twelve o'clock the bell rang in the back yard, and we sat down to dinner. We washed our faces and hands, combed our hair, and we ate dinner at all of our houses in the middle of the day until one of our cousins came back from Paris and told us company would be coming for lunch. Very often we had company at our houses — always politicians and preachers were dropping in, and there was a steady procession of arriving and departing kinfolks. We did not care who our guests were — Senator Pitchfork Ben Tillman could stay for dinner if he liked, and so could the presiding elder — no one caused us much trouble as all we had to do was kill another chicken. Everything was placed on the table, and we helped ourselves, and ate.

I remember the time one of my aunts tried to make one of our meals more stylish; it was my Aunt Bettie, and she had decided to serve a dinner in courses, for a famous preacher was coming from one of the biggest cities in the South. She got out all the best china and linen and silver,

and when we came in, there was no food at all on the
table except a little soup. " Where's the dinner? " inquired
my Uncle Wade. " Mattie," yelled he to the cook in the
kitchen, " bring on the dinner." My Aunt Bettie was so
angry that she got up herself and, going to the kitchen
door, said in a very quiet and meaningful voice: " Bring
on the dinner." Mattie was so mad that she flung dishes
of food on the table. My Uncle Wade burst into laughter.
" Putting on airs," said he.

At my grandfather's house at noontime we had soup
and two or three kinds of meat, fried chicken, fried ham,
or spareribs or liver pudding; and we had four or five
vegetables and a dessert or so and fruit. We all were fond
of fried chicken, but the chicken had to be very young and
small — we did not fry old roosters, we fricasseed roosters.
We threatened to send to the cotton patch cooks who
fried tough chickens. To fry chickens, to boil coffee, to
boil rice, and to make good biscuits were the four require-
ments we demanded of cooks. I don't think I ever had all
the fried chicken I could eat until I was twenty-one years
of age. I never got enough because I liked the thigh and
the gizzard, and half the others also preferred those pieces.
We never expected ever even to taste the liver — the older
men were served the liver. My Aunt Bettie always declared she liked the back, and my grandmother took the

And Cotton

wing, but I did not believe they liked those scrawny pieces of the chicken. They ate those bits because they loved us and did not want to take what we liked best — that was their charity. We liked ducks next to chicken and we sometimes ate a goose or a turkey, but it never occurred to us to eat guinea fowl. We kept guineas at our houses because they were decorative and because we liked the way they cackled. It astonished us once to read in the newspaper that in New York the President of the United States had been served a guinea for dinner. We kept peacocks, too; we were fascinated by their pride.

We were fond of red-pepper sauce, fiery hot, of sage in sausage, of cloves in peach pickles, of nutmegs on clabber; we liked turnip greens, collards, possum and sweet potatoes, roasting ear corn stewed and thickened with flour, cornbread with chitterlings, ambrosia, stuffed eggs, pound cake. We were required to eat something of everything on the table at our grandfather's house, for our grandfather said it was nonsense to pick and choose, to like this and not to like that. He said we would get to like anything if we tried hard enough and kept trying long enough. Eventually I got so I could eat everything under the sun but it did require discipline and persistence to relish parsnips.

When the cooks among our kinfolks did not fry, they

boiled. They believed in long cooking over slow fires, and in all of our kitchens the open fireplaces had cranes to swing iron pots from. Beans to be eaten at noon had to be on the fire by eight o'clock in the morning. So did cabbage. My grandmother said cabbage boiled less than four hours would kill you. We boiled beans, potatoes, cabbage, turnip greens, with a chunk of fatback. Our folks have boiled vegetables like that clear across the United States, from South Carolina to Texas, and up the Texas trail right into southern Montana. Either we boil vegetables or we eat them raw — we have never put any stock in the scalding school of vegetable-cooking.

At dinner time we ate until we felt drowsy; then we would say: "Excuse me, please," and would go out and take a nap. There were three occasions, however, when no amount of food could make us sleepy; those were the dinners when as guests we would have a distinguished preacher named Mr. Turnipseed, a tramp whom we called Uncle Bob, or a politician whose face was like a parrot's. There was always excitement when any of those three were present; those were our favorite visitors.

We liked Mr. Turnipseed because his name was Mr. Turnipseed, and a turnipseed was such a tiny seed. We were entranced by the tramp because he was the only tramp who ever sat with us at the dinner table — he ate with us because, tramp or not, he was kin to us; he was one of our cousins. We liked the politician with the parrot face because we constantly hoped to see a miracle — to see a man's chin touch his nose. This man was a clerk of court and he had a concave mouth with no teeth and a goatee beard that turned up and a nose that turned down. We still talk about that man — we talk about him as a generation of the present small boys talk about the freak at the circus who swallows a live mouse.

My grandparents never forgot Lee's surrender and the days of starvation in the South, and neither of them ever allowed any of us at their house to waste rations. "You can eat whatever you like and as much as you like," my grandmother told us, "but what you take on your plate you must finish." My grandmother did not mind if we cleaned our plates with a piece of biscuit. "Don't be dainty," was her motto.

Supper with us was simple. We sat down to it at dusk, tired out from the long greatness of the summer day, and often all we would have would be milk, cool from the springhouse buckets; cornbread, sliced thin and almost sizzling hot; soft salted fresh butter; and sorghum molasses. Soon after supper we washed our feet and went to bed. We believed we slept better if at our last meal we had eaten but little. We did not bother really about sleep, but if for any reason we should lie sleepless we did not much care. Most of us by nature were light sleepers, and we often enjoyed lying awake for an hour or so at night. Sometimes we would stir about in the darkness — in the stillness and coolness we would go to the well for a drink, or we would write down something we had thought of. Mary, the colored woman, says there are times when she sips black coffee at night, deliberately to stay awake. " It is very watchful to lie sleepless through the dead still hours of midnight," Mary often declares. "You will hear many little things, both within and without. Everybody ought to try it."

It has never mattered much to any of us where we sleep — a featherbed, an inner-spring mattress, a trundle bed, a pallet, all are the same. Up until twenty years ago, we thought very little of camping out, for we still had that pioneer habit, and besides, our grandfather was a Confederate veteran and he brought us all up like soldiers — we were to sleep wherever night found us. My grandfather was hardened by the campaigns, and after dinner when taking his nap he would turn a straight chair upside down and lie on the floor of the front piazza with his head resting against the back of the chair. He was like Daniel Boone, who preferred to sleep on the floor at Audubon's house. It is a little difficult at first to sleep on a soft

And Cotton

bed if you have been used to a hard one — a hard bed you
find has its advantages; for one thing, it is cool.

When we stay awake an entire night in our valley, we
are never in doubt at all as to the complete reason —
we have done something we should not have done, and we
are having to struggle with the voice within, to answer to
our conscience. Mary says when she finds she is not going
to fall asleep at all, she just gets up and takes a drench
of wine.

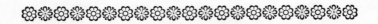

CHAPTER IV

Our stern Grandfather Bowen was a Southern gentleman, a leader in South Carolina, and he worked in the fields all his life along with the rest of the hands. On week-days except Saturdays he wore linsey-woolsey breeches and a loose blue shirt, open at the neck, and from sunrise to sundown, except for the hour of his nap, he would plow and hoe cotton, pull fodder, thin corn. In the autumn he could pick two hundred pounds of cotton in a day. On Saturdays, the year round, he would put on a white shirt with a black shoestring tie and a black frock coat and black trousers and would drive in to the Courthouse in the carriage to attend to public affairs. It was a three-mile drive from our house to the town over a crooked rutty road called the Black Snake Road, and very often our grand-

And Cotton

father would take some of us to sit beside him. Always it impressed us to see the manner of our grandfather's reception at the Courthouse — the deference that was shown to him and to us, the children of his children.

Our grandfather was a dignified man, solemn, courtly, severely grave. He was lean and spare, with great square shoulders — an erect man, a soldier. He was a hill-country man too; he had that gauntness which so many men of the Blue Ridge region have, that aloofness and aloneness which never leave them no matter how large the crowd is about them. He had fine blue eyes that often lit with gentleness and kindness, eyes that relieved the severity of his classic face; and his hair was sandy and his sandy beard was like General Robert E. Lee's.

In the rowdy days after the war, our grandfather took part dutifully in the first Ku-Klux Klan — he had ridden at night like all the rest of our kinfolks, he had gone to the South Carolina House of Representatives as a Red Shirt. In his later days, after the Reconstruction, he sat for our county in the South Carolina Senate, alternating in that office with our other grandfather, the drummer boy whom we called Grandfather but who really wasn't. Both my grandfathers regarded office-holding in an old-fashioned manner: it was a duty.

I think our folks sent my Grandfather Bowen " down

thar to Columby" when they were firm for no compromise, and I think they sent my other grandfather when they realized that compromise was their only practical course. My Grandfather Bowen was forthright and direct and simple; he trusted men, put them on their honor. I think the ever-nearness of death during the four years of the war had developed those qualities in my grandfather. He had faced himself on battlefields, had been tested and tried, and the ordeal had made him gentle and good. The war had hardened his gaunt physical frame but not his heart. My grandfather would not bargain with men, he would not check on them, he would not retaliate even if they cheated him. "It doesn't matter if others cheat you," he would say to us, "but don't you cheat." An attitude such as that in a man as strong as my grandfather sometimes created sensational effect. Even rascals were honest with him. Sometimes I think my grandfather got more by goodness than others in our family did by even the shrewdest guile. My grandfather succeeded because his dealings in his lifetime were as man to man. He would have been taken advantage of immediately by the impersonality of a great corporation — he knew that, he never forgot it. A corporation is beyond emotion; it was organized for that reason. A corporation is like a dynamo, a motor. It is a machine.

And Cotton

Even horse-traders softened when my grandfather approached them. Once my grandfather got carried away with a horse; he wanted to buy the horse, but Mr. Crain, the trader, said: "Brother Bowen, that horse isn't for you — it balks when you least expect." Brother Crain would not sell that horse to my Grandfather Bowen, but that afternoon he sold it to my other grandfather. My other grandfather did not trust horse-dealers.

Even my Uncle Wade would not bargain with my Grandfather Bowen, and my Uncle Wade loved to trade horses and mules with his kinfolks — nothing pleased him more than to make the most of a horse deal with an uncle or a brother or a cousin. One day when my grandfather said he needed a mule, my Uncle Wade without thinking said: "I have just the mule you are looking for." Instantly my grandfather said: "All right, Wade, I'll just buy it." That surprised my Uncle Wade, for to him mule-trading was a ritual — it took time and bickering and you offered delays in order that both sides might enjoy the conditions. That same day my grandfather arrived at my Uncle Wade's house and, taking out his checkbook, said: "Wade, how much do you want for that mule?" Well, my Uncle Wade had been offered two hundred and fifty dollars the week before for the mule, but since it was my grandfather he said all he wanted was two hundred and

77

twenty-five dollars. My grandfather wrote out a check and started home with the mule. As he turned the corner, however, my Uncle Wade suddenly to his horror saw that the mule was lame in its left hind foot. In agony he said to my Aunt Bettie: " I'll bet your daddy thinks I have put a lame mule off on him — that mule wasn't lame last night, it has never been lame before." My Uncle Wade worried so much about the mule that next morning early he started off to my grandfather's to see how it was faring. On the way he met my grandfather hauling a load of cane to my Uncle Tom's, and my grandfather was not driving the mule my Uncle Wade had sold him, he was driving another mule. " That mule I sold you — it was lame in the left hind foot, wasn't it? " said my Uncle Wade.

" How did you know that? " asked my grandfather. " Who told you? "

" Nobody told me, but I saw it when you turned the corner." My Uncle Wade got out of his buggy. " I want to take that mule back. I don't want to sell you a lame mule."

" The mule will be all right — there's nothing wrong with the mule," said my grandfather.

Eventually the mule did recover completely, but for weeks after that my Uncle Wade worried. A mule was a mule, and he was afraid it would develop some new kind

And Cotton

of indisposition. My uncle said to us: " It made you uneasy when a man trusted you like your Grandfather Bowen."

My grandfather helped draft the present Constitution of South Carolina — our kinfolks sent him to Columbia to sit for us at the Constitutional Convention. Our grandfather aided the agrarian revolt in the state; he worked fifty years for the spread of education, holding that American hope that education would solve every problem. He believed without ever a doubt in the people. He held that something divine guided the plain common people of the United States, that something instinctive in them always in time of trouble led them to men like Andrew Jackson and Woodrow Wilson. He believed literally that men were born equal, he stood for their retaining their equality after their birth — for all being given equal opportunity. My grandfather believed in the Baptist church, in the Democratic Party; and whenever either of these erred he said it was from lack of knowledge, not from willfullness of motive. Always my grandfather was for knowledge and more knowledge — for the rich man, the poor man, the black man and the white. His faith in the good intention of most people was basic. Therefore, he was for education at whatever cost for us, at whatever sacrifice, and he was for the highest, the most absolute forms of education —

for philosophy and logic, for all the subjects that trained the minds of people to question. He wanted the Southerner to learn to think — to follow his heart but also to listen to his mental prompting. Once at an old Confederate reunion at the Courthouse, he said in a speech that the children of the United States possessed the finest, roughest, toughest inheritance in the world, that all they needed was a chance. He said the most illiterate and remote in the Blue Ridge Mountains had the fire and the spark, their heredity was great. Like an early American, my grandfather believed in setting a goal for this country higher than any goal any country had ever aimed at in the history of creation. There was nothing too great for him to expect from this country. Like many Southerners of the hill country, he dreamed of America as a perfect state. My grandfather had faith; he believed.

He preached "money for the schools." My grandmother piled rocks in gullies; her thesis was "the country is washing away."

My grandfather hated banks. He was against liquor. He hated bankers personally, but not drunkards — he was not hard on individuals who drank whisky unless they belonged to our family. It would anger him intensely if word got to him that any of us had been seen sniffing a jug. He would do something about it too. We all have

And Cotton

been the kind of people who have believed in doing something direct and immediate about whatever it was that
angered us — in doing something with our hands or our
tongues. We can settle down better after there has been
a battle.

My grandfather, during his day in the legislature,
helped establish the South Carolina Dispensary, a system
of liquor control that failed and failed scandalously a few
years later; it failed as all other attempts to curb the sale
of liquor have failed in our state, and it failed in the
same way and for the same reasons. Some time after the
dispensary had been abolished, a politician said to my
grandfather: " Didn't you know it would fail? " My grandfather answered: " I knew we couldn't succeed, but I was
about it like the boy was who was holding on to the tail
of a calf — the calf was running and dragging the boy
along behind it, and a man said to the boy: 'Don't you
know you can't stop that calf by holding on to its tail?'
The boy replied: 'I know I can't stop it, but I sure can
slow it down.'"

Twenty years after the collapse of the dispensary system I was suddenly attacked one day in Charleston by
a one-legged colonel for being the grandson of my dry
Baptist grandfather. Since this gentleman chose to base
his assault on that ground, I did not in the least mind the

abuse — I was my grandfather's grandson. My grandfather and I belonged to the Upcountry and this old Charleston colonel belonged to the Lowcountry, and Upcountry Carolinians and Lowcountry Carolinians at that time had been fighting each other about almost everything for a hundred and eighty years. I do not mind even today what anyone in Charleston says about me or about any of my kinfolks.

All of us hated bankers and we hated merchants. We hated them because they had robbed us — they should have been shot and we should have shot them, but always they had been so legal in their dirty business that we never felt quite justified in going after them with a gun. We would have felt better about them if we had killed a few, but we do not as a rule shoot people over property matters; when we shoot we do so because of passion. We shoot on the spur of the moment and do not often meditate a murder. Often it is a good way to shoot — to shoot on the spur of the moment; it clears the atmosphere like a thunderstorm.

We were farmers in Twelve Mile valley, and we intended to be farmers, and we intended to grow cotton on our land. But cotton is hard on the same fields for over a century, year after year; we had to fortify our soils with heavier and heavier applications of artificial fertilizers.

And Cotton

Cotton had exhausted the phosphorus, potash, and nitrogen in our lands. These had to be supplied, and these fertilizers were costly to buy. The nitrates that we used had to come all the way from Chile. Some of the potash reached us from the South Pacific Ocean. Often we had to borrow money to pay for these products. We had to borrow in March, when the seed was planted, and we would not be able to repay the loan until October, when the new cotton had been picked, ginned, and sold on the markets for cash.

Bankers, when I was growing up in the South, did business on a ninety-day call-loan basis. It was a contraption that suited them. Manufacturing concerns could deal with banks on a three-month setup, but not our cotton farmers — we had to borrow for six months or for seven. The banks would not lend us money in those days, but they would lend to merchants. Merchants would lend to us, but first they would take a lien on our cotton crop, on our land, on our stock, and on all of our equipment, and they would require various charges; sometimes the interest we were forced to pay would amount to twenty-five per cent. They were usurers and thieves, and we fought them and the bankers behind them in our counties, in our states, at Washington, and at every national convention of the Democratic Party. President Wilson did us some good,

Red Hills

but in general the banking system of the United States never helped us really until Franklin Roosevelt was elected and started the New Deal. For a hundred years we considered it a public disgrace for a man to make his living in a bank or in a big-town store. We scorned men "in trade."

Time and again our grandfather said to us: "Never mortgage a foot of the land — no matter what happens, don't mortgage it, and if you haven't cash money, don't buy; and if times are hard, do without." We were hamstrung and curtailed by such a policy; we had to live plainly and simply, to stay at home, but we have come through a hundred years in spite of bankers, and still in 1941 we in the valley are free. We have come through because of character, because of sacrifice, because of our owning estates from the beginning, and because of our blood relationship — often our kinfolks have pooled all their resources, they have stuck together.

You do not often find stern men who are gentle, but with his grandchildren our grandfather always was gentle. He would wind us twine balls, talk, take us to the creek wading. Like all adults in our family, he spent much of his time with the children, giving much of his thought and care personally to our education. He taught us much him-

84

self. He gave us time, energy, his money. He seemed to think that the purpose of one generation's living was to help the next — a generation was obligated to all past generations for what it had, it was obligated to the future generations in that it must keep up and improve and pass on the land and the tradition. We were all a part of the procession — the past, the present, the time to come.

When we were small, we would travel to our grandfather's house by the Southern Railroad from Calhoun to Easley, where we would change to the Pickens Doodle. Always on the Doodle we would tell Mr. Partridge, the conductor: "We are going to our grandfather's, so will you please let us off at the house?" The train would stop at the foot of the long red hill, and there our grandfather would be in the buggy with a big sun umbrella. When our mother was dying and we sent for our grandfather to come, Mr. Partridge stopped the train and walked up the hill and waited until our grandfather could dress in his Courthouse clothes. The trains always stopped for all of us in our valley, for my grandfather had not charged the railway for its right of way; he had given the company the land. Everything was personal with my grandfather, even his relationship with a railroad.

My grandfather enjoyed small pleasures — talking, watching crops grow, attending Confederate reunions.

Red Hills

He liked to make cider. We all enjoyed that occupation —
it was pleasant and memorable. How good the juices
smelt, how they dripped, brown and foamy, into clean oak
buckets! New cider is one of the cleanest things in existence. It has what we admired in everything in the open,
that something never captured or got into a bottle. My
grandfather did not mind if we climbed the trees, and he
gave us pets — chickens, rabbits, goats, pigeons, bantams,
frizzled hens, and once an alligator that we kept in a
washtub by the well. He let us ride any of the mules and
we could ride the steers and heifers, but not the milk
cows. Once when I rode a milk cow anyhow, I had my
head struck against a beam above the barn door as the
cow dashed into a stall. That night at the supper table
after grace my grandfather said he did not believe I was
feeling well. Suddenly the entire table became silent; a
dozen of my cousins stared at the hominy in their plates
and said not a word. My grandfather did not inquire any
further. He let us go anywhere on the farm, and in August,
when the crops had been laid by, he would let us drive
in an open wagon to the night preaching services at Mount
Tabor Baptist Church with Mr. Beasley, one of the tenants, and with Nora, Mr. Beasley's huge half-witted
daughter. It was fine to sit in the body of the open wagon
in straight chairs, to drive along the winding road in the

And Cotton

cool. At the church the preacher would describe hell in vivid, terrifying words and he would threaten every one of us with the possibility of burning there forever and forever — we would burn on and on in that fire and there would be water within sight but we would never be able to touch it. Always Nora would become frightened; she would jump to her feet and shout and sob and dash up to the mourners' bench, screaming to be saved. We knew Nora would do this, and we always waited for the climax. The preacher would plead: " Won't you come to Jesus? " and Nora could not stand it. We never told our grandfather why we liked so much to go to Tabor with Nora and Mr. Beasley. Some years later Mr. Beasley was elected coroner of our county — he could hardly write his name, but he made a good coroner for he had judgment by instinct and common sense. We have never been so fearful of illiteracy in the South as others have been in other sections of the Union — after all, General Forrest could barely spell a word. We believe in education, but we realize that we must pay its price — many bright flowers of the mind have been crushed by a public education.

During all of my early years my grandfather punished me just twice: once when I called a colored boy a nigger, and the colored boy called me poor buckra and white trash, and I hit the colored boy and he hit me; once when

Red Hills

I bit my cousin Ira, and my cousin Ira hit me with a brick. My grandmother would switch us when she took our punishment in hand, but our grandfather would just take us into the parlor and sit for a while and say nothing. A hurt look would come over his strong stern face and that would bow us down with remorse. It was better to be switched than to sit there in that sort of silence — it was quicker, less accusing. My grandmother switched us with peach-tree switches. They stung and humiliated, but peach-tree switches did not really hurt.

Many people in trouble came to my grandfather for advice and help — the politicians, the preachers, the kinfolks, the colored folks, the tenants. He talked to them all on the piazza. Once I remember my Uncle Jule came to tell my grandfather and all the rest of us that we ought to go right away to the Panhandle of Texas. My Uncle Jule had caught Panhandle fever, and he wanted the last one of us to sell out in Carolina, pack up, and head straight for Texas. This was a kind of fever we have always been susceptible to — we have always been tempted by panhandles and gold mines and far-off bottom lands and distant valleys, by western places that have just been waiting for us to come into them and make a million dollars. Often too it has been easier for us to go somewhere than it has been to stay at home. My Uncle Jule this time was excited; he was sure that the Texas Panhandle was the coming country, things were bound to boom in that country. So he talked and we sat on the piazza and listened. He said: " I'm going." Turning then to my Uncle Jim, he asked: " How do you feel, Jim? " My Uncle Jim was a rambling man; he too had been having problems at home — cotton was under seven cents, bills for fertilizer were owing. " I'm interested," said my Uncle Jim. With that assurance, my Uncle Jule then turned toward my Uncle Wade. But before he could say anything further, my grandfather interrupted. " Boys," said he, " now just you hold on — I don't want too many of you going out there at one time. If too many of you go, I might not have money enough to get you all back."

Out on the wide quiet piazza, my grandfather always sat in a low straight chair — the chair he turned upside down whenever he took his nap. My grandmother was a lady who liked a rocking-chair; she would sit in a broad hickory rocker and rock. The rest of us would sit on the slabs of granite that composed the front steps. Shortly after dusk, our Great-Uncle Bob would arrive from his house down the creek, and he would drop down on the edge of the porch with one foot on the hard sandy ground. The immense Southern night would descend on us all and then the talk would start — my grandmother would rock, and we would listen, and our grandfather and our Great-Uncle Bob would tell us about the Civil War. We would sit in the tremendous starlight, and sometimes a warm, worn breeze would stir, and we would sit still and listen to the story the two men loved to tell. Thirty years have passed since then, but I can still close my eyes and hear them — hear their Southern voices, hear the katydids in the oak trees, the droning chorus of the crickets; hear a hound dog howling, a lean mourning sound; hear still farther away the lonesome remote rumbling of a train.

" After holding ourselves in readiness for battle through the night, on Sunday a.m., just at sunrise, General Scott opened fire on us from the opposite side of the stream. By eight o'clock we discovered his army had crossed the steam — the Civil War had started." My grandfather would hesitate there for a full effect. He had a feeling for story-telling, for the effects. " Two companies were left to guard the bridge and the rest of us had no more sense than to go for them at a double-quick pace. We soon found ourselves facing the enemy in an open field where the battle was on in earnest. Your Cousin Taylor was killed in the very first volley." Again our grandfather would pause. " Elisha Ferguson fell mortally wounded. It was soon discovered that the enemy was endeavoring to surround us. At this juncture General Bee made along our lines ap-

parently as cool as if nothing serious was on hand. General
Bee gave orders to fall back on the Henry house, a distance of eight hundred yards, where we would continue
the fight. General Bee was killed before we reached the
Henry house." We all knew about General Bee — they had
brought him back to South Carolina for burial, he was in
the burying ground at the foot of our valley. Our grandfather would continue: " Well, by two o'clock in the afternoon if we had known anything about war, we might
readily have concluded we were in on the eve of a mas-
sacre, but we didn't know anything then about war. An
hour later we were wiser — a man learns a lot about war
even in the first battle."

On and on. The Seven Days' Battle, the Wilderness.
General Jackson in the valley of the Shenandoah. General
Lee. The sound of the Yankees' pickaxes, digging under
Petersburg. And Richmond, always Richmond. To save
Richmond. It became a holy place to us, a place to be
loved forever like Plymouth Rock and Valley Forge and
the Mississippi River. On and on. The katydids and the
crickets. The hound dog. Another train, echoing through
the sleeping hills. My grandfather would finish. My Uncle
Bob would start over. " We were at Fredericksburg, and
our men held their fire until the Yankees were almost on
us . . . the slaughter was desperate. I passed over the

Red Hills

field of battle a few hours later and the dead were so numerous that many of them were being placed in a common grave."

The campaign would turn to the Tennessee. " Chickamauga, and that was the bloodiest battle of the war. In Virginia we often fought foreign-born men whom Northerners had hired to take their places, but there at Chickamauga it was us against men from Ohio, Indiana, and Illinois — it was us against our brothers."

Whenever our grandfather and our Great-Uncle Bob had finished talking, we would sit on for a while, alone on the piazza in the great motionless night, and our hearts would nearly break within us. We had lost, we had lost.

Very often they would talk to us about Jackson and Lee. My grandfather and my Great-Uncle Bob had been privates in the armies of those generals, but they had known them — sometimes they had talked to them, often had been near by. The relationship between everyone in the Confederate Army seemed always to have been intimate, to have been brotherly and close. Often Confederate privates had brothers who were colonels — our Cousin Bob had been a colonel, and my grandfather had saved him at Lookout Mountain. He had placed the cousin colonel, wounded, on the back of old Grayboy, one of our horses,

And Cotton

and, being himself too tired to walk, our grandfather had held on to Grayboy's tail and the horse had brought them both to safety. Within our own family, there were privates, sergeants, captains and a colonel in the Confederate Army. It was a democratic army, a personal army, and my grandfather and my Great-Uncle Bob all their lives loved Lee and Jackson like their father. They seemed to have felt when those generals were camped with them that they and the rest of the Confederate Army were their personal protectors. It is the way we have always felt in the South toward our leaders. Once one of my aunts went to the battlefield at Kings Mountain when President Hoover was there to dedicate a memorial to our people who had been killed in 1780 in that battle. My aunt came back home astonished at the number of secret-service men and guards that had been thrown around the President. "Who did they think they were protecting him from?" asked my aunt. "There was nobody there except us — just the Governor and the president of the university and a lot of home-folks from the cotton mills and the farms." It was shocking to my aunt to see a President of the United States surrounded by a guard in South Carolina. She and all the rest of us have always regarded ourselves as the protectors of the President — as protectors even of President Herbert Hoover.

Red Hills

One summer day, with the heat at a hundred degrees, my grandfather died of old age, and we buried him with my mother and some of the others in our burying ground at Liberty — on a brave open slope with the Blue Ridge Mountains in the distance. Twenty years have passed since then, but we often visit his tomb. Sometimes we take the wild fragrant flowers that he and my mother were fond of — the star-of-Holland roses, the wild peach-tree blossoms, the mimosas. Sometimes we go there without anything at all — we just stand and maybe walk for a while and think. We like to visit cemeteries. We do not feel we are strangers among tombs. The dead in their life-times had lived a full life; they had had no complaint, neither the young nor the old. They had lived on frontiers, and men on frontiers prepare themselves in life for death. Men do not fear death once they have made up their minds to face it. The dead had lived, and when their time had come, they had gone on. The dead now are resting, they are sleeping — this one is our grandfather, and here is our cousin Taylor, and this one is our Great-great-great-great-Aunt Narcissa, whom the Indians scalped. Grave-yards in the South are like the Southern hills: there is the same looming eternity about them, and we understand eternity in our lonely country. It gives you a proper per-spective to spend an hour among tombs.

And Cotton

My Aunt Bettie wished to put a number of things into an epitaph for my grandfather — she said one of the dull things about modern tombstones was that they had so little to read. She wanted to put something on the stone about the battles and something about my grandfather's goodness and strength of will. But finally she gave in to the rest of us when we held that nothing we could write could do our grandfather justice. We had his name inscribed on a slab of white marble and beneath that were the dates of his birth and death. We intended to leave the marble with that, but my Aunt Bettie insisted we include the name of his outfit in the Confederate Army. So we did add that.

My grandfather had austerity and severe self-discipline — rare qualities to flourish in a country of hummingbirds and pink mimosa trees. At his house we always found great love and affection and repose. There was a deeper rest about that happy house than about any other house in our valley; it was as quiet there in the high front hall as in a forest. My grandfather was certain about many things, sure in an unsure time; and in an age that was grasping, he advised us not to grasp. He believed in success, but he had his own quiet definition of that term — success was a thing within, it was the how of achievement.

My grandfather did not believe in his age in America,

and he made no attempt to equip us to succeed in it. Some people hold that it is never wise to fend against your time, but my grandfather was seeing beyond the vision of those people. He did not believe in the new factory system of the North as a civilized way of living, he did not believe it would last, it would have to be scrapped or modified. The factory system smothered the individuality of life, it killed a man's inner glow. He was afraid of the power of the great factory, afraid of the wealth it accumulated in the hands of a few — a sort of few whom he did not care for. He believed men should control their own time; he did not believe in work as the purpose of existence; he believed in work as a means to an end, and that all men should have time after their work to sit on piazzas and talk to one another, hours to walk alone in the fields, time to think. He believed that eventually the United States would come back to the South for the key to its culture. So he told us to wait. That was why he always pleaded with us never to mortgage the land. We could hold on so long as we owned our land.

We have had few men like our grandfather. There have been a number with his strength, with his steadiness, but few with his gentleness, his self-denial. According to the standards of the South, he lived a true life, for he was at

And Cotton

rest with himself, and he was as happy as any man could ever be who was not in sympathy with his time. I do not know of a single thing my grandfather ever did that actually was evil. Once, however, he did buy some wild oil-well stock.

CHAPTER V

My kinfolks did not live in magnolia groves with tall white columns to hold up the front porches. We did not care for magnolias — they were swampy; and as for the white columns, we considered them pretentious. We did not call our farms plantations in the Upcountry, and we did not call ourselves old Southern planters — we were old Southern farmers. We were plain people, intending to be plain. We believed in plain clothes, plain cooking, plain houses, plain churches to attend preaching in on Sunday. We were Southerners, native-born and of the heart of the South, but we preferred the ways of Salem, Massachusetts, to those of Charleston, South Carolina. Charleston was a symbol to us — it represented luxury and easy soft living and all the evils of Egypt. Charleston believed in a code that shocked us. It was Cavalier from the start; we were Puritan.

The leading Charlestonians were descended from gentlemen in England, and they actually talked about who was a gentleman born and who was not. We said God help us if we ever became that kind of gentleman; a gentleman with us had to win his title by the quality of his acts. Charlestonians had come to the colony of South Carolina with money and china dishes and English silver. We had come down along the mountains from Pennsylvania with nothing — we had walked. The North was our mother country — John Knox and Plymouth, the church without a bishop, the country without a king, and when we named a town in South Carolina by the name of Chester, we were naming it for Chester in Pennsylvania, not for the Chester in Britain. We gave our places Northern names and Biblical names — Chesterfield, York, Ebenezer, Mount Zion, Bethany Grove, Pisgah; and we called places for whimsies that struck our fancy — Nine Times, Lickety Split Creek, Honea Path, Due West. Once in the early days our kinfolks named a creek for a good, faithful hound dog — it is still called that on the map. It must have been a magnificent feeling to march down a continent, giving names to town sites and to mountains and streams. That

Red Hills

must have marked the start of our real feeling for freedom. We understand in our country why Walt Whitman
liked to sing the names of American rivers, why for apparently no reason at all he listed them one after another.
We know what swept Thomas Wolfe when he wrote of
the golden Catawba, of the Swannanoa, of the Little Tennessee — it was lightning from his heart.

Charlestonians too had the same sort of love for place
names that we had — they gave good original names to
Hell Hole Swamp, to Christ Church Parish — but they
named other swamps and parishes for Lord Colleton and
Lord Ashley and for the Earl of Craven. Charlestonians
settled a lowland; we came into a hill region — it was inevitable that we should have fought. From the beginning,
the difference in our views was fundamental, and the time
was bound to come when there would not be room enough
in Carolina for two such conceptions of a state. There
would not be space enough even in the South, nor even in
the whole of the West. One of us had to whip the other
to a farewell and a frazzle. In Carolina from 1750 to 1860
we lost to Charleston; since that time Charleston has lost
to us. The Charleston idea, which also became the Mobile-
Natchez idea, the idea of all the low countries and deltas,
was beaten by the troops of the Federal Union, and
Charleston in losing took all of us in all of the upcountries

100

And Cotton

along with it. Our Upcountry idea is an idea within a beaten idea, and has been a conquered idea too for eighty years, but we have not let it slip from us. We know what we want. We are Southern Jeffersonian Puritans who have never given in to Alexander Hamilton's state. Sometimes I think there is more of Salem in our Southern hills today than is left even in Salem. We still believe in reform — in reform and more reform, slow and steady and never letting up, and when necessary we believe in revolution. We are not fearful of revolution. It has its place.

John C. Calhoun lived at the foot of our valley, where Twelve Mile and Keowee come together to form the Seneca, but Calhoun was not popular with our kinfolks. His land came almost up to our land, but that did not matter. His people were the same sort of people ours were, and our feud with him, like every other kind of feud we ever had with anyone, was personal. Our kinfolks and his had traveled together in the same caravans for nearly a hundred years before Calhoun became Calhoun; we remembered when his grandmother was scalped at Longcane in 1760; we remembered his father, Patrick Calhoun, who was as afraid as we were of voting for the new Federal Constitution. John C. Calhoun was an Upcountry Carolinian, but he also was a politician, and everybody knows what often happens to a politician. He sold us out.

The cause of the Lowcountry became his cause — we were not important enough in 1815 for Mr. John C. Calhoun.

Personally and politically we opposed Calhoun; we personally disliked his wife. She made fun of Mrs. Rachel Jackson for smoking a corncob pipe, and Mrs. Jackson was a Donelson — she was one of our cousins, and we did not stand for any public ridicule of our kinfolks. My Great-Aunt Narcissa said: "We certainly did not stand for a Charlestonian making fun of our kin." Mrs. Calhoun was a Charlestonian.

Calhoun very early in his cold and ambitious and great political career married his Charleston wife; she had a plantation and some money. He kept his legal residence in the Upcountry in our district — our Courthouse continued to be his Courthouse, but that became merely a technicality, for after his marriage we never again saw him very often. He built columns on his house at the foot of our valley, planted magnolias in his yard, and our Great-Aunt Narcissa told us: "He even had himself sprinkled in the church of Charleston," the Protestant Episcopal church.

We preferred the Baptist, Methodist, and Presbyterian churches in the Upcountry to the church that copied the royal church of England. We were opposed to Episcopal ritual, to vested choirs, to stained-glass windows, and we in the Baptist and Presbyterian churches completely loathed the idea of an American church creating bishops. "Bishops," my Great-Aunt Narcissa said, "are kings — they even dress in purple." Mary, the colored woman, told us once that the reason the Charleston folks belonged to the Episcopal church was that they ran about all the week having such a good time that when Sunday came they were so worn out they wanted to rest, they wanted a church that would not disturb them, that would leave them to their quiet. The Upcountry folks, said Mary, worked through the week, and when Sunday came, they wanted to enjoy themselves, so they liked the Baptist church, which gave to everyone the liberty to rise up and shout.

Charleston as we looked down upon it was a worldly place, a sea city trading with remote London and Canton in heathen China. It had silks and a theater and artists came there to paint the portraits of the Rutledges and Ravenels. In the hills we were continental, pure backwoods, and we had determined to turn our backs on all foreign countries. We were going to get rich quick somehow in our Upcountry. We were going to accept Christ as our personal Saviour, and forget Europe with all of its

Red Hills

squabbles and wars and worn-out religious faiths. In America we were going to build the greatest, freest, best nation the world had ever known.

Our spoons in the Upcountry were pewter, our clothes were spun on the loom, our beautiful curly maple and solid walnut furniture was made by hand, by some of the kinfolks. We lived only two hundred and fifty miles from Charleston, but we seldom went there unless there was a constitution to sign or a charter was up for discussion. We knew more about Texas and California than we knew about Charleston. We were a land people in the hills, were inland in our mind and in our experience, and our knowledge of Charleston's ocean was limited to the sound we listened to in the pink conch shell that held open the front hall door. The sea to us was a mystery. It was far off and we never forgot what our Grandmother Bowen said to us about it — that she would wait until she reached heaven to see the sea; that the first places she would look down upon from on high would be the Holy Land and the ocean.

Charleston was worldly and sumptuous, with the wicked walking on every side, but it too was American and Western, standing for a country without a king. It was Southern also and its relationship with us in the hills was always a family affair. It was hard on us for a hundred and ten

And Cotton

years, and we have been hard on it for the past eighty. An Upcountry politician, running for the United States Senate, told the people of Charleston once that he did not care for their vote — the grass could grow in the Charleston streets for all that it mattered to him. And there was an Upcountry woman who had engraved on her tomb: " Born 1810 — Died 1890. Lived Fifty Years." The other thirty years, it was explained, had been passed in Charleston. We have hated the lovely old city, but at the same time we have admired it — it has always had strength of mind and sometimes it has had genius. During the harried generation before the Civil War, it developed into a city state, into a sort of American Athens; it all but ruled the whole nation and bidding for glory, it swept us and all the rest of the South straight into secession. One of our tragedies in the hills was that we did not hate Charleston enough; we were not opposed to it with complete violence nor with absoluteness of conviction. Our relationship with Charleston was like that of our Great-great-Uncle Billy and our Great-great-Uncle Alf — we did not speak to Charleston but we would knock down any stranger who spoke of it with a jeer. After all, Charleston is Carolinian — even if its streets are flat. It does not please us even now to hear Yankees ridiculed in Europe.

The Charleston idea and the hill idea of the Southern

Red Hills

Scotch Irish have had this in common throughout the South since the beginning: both have been against the Northern factory system, both have been fearful of the sort of state the Northern capitalists intended to set up in the United States. Almost all Southerners still are afraid of letting themselves fall into the Northern power of money. Even now we put more faith in a cotton bale than we put in money. We are primary people, we believe in tangible things — in abstract thought, but in tangible things. In faith, in love, in cotton bales, in acres of lands, in mules. We do not understand shares and stocks, the use of money to make money. We want to own our own jobs, to work for a man whom we know personally, to live in our own house or in the house of a person with whom we are acquainted. We do not believe in a system that forces us to deal with an owner's agent. Again and again we come back to the central focus of all our economic fear — to the impersonal life, to the mechanical that kills you.

Our tragedy in the Southern hills was that before we had been beaten by the North in the Civil War we already, within the South, had been beaten by Charleston. Even before Fort Sumter was fired on we had lost in the hills. We had lost and all the time we had been as fearful almost of the sort of national life Charleston stood for as

And Cotton

we had been afraid of the money-harnessing schemes of the Yankees. In the South both the hill people and the Charlestonians wanted a rural nation, but Charleston believed in a country of great estates, we in one of small ones. In the Upcountry, however, we lacked the absolute courage of our conviction; too often we also had coveted great estates. Ours seldom were as great as the plantations of the lowland gentry, but very often they were great enough — we would own a thousand acres of land. The Charleston system was based on slavery, ours on our own hands, yet we also bought slaves — we gave the sons land when they married, and the daughters slaves as their dowry. Sometimes we bred slaves as a crop, raising and selling them like cotton on the market.

My Great-Aunt Narcissa was a fierce Upcountry democrat, yet she had a personal servant. That personal servant, that slave, that thousand acres of land was the clay link in our fine steel chain; so when the pressure came we gave way. The folks in Salem said slavery was a nightmare, a crime, a horror, the sum of all wickedness; they said we were dirty, unkempt, poverty-stricken, ignorant, vicious. Our Baptist church in our valley was called Salem Baptist Church, but when 1860 was reached, we sent our delegate to the Carolina convention to vote with Charleston. Upcountry and Lowcountry — we seceded.

Red Hills

We had never intended to fight that war on a question of Negro slavery; we had wished to fight it on the proposition of a rural against an urban civilization, on human rights against money rights. We wanted time to abolish our slavery and we did not want another slavery thrust upon us. We were Puritans in the hills, spiritual people, and it was a profound blow to find ourselves maneuvered into a position of being obliged to defend Negro slavery with guns. Secession, too, smote us to the depths of our conscience. We loved the United States, the Union was like the Ark of the Covenant, it was holy. Our leaving the Union still troubles us in the true Biblical manner — into the third and fourth generations. It grieves us because we have always believed in the final triumph of good, and we have never been able to defend secession to ourselves after our losing the war. Right somehow makes its own might. It is evil that loses, and when God let us lose, it bowed our spirit to the dust. The surrender at Appomattox broke us economically, but it did us a far deeper injury than that: defeat put us spiritually on the defensive. We have been punished for eighty years for defending black slavery, but we still have our original conception, and we know in our hearts it is right. For us in the South, it is not complicated this time by slaves.

And Cotton

Our Grandmother Bowen would talk to us through the long summer heat at the house on Wolf Creek about our cause that had lost and had not lost. To justify secession seemed always on her mind, an essential that she must explain. It disturbed her incessantly, and she would repeat to us time and again the legal reasons that had made it lawful under the Constitution for us to dissolve the Union. The Union had been a pact, a mutual agreement, and in any court of law a compact under circumstances could be abolished. This was a sad predicament in which to find my grandmother, for she in her inner being did not believe in legal arguments, in appealing to courts. She believed in absolute right and wrong, in moralities, not in legalities. Furthermore, the arguments she gave to us about secession were not hers at all, but had been concluded for her by the cold expedient mind of John C. Calhoun, the man she had never admired. My grandmother trusted the heart, not the mind. She believed in the flame within, in touching the secret life, in inspiring human beings to act because of love and generosity and pity.

She held, like my grandfather, that the United States under the rule of the North had mistaken its great purpose in the world. And like my grandfather, she too cautioned us throughout her life: don't give in, your time will come,

Red Hills

work and hold on, wait. My grandmother loathed the
crudeness of the system that had developed the new cities
beyond the Potomac River. This system existed on ruth-
lessness, on wealth and power, rather than on duty, and
it had to win at any cost. Any cost. She had rules, a set of
standards, and if success did not come within these, then
she believed in accepting failure. There was a time to
lose, she said. The passage she quoted most from the Bible
was from the third chapter of Ecclesiastes: "To every
thing there is a season, and a time to every purpose: a
time to be born and a time to die; a time to plant, and a
time to pluck up that which is planted; a time to kill, and
a time to heal; a time of war, and a time of peace."

The new Northern system shocked my grandmother by
its lack of social responsibility, by its lack of obligation —
it took profits, it attempted to shift on to others its rightful
losses. My grandmother could not understand how a corporation could hire men when times were good and then
drop them from the payroll when times were hard; she
held to the old rural relationship of landlord and tenant.
A landlord provided a tenant with a house and fatback
and meal, the ultimate necessities, no matter what happened to the price of cotton. Factories, like farms, said
my grandmother, should be small; ownership should be
dispersed. It made her sad to see more and more families

And Cotton

from our valley move off to live in the strangeness of big cities. Her entire instinct warned her against leaving the fields, against working for organizations controlled by the new leaders who had organized vast accumulations of dollars.

A human being, my grandmother said, was responsible to others than himself — to the general community. And my grandmother's Southern individualism never included the individual right to make money at the community's cost. She was an old-fashioned Southern woman, conservative in a Southern way and radical; she had that very old radicalism that has always been latent in the South.

Yankees, according to my grandmother, lived off the sweat of human beings, and to impress upon us how intense was her disapproval of such persons, she sometimes would assemble us and say in a pleading, commanding voice: " Don't you dare marry a Yankee — marry someone in Carolina if you can, and if you can't find anyone suitable in Carolina, then look for someone in Georgia, but don't you marry a Yankee. They are just pigtracks." The grimness of my grandmother's life was Yankees.

Our Grandfather Bowen, on the dark front porch during the stately motionless nights, told us about Confederate battles; our grandmother, during the sultry days, would tell us about the women, alone at home through the war. In a sad soft voice she would remember her brother Joel. A crowd of us would sit about her on the cool back piazza, peeling peaches to can or apples to dry, and our grandmother would talk. It was a queer sort of pacific militancy she preached. She would tell with deep sorrow of the despair of war, of the desolation and death, of the bitter destruction of love, and yet she never told us not to fight. It did not seem to be the fight that she regretted so much as the inevitability that made the fight unavoidable. Once she said to us: " Wars cut down the flower of the country's manhood — they leave scalawags and rascals to inherit the earth." But when the United States declared war against Germany in 1917, she told her grandsons who were of age, after weeping, that they must go, to fight would be their duty. My grandmother regarded death as all veterans of wars regard it. The pricelessness of life must be paid for with corpses.

My grandmother had serenity and a wonderful tranquillity; nothing petty could ripple the sweet pool of her disposition. Grandchildren could fret and yell, dogs could bark in the yard, the pigs could break into the sweet-potato patch, cows could get out of the pasture, but my grandmother would not harry herself nor worry. Hawks were the only thing that could automatically ruffle her com-

posure. She hated hawks, and whenever they would swoop
down on her chicken yard, she would grab a shotgun. She
shot at many hawks in her lifetime, she killed quite a few.

My grandmother and many Southerners like her became serene in their old age because during their days
they had faced every sort of tragedy and desperate trouble and had survived — there was no terror left that could
try them. They had fought a gigantic devastating war and
had lost it; they had seen the country stripped and looted,
had lived under the unreasoning despotism of soldiers,
under a radical black government; almost starving, they
had taken the law into their own hands, had ridden at
night and terrorized, had not hesitated to vote tombstones
in elections; they had nullified an amendment to the Constitution, had reconstructed a state, and in their old age
their strength was firm; they were stoic in repose.

My grandmother was a short, round lady, all curves, with
long wavy snow-white hair, and clear eyes as blue almost
as the sky, and she had a notable complexion. When she
was more than seventy years of age, old Confederate veterans would come up to her at reunions and tell her ten-
derly that for fifty years they had remembered the beauty
of her skin. She put buttermilk and cucumber packs on
her face.

She was not stern like my grandfather. She was sunny

and light of heart, and she wore black taffeta dresses with long, full skirts that rustled. My grandmother liked to arrive late at a church and rustle up an aisle. Sunday, I think, was her favorite day. She liked to dress up and listen to good preaching, and she liked to see the people. When the service was over, she would stand in the yard under the shade trees and shake hands as though she were present at a great reception. She and all the rest of us would spend the whole of Sunday in the churchyard. We would get there early, listen to the preaching, enjoy the singing, join in the prayers, and then we would eat a picnic dinner together in the grove. My grandmother did not believe in working on Sunday unless an ox were in a ditch — it was a day of rest, a day given over to the spirit. She liked the preacher to lift her up, to inspire her to do more good, to live a better life. She enjoyed sermons, preached with bluntness and vision, on such subjects as renunciation, self-denial, temptation, hypocrisy. Everyone in our country, white and black, enjoyed a strong sermon, and we demanded ability from our preachers. One time I remember Mary our cook coming back from Big Abel Church, tired out from a long-winded dreary service, and of her saying to us: "Damn a preacher as sorry as Reverend Durham."

The curiosity of my grandmother was intense. All her

And Cotton

life she was interested in the passing by our house of every carriage, every wagon, every buggy, and every rider on horseback. She would speak to all if she could, and if she missed them she would wonder who they could be, where they were going, whom they might be kin to. Often she would put her glasses on and go look at the passers-by through the parlor windows. It was the only thing she enjoyed about a town, she said — to watch so much coming and going. She was a real patron of peddlers. The clock boy, the pot and pan man, the lightning-rod man, the scissors-grinder, the umbrella-mender — all were her friends, and she did a little business with them all, for she said they would not make a living peddling unless they badly needed cash. Besides, she liked to encourage them to come again, for peddlers brought news, and my grandmother was interested in news of every kind and especially enjoyed gossip. Once an itinerant peddler, selling aids to the deaf, came and sat down on the piazza. My grandmother came out and sat, too. The man was embarrassed about bringing up the subject of his visit. He said it was a fine day, my grandmother said it was. He said the crops were looking mighty fine, my grandmother said they were. Suddenly then the man whispered: "Can you hear what I am saying?" My grandmother leaned forward and whispered: "Yes." "Well, ma'am," said the man

in a loud voice, "then you don't need what I'm peddling."
My grandmother laughed and helped him make a list of
everyone who was deaf in Twelve Mile valley.

At my grandmother's we were required to take a light
bath every day and a heavy bath on Saturday. Often my
grandmother washed her long, beautiful thick hair. Once
I remember her drying it; it was winter, and she was sitting in the sunshine before a window in the little room
that we called the apple room. She was telling us about
Ruth in the Bible, about the wheat sheaves, when in came
a woman who was visiting — an old thin woman, none of
our kin, just someone we knew who stayed a day or so at
our house while making slow progresses from somewhere
in North Carolina to somewhere in Georgia. "Why,
Becky," shouted this woman, filled with amazement,
"washing your hair in winter!" "Yes," said my grandmother calmly. "You'll die," said the woman. "I have
arthritis so bad in my face," she continued in a lordly
tone, "that I don't dare touch water to my hair. I haven't
washed my hair in four years." My grandmother looked
sternly at that woman, and a few minutes later, excusing
herself, she went over into the main part of the house and
hid every one of our combs.

My grandmother tithed — she gave a tenth of what she
had to help others; she gave to foreign missions, to home

missions; she fed every tramp at the door. She cooked, canned, sewed, quilted, cared for the flowers, worked in the garden, smoked hams with hickory smoke in the smokehouse; she always kept cookies and blackberry jam for us in the pantry, a pound cake in the dining-room safe. She taught motherless calves to drink milk from a pan; she always kept a collie dog, and called a whole line of them by the same name — Dixie.

She worked all of the time, she kept herself busy. My grandmother had raised six children of her own, and two others besides: one day two small boys, hungry and home-less, had come wandering by, so she had just kept them. She was grandmother to about thirty-six of us, and I am sure we must have been the center of her existence as she was always talking to everyone about Joel's children and Lillie's children and Tom's children. Always when we reached the house on Wolf Creek, there on the granite slab steps would be our grandmother, waiting to greet us, and if we ever got seriously sick, no matter where we might be, our grandmother would come rustling in, wear-ing the taffeta dress. She had often to be away from home because of our illnesses — small children in the South in those days in infancy were fed by their mothers and often they had colic and died. Small white children in the South in those days sometimes starved. It was the black children who thrived — black women would feed pot liquor to their babies. Sometimes the black women would slip a spoonful of pot liquor to the white babies, but they could never let the white women know.

The life my grandmother led was lived in the midst of bustle and disturbance, surrounded almost always by children, kinfolks, colored folks, and company. She seemed to like activity about her and pleasant commotions, but at the same time she cared immensely for solitude and silence. All of us in our country must spend hours alone; there are sensations that can come only in solitude, thoughts that can only be thought in secret. So often our grandmother would leave us all for an afternoon. Off she would go to the fields, and we would see her staring long and intently at the clouds and the sky, at the distant brooding ancient mountains. There were times when she would sit alone on the front porch and rock and sing about burdens and cares and about this world not being her home. In the midst of all her happiness she lived a life of her own, within, and as to what it was like she said never a word.

When our grandfather died, our grandmother told us she was glad he had gone before she had. She said when two people had lived together for fifty years, the first one to be called was the fortunate one. She said she had rather

And Cotton

grieve alone for our grandfather than to have him grieve alone for her. So she sewed on and knitted and sat in a chimney corner for six years. Times have changed since our grandmother's death. Distance has lost its former meaning, speed has increased, we have furnaces in the houses in Carolina and electric lights and refrigerators. We have many inventions intended to make our living an easier existence. She would be curiously concerned about these improvements, they would interest her, I know, but they would not greatly impress my grandmother. She would be interested in our faces, in seeing what quality of life we could show her. She would look for goodness and happiness in us, for those were the virtues she sought through the whole of her years on the earth.

Sensitive, eager, my grandmother was a real Southern woman. We loved her, respected the richness of her glowing character, we admired the pattern she had made of her uncompromising life. Our grandmother taught us more than she ever knew.

Our grandmothers and grandfathers in the South influenced my generation more than all the schools and universities. Sometimes, I think, they had more to do with defining purpose for us than did even our fathers and mothers. They had knowledge and intuition and the

Red Hills

power to inspire. And they never gave up, they never lost hope, although to them the land was a land of darkness, as darkness itself, and of the shadow of death, without any order, and where the light was as darkness.

They are a voice to us, a cry.

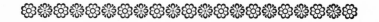

CHAPTER VI

WE are what we are because we are what we are, and because our Southern country is what it is. We are stark Northern people, bitten in spirit by frosts and hard winters, hampered in memory by darkness and ice, and our country is warm and sunlit and Southern, an easy-living violent land, threatened with magnolias. To eat is easy in Carolina, but to live a religious life is often very hard. There is a wildness about our characters, a ravaged quality that always threatens to well up, to give way, to explode. Whole branches of our kinfolks have withered in the heat, have lain themselves down in the sunshine, have listened to the eerie whippoorwills calling from the shadows at sundown. They have sat on piazzas, smelling the mimosas. They have lolled and been lulled. Sometimes, I think, we are like the Blue Ridge Mountains — we are a Southern range of granite with monolithic peaks like our grandfathers, but all about these peaks are hundreds of fallen rocks and flimsily wedged boulders. Some of the loveliest of our rocks are boulders, glowing and glistening and flecked with mica and warm in the sun. The most beautiful of our lilies grow entirely wild on the terraces of the cotton fields. Sometimes it is sad to be a Puritan in a country like South Carolina. A Puritan must have a purpose, he must set himself a goal, he cannot tolerate a shiftless grasshopper existence, and it disconcerts him to discover that there are localities where grasshoppers seem born to thrive. That is why we are taught with such insistence to control ourselves, to hold ourselves in, to do our duty and to accept our obligations. We must make something of ourselves and be somebody, we must not fall with the rocks.

We have broken dams and dried up wells. So many of us have been wasted, have drifted with the river. It is sad to think how many of us have whittled ourselves away. Still there is our range of mountains, and it is worn and strong, one of the oldest in the world. Mount Mitchell in the Blue Ridge Mountains is the highest mountain peak east of the Mississippi River.

And Cotton

One time in our hills we had a boulder of a cousin who ran for sheriff on a platform of being one of the kinfolks. On every stump in Twelve Mile Valley he told us who he was — about his people being in the Revolution, in the War of 1812, in the Mexican War, and coming on down, there had been his poor old father, who had fought through the whole four years against the Yankees — his poor old Confederate father who was lying with the rest of our kinfolks on a high hill above the tinkling waters of the Keowee. Our cousin had himself volunteered for the Spanish War. "Folks," he would cry, "the blood that flows in me flows in you, and I would like to be sheriff." This cousin disliked farming, he would never care for his crops, so we thought we might as well give him a chance — why not see what sort of sheriff he would make; to be sheriff was a wandering, traveling sort of life. Maybe it might suit him. So we elected him, but our cousin had to resign before his term was up.

"He had to resign," said our Cousin Billie, "because he shot his own son when he was drunk once."

"Drunk once?" said my father.

Laughing, our Cousin Billie corrected himself: "Once when he was drunk. . . ."

We had another cousin who campaigned our county as a candidate for the legislature on a platform of perfect failure. He told us he had failed at farming, at sawmilling, at store-keeping, at cotton-ginning. He told how much money he owed that he had no hope ever of repaying. " I want to go down thar to Columby," he said earnestly, " and have a trial at something new. Of course, I might fail down there, too, but it might be just what I was cut out for — legislating." We tried him as we had tried our other cousin, we gave him the chance. But it was to no purpose. Once again he failed.

Many of our people, like our grandfather, like our cousin the sheriff and our cousin the legislator, were not happy in their time. Unlike our strong grandfather, some of these others never found themselves; they only knew what they did not want to do, not what they did want, so they groped and wandered and whiled their lives away. Odds and ends interested them, outer perimeters, the misty, the remote. Throughout their lives they were unable to discipline themselves to the monotony of routine — it was not in them to punch clocks, to turn nuts. They were adventurers of the wrong kind in the wrong age, I think — there was no open West for them to disappear into, no Daniel Boone to follow, and they had not the knack of adjusting themselves to the adventure of the flying plane. Shiftless, restless, they were ourselves at our

And Cotton

worst, and we knew it. We knew why they took to whisky.

There was an entire family within our family, a whole strain of kinfolks, who spent their time fiddling at break-down dances, hunting possums, picking banjos, and planting popcorn and watermelons instead of cotton. They were weak people, born weak, and we scorned weakness, but at the same time we knew they could do no better; the quality of strength was not in them. They were shiftless, trifling men and women, as happy as larks, and the wittiest folks in Twelve Mile Valley. "But wit was all they did have," said my Great-Aunt Narcissa. "After they had contributed their wisecrack, they had nothing more to add to a conversation."

A stranger came once from Texas to a house of one of these kinfolks and announced to one of our great-uncles that he was a brother-in-law.

"You are?" asked our great-uncle.

"I am," said the Texan.

"Can your wife tell through a brick wall twenty feet thick if you have had a drink of liquor?" inquired our great-uncle.

"She can."

"Can she tell it two days later?"

"She can."

Red Hills

Our great-uncle shouted with wild laughter. " You're my brother-in-law all right," said he. Then reaching into a meal bin he pulled out a jug. " Help yourself, brother," he said. " Just help yourself."

We fussed with those kinfolks. We had to give them meal and flour and molasses, give them hay for their live-stock, we had to care for their children in illness. Still we loved them. We especially loved them because again we understood them; volatile, quixotic, they had given in completely to the South, to leisure, to the freedom even of idleness as they chose. We loved them, but at the same time we feared these kinfolks — they were a living object lesson of what we might all become if we lost our self-control. There was no hope for these kinfolks who had given in. They were lost.

There is something lost in all of us — lost in us as a type, I think. It is that something that sometimes strikes us with a pang when we see, high and free in the sky, a wedge of wild ducks flying — that something that disturbs us when we listen to the lonesome rumbling of a train. It is that quality within us, I think, that always has sought perfection and that never gives up searching. It is all or nothing for so many of our kinfolks, and that perhaps is why we are so restless — why flight, why motion disturbs us. We feel that somewhere there exists the complete unity we long for, we feel that if we keep on looking for it, surely somewhere we will find it. It is at the base of our strength and of our weakness — this desperate craving we have for the absolute in existence.

We do not always fail because of weakness either — sometimes we lose because of strength. A cousin said to me once, in tears, that if she won the man she loved she would have to play all the feminine tricks, turn loose on him all she knew of lure. "But," said she, "I won't win him that way — if I must win him that way then he isn't the man I wish him to be." Bitterly, she said: "I am going to give him up."

Our strong characters usually are very strong, our weak ones often are exceedingly weak. Once in one of the houses of our fiddling branch of kinfolks they divided the household goods before they buried their father. And at another of their houses the father brought home a new wife before the tracks from the hearse had dried in the road. If those people had not been our kinfolks, we would have called them trash. They were on the way down, travelers on the wide and open road, and unless they could find themselves nothing in the world could save them.

Again and again, it is evident to us in the South that we have no understanding at all of temperance, of the half

Red Hills

evil and the half good. The dam within us either holds or it bursts. We are a sheep or we are a goat. The standard we have set for ourselves is stern and hard; it is intended for the strong, for those who can deny and renounce, who can resist, and it leaves the weak dangling and lost and outcast, it leaves them excommunicated by the Southern church and by the Southern state. Adultery does not exist in our code, prostitution does not exist, the marriage vow is irrevocable in South Carolina, there is no ground for divorce, to drink whisky is a sin. There is no hope for the weak in our system unless they have the strength of their weakness, no hope unless they move through the whole gamut of sin and finally through satiation arrive also at renunciation — arrive too at the foot of the cross. We travel round the great curve of a circle, and whether we move toward the right or toward the left we aim ultimately toward the foot of the cross. We understand the struggles of St. Francis, of St. Simeon the Stylite, of both Mary Magdalen and Christ. We flay and persecute but, by paradox, we understand and finally we forgive — that is the saving grace of our unforgiving, unrelenting religion. We know that in the end there is no difference between the great sinner and the pure saint. The corrupt machine politician wills to do final good as earnestly as the Baptist preacher. The standard for all of us is always there — perfection.

And Cotton

We are the people who denounce the girl in *The Scarlet Letter,* who brand but at last are ashamed of the branding. We know by instinct what Emerson is preaching, and we take Thoreau to our hearts — the place all of us would like to inhabit is Walden. We understand the unsaid in Melville's books. *Moby Dick* is as real as creation. And we are moved to the depths by Thomas Wolfe. We must attempt to carve the face of the angel even if we know we shall never be allowed. That is the great strain that we believe in, that we trace in everything and follow. We believe in transcendentalism.

The wonder about the South is not that so many have fallen, but that so many have not fallen. Thousands of Southerners keep their faith. They live hard celibate lives; they do not touch whisky. They have chosen denial rather than indulgence; they believe that finally it brings greater happiness to an individual. Denial may warp, but there is no flabbiness about it. No love is better than all love.

I think we are afraid of ourselves — we are afraid of our emotions. We know that to lose self-control is the greatest of our temptations. So we clamp down, we tighten, and there is no middle ground, no temperance. I do not know whether we are intemperate because of our religion, or whether our religion is intemperate because of us. I know, though, that the basis of our character is derived from our spiritual outlook and from our living alone in the open. We have inherited the direct Protestant Reformation, strengthened by the effect of a great religious revival which swept through the South in the early 1800's and influenced our lives like a tidal wave for more than a hundred years. We live in the fields among the growing cotton and the green corn, and we are face to face with ourselves, with all of eternity and its problems. We try to explain the wind and the sun and life and death, the here and the hereafter. We cannot explain, so we turn from the natural to the supernatural. In solitude we reach our own conclusions. We have arrived at many things alone. So we are personal, we are emotional, we have learned to dream, we are romantic. And because there is pride within us and a certain elemental wildness, we sometimes fly off the handle. Some of our people, before they know it, have shot, have slashed someone with a knife. We must attempt to control ourselves, we must be on our guard.

Then too we have a sense of self-reliance, of independence, that sometimes we must curb. This quality again is fundamental within us. We have lived far from the center of help for so long that we have become accustomed to taking things in our own hands. We have had to be the law, we have had to put bones in splints, to prescribe for

And Cotton

sudden illnesses, we have had to make coffins and recite prayers and to do the preaching at funerals. We have a sense sometimes of being the church and the state. We further have an Old Testament attitude toward sin. We believe we can commit a sin if we are willing to take the consequences, if we are willing to stand the punishment. Jonah sinned. David sinned. We can kill a man if we believe he should be killed, and if we are willing to thrash out the killing with God and to submit to jailing by the state. We are capable of making a peace with ourselves that is beyond the power of the state or of the earthly church to touch. We have a ballad: " I don't worry, 'cause it makes no difference now."

Once Ninny came into the kitchen and told us she had bought some Rough on Rats at the store and had planned to kill her husband. Her husband was so sorry and no-account, he gave her so little help and ran around with so many women, she had decided to kill him. She had been to tell her sister what she meant to do, so if the state sent her to the electric chair, she would know that her sister would understand and would care for the two children. Her sister, she said, had wept and had got down on her knees and begged Ninny to think twice. She had told Ninny that she could not care for the children; she had a mean husband too and he would not allow her to care for anyone else's children. Well, said Ninny, the children would just have to care for themselves, for she was going to kill her husband anyhow. With that her sister had told her to pray; so she had prayed, and Ninny said after a while she had decided she would give her husband one more chance, she would give him one more chance because of the children.

Many devious things are apt to happen to a people such as we — to us as white people and as black. Living is not often dull in a country that moves from extreme to extreme, and anything is liable to happen with the swinging pendulum. We are apt to move from strange premises to sound conclusions. Not long ago a colored preacher said to me: "We haven't had to call in the law at our church for the last three Sundays, and that speaks well for our young folks."

The other Monday morning Mary said at breakfast time: "Miss Mattie certainly had herself a Sunday."

"What did she do?" asked I.

"I ain't saying. I'm scared of Miss Mattie," said Mary.

I went on eating. "What did she do, Mary?"

Mary dipped a biscuit into a coffee cup. "Aunt Nan and Aunt Neat," she said, "were walking home from Little Hope Church, when, bless God, there came Miss Mattie tearing down the road right at them. Miss Mattie grabbed Aunt Neat by the neck with one hand, and with the other hand she pulled a knife from a pocket and said she was going to cut Aunt Neat's throat. Aunt Neat said: 'Please, Miss Mattie, don't cut me.' Aunt Nan then picked up a rock and pretended she was going to hit Miss Mattie on the side of the head if she didn't let Aunt Neat go, but of course Aunt Nan wouldn't have hit Miss Mattie — Aunt Nan wouldn't hit white folks."

"Mary," I said, "was Miss Mattie drunk?"

Mary ducked her head and covered her mouth with one of her big broad hands.

"Well, what happened next?"

"Well, Miss Mattie turned Aunt Neat loose and grabbed Aunt Nan and yelled at her: 'Put down that rock.' Aunt Nan, with that, dropped the rock, and Aunt Neat left. Aunt Neat tore out across the cotton patch and left Aunt Nan to take care of herself. Aunt Nan fell down and Miss Mattie jumped on top of her, but Aunt Nan yelled so loud that George came running. When George saw what was going on, he shouted: 'Miss Mattie, is that you?' Miss Mattie looked up to see who it was shouting at her. 'Who is that?' she said. 'This here is George, Miss Mattie.' Miss Mattie then said: 'Well, George, God damn your soul, you come here.'"

Mary said George ran, and Aunt Nan ran, for Aunt Nan

by that time had got loose. Mary said Aunt Neat was nearly out of sight.

Mary began a quiet laugh. " Them two old sisters," said she, " hadn't done any running like that in forty or fifty years.

"Miss Mattie," Mary then added, " went on home and not long after that her husband came running out into the yard. Miss Mattie," Mary said, " was right after him, and she shot him in the right arm with a forty-five."

We pay for the strictness of our Southern code with Matties.

The pebbles are the pebbles. It is the range of mountains that endures, the solid wall of rock. I think of gauntness, of leanness, when I think of my kinfolks and of the Southerners who are like them. Of high cheek-bones, and thin yellow hair. I think of a hidden hungriness, of moodiness and melancholy and wild ecclesiastical power. I think of the ecstatic singing: " I am nothing but a poor child in this world." Of the troubled singing: " I got drunk and I got in jail, and I had nary person to go my bail." I think of the Bible, of the haunting beautiful melodious words we know by heart: " He that believeth in me though he die " . . . " If it were not so I would have told you." In our hills we have walked where no one else has walked, we have rested upon the gray granite, upon the oldest strata of rock in existence. Sometimes we have seemed weary, resting there on the edge of the world, silent, still, waiting for time to change. The wind blows, the sun shines, and we live whole days alone, weaving our own fancies. We were a pruned tree when I was growing up in the South. We had been cut back by a war, and it had taken us eighty years to grow strong again, to flourish with keener insight, with deeper wisdom than we had ever known before the pruning. We were a laughing, rollicking people on the surface, but when I think of our true selves, I always think of sternness, of austerity, of the real solemnity of our existence.

But when I think of the country we lived in, I always recall the exotic. I remember sleeping on a pallet in the parlor with moonlight streaming in and mockingbirds singing at midnight; I remember the smell of boxwood and myrtle, of wood smoke from upstairs when we first woke in the morning; I remember purple mulberries that came from China, and pines and the springhouse and the coolness of the interior and the clearness of the spring, and the colored people about us — the willingness of their hearts. The hollyhocks, the hummingbirds, the bees. And the jasmine and hyacinths and roses, the buckets of warm foamy new milk and the smells of the hay barns, of clean

Red Hills

clothes boiling, of tomatoes cooking, of fresh cornbread and beans boiling, the scent of tallow and wax and steam from the irons. I remember looking for stills, remember the creepy feeling of wading down the spring branch where leaves were so thick on each side, and of finding deep well-like pools; of actually walking into a still, and of walking on and never telling — I knew by instinct the country I lived in, and although the still was on our land, I knew never to say a word. I remember thunder, lightning, tremendous and sudden storms that filled us with vague alarm — the old burying grounds, so windswept and lonesome. The kerosene lamps. The dusty unpaved roads. Sometimes in the evenings Windy Bill would pick a banjo and sing a long, endless ballad about a lost boy, ten thousand miles from home. Old Bill would pluck the strings, singing in a mellow bass: " I'm going to send you to the pen, poor boy — yes, send you to the pen." Sometimes our Great-Aunt Narcissa would tell us about the stars.

We lived in a wild, wonderful country. Sometimes you might think that people such as we, a spiritual half-ascetic stock of men and women, would be puzzled by such a land, that we would always regard ourselves as strangers. Our country is so easy on us and so hard. But it is ours, it is home, and from the depths of us we love it.

And Cotton

All of our lives it has been a sheer pleasure for us simply to look upon our country — to watch the cotton growing, young and green and growing like satin in the rich silky fields, to watch the great Southern clouds, to stare at the dreaming mountains. We never forget the hills and the woods and the fields, and at the old house, among the trunks, there are letters that are filled with tears of homesickness from Tennessee and Mississippi and the Panhandle of Texas. "Oh, I long for a sight of the dear mountains. My mind wanders all the time back to lovely Keowee Valley. Oh, the dear cotton fields. Oh, the dear blue hills." One of the kinfolks, who died in Alabama and finally was brought back to be buried in the valley, wrote for her epitaph: "Among my own, in my own country, I sleep." At the old house there are letters from Europe: "Dear Mother, I think of home."

It was a moody country, now quiet and calm, resting after one of the storms, now violent and disturbed; a region of droughts and swirling rains, hardly ever given to moderation. A lovely beautiful valley, draped in a delicate purple haze. The valley was deep and of hornblendite among the granite, of gneiss and shale, and the soil was red, being tinged with iron. We had tornadoes and rattlesnakes and buzzards and whippoorwills — screech owls, snake doctors, water gliders so light they could walk on the top of water. We had fine sunsets and the west wind, and polecats and corpse flowers and mica and wild lilies in the field. It was a land of heat and sweat, and always off on the horizon there hung the mountains.

There were echoes in our valley. We could shout and hear the shout repeated, rolling and reflected in the hilly distances. And at night we could hear the lonesome rumbling of the trains — the most disturbing of all our sounds. All that was dissatisfied within us was wrought upon by that rumbling, all that soared and searched and sought. That groped and reached beyond. The trains that screamed through our lonesome country were not bound to schedules — not in our imaginations. They were not plodding cars making their way, over and over again, from station to station, working like a clock. They were free agents, roaring through the night, speeding off into distance. They had shed the routine of existence, the humdrum, and the everyday and had struck away into the depths. Trains made us realize how much there was to do that we would never do, how much there was to tap if only we could touch it. How our spirits were bound to our bodies, to crumbs and the ground.

Throughout the South in the darkness we listened to the trains, and longing and restlessness would stir within us. Something would make us want to get on our way, to get on with the principal thing that we lived for, to cut through all that held us back, that delayed. Often during the daytime, we would ride down to the railway and wait until train time; we would watch the train go by. We dreamed of trains, wrote ballads about them: "When a man gets the blues, he boards his train and rides," and "You're traveling home to victory on No. 29." We wrote songs about the men on trains: "Their hands upon the throttle, their eyes upon the rail." Jim could imitate a train on a harp, Windy Bill could make rumbling train sounds with a single banjo string. We knew the names of the engineers, we could tell who was driving what by the way their whistles blew. Railroad engineers were heroes and they knew it — sitting in their cabs, speeding through the darkness, they knew that for miles the South was listening, and they would blow and blow, filling all the valleys with long, sad trailing echoes. They too were entranced by the drama of railroading; they would blow for crossings that never existed, they signaled phantoms in cotton patches, traveled in their cabs through a country in a dream. Gypsy Smith, the famous engineer on No. 37, was an evangelist on Sunday, and his train was "The Gospel Train" that the colored people sang a hymn about. Gypsy Smith's train was on its way to glory, and only saints would ride the cars — sinners and hypocrites and backbiters and pharisees would be left standing at the station, by the Gospel Train.

Old 97 blazed its celebrated way through the heart of our hills. It carried only mail, and at ninety miles it came on south from Lynchburg to Danville, to Charlotte and Greenville, and roared off toward Atlanta. It ran faster than anything had ever run in South Carolina, and we would gather from everywhere to watch old 97 go through. " Boys," Jim said the other morning, sipping a little government whisky for his rheumatism and talking about old times, " old 97 looked like it was flying." All tracks were cleared for that train. It took right of way over every train on the line, and it was a sight to see as it swerved round the bend above our house and gathered speed on a long down grade that led to the high trestle over the river. It hit our country just after daylight, and the Baptist preachers in the small white chapels along the railroad compared 97 to divine things — to God's wrath, and to the terrible swift sword.

Like every other instrument of progress, old 97 killed more men than any train the Southern ever operated. The time it was wrecked near New Market, Virginia, it killed everybody aboard except the baggage master, and how he escaped nobody ever knew. The baggage car was broken in half, yet the baggage master came out without

And Cotton

much more than scratches. It was a miracle, the preachers said — the hand of the Lord, said the men in the cotton fields. The rails in that day were lighter than they are now and trains were of wood and light too — old 97 like many other original creations of the will was too frail for the speed at which it had to travel. So after the New Market wreck it went into oblivion — it passed into the immortality of a song, and never again has the Southern Railroad tried to fire the imagination of the South. Southern's glory and greatness somehow vanished with that train.

Often during my childhood trains were wrecked in the South. Once the Gospel Train jumped the track on a long bend between the stations of Norris and Central on the edge of our valley. It plunged into a cotton field, scattering a shipment of dollar watches for a quarter of a mile, sending a bronze coffin flying into a red gully — the coffin containing the corpse of Vardaman, the violent senior Senator from Mississippi. Pitched into an aisle in one of the Pullman cars was a delegation of living senators, including old Senator Bankhead of Alabama. The house of one of our cousins was located in a grove of red oak trees on the inside of the bend, and trainmen burst in and tore up sheets to bandage the injured. My cousin was not at home, so they broke down a door. My cousin returned a few hours later, very angry, and Gypsy Smith quickly apologized for intruding and promised that the railroad would pay for every sheet. "The sheets!" shouted my cousin. "You're welcome to the sheets. What burns me up isn't sheets — it's that I should live in the bend of this road for thirty years and not be at home when an accident takes place."

Some time after the derailing of the Gospel Train, we had another fine wreck in the valley. One cold winter morning the station agent at Calhoun let the northbound passenger train pass through on its way toward Central, the next stop, and a minute after he had done this, he got a message from the station agent at Central to hold the passenger train as he had just let the early morning freight depart from Central for Calhoun. The station agent at Calhoun said he raced out helplessly into the yard and prepared himself to hear a crash. A few minutes later 46 and 35 ran head into each other two miles north of Calhoun.

My father was in a wreck once, somewhere in Virginia; Jim was in a wreck; our cousin Stephen John was derailed on the P. and N. Another of our cousins was engineering on the Western Carolina when a lynch mob ordered him to take them immediately to the next town. "You can't take a train out of a station without orders," protested our cousin. "It's dangerous to do a thing like that." A man with a mask over his face yelled: "It's dangerous not to, brother."

When we had sold the cotton for cash in the fall of the year, we traveled. We took trips on trains, exploring the states about us — we went as far into the unknown as our cash would allow us. Often we traveled on the special excursions. The Southern Railroad in those days was always staging an excursion to somewhere — to Lookout Mountain, to Tallulah Falls, Georgia, before the Georgia Power Company ruined the beauty of that wildly gorgeous place; to Johnson City, Tennessee; to Bristol, Virginia-Tennessee, where we could stand with one foot in one state and the other foot in another. We did not care much where the excursion went nor what was the occasion; we went along for the ride, for the joy of traveling on a train. The cars would be packed, but we did not mind — discomfort never kept us from doing anything that we really wished to do. Discomfort was only a temporary thing and we would always have the satisfaction of having gone on a trip, we would always have the education, the permanence of memory. We had one cousin who never missed any excursion, and our Uncle Wade did not miss many. Once the cousin who went on them all told his wife he was going to Greenville in a buggy to buy some fertilizer.

Red Hills

In Greenville he boarded an excursion train for Chick Springs, and on this trip the train turned over and our cousin was caught between the back of a chair and a wall. When his wife came to see him at a hospital, she said: "John T., what in the world were you doing on that train?"

One time my sister went to Charleston in August on an excursion because it was so cheap; anyone from anywhere in South Carolina could go to Charleston and back for two dollars. My sister said it was a bargain she could not miss. She boarded the excursion train at Calhoun with her ten-month-old son, and everything was fine until they arrived in Greenville. At Greenville, my sister said, there were more people at the station than there had been the time President Wilson came through during his second campaign. My sister had no chance among that crowd with her baby, so she had to take a seat in the Pullman and pay regular fare. But even so, she said, she had saved a little money, and she had had the ride, she had taken part in the mix-up of an excursion.

I heard Jim, the other morning, calling to a friend who was passing. "How you feel, jaybird?" I heard him shout. "I'm tired, Brother Jim," came the answer from the distance; "I'm tired and I been tired." "Yeah, man, I know how you feel," shouted Jim in reply; "we got bends in

And Cotton

our backs we'll never get out." Then Jim raised his voice
to the tone of triumph: "It was railroading that ruined
you and me."

Trains had speed, power, purpose. They were symbols
to us in our country, and it would have been wonderful if
we could have lived our lives like a train — if to guide us
into the unknown, there had been a railway track.

At breakfast this morning Mary sat warming her feet
before the kitchen fire. Aunt Neat, she said, had held a
goober-cracking last night at her house on the Stone
Church road. Aunt Nan and Aunt Neat had to raise fifty
cents somehow for Little Hope Church, and all they had
to work with was peanuts, so they bagged a peck and in-
vited all the folks along the line to come in, buy a nickel
bag, and crack goobers before the fire.

Mary said Titsy told Aunt Nan that Miss Mattie was
out looking for her again. Titsy was teasing, but Aunt
Nan told her to shut her mouth about Miss Mattie. "We
ain't going to say a word about that lady. You all know
very well what'll happen if Miss Mattie hears we been
talking about her. She'll light up the road — that's what
she'll do." Mary said they all laughed at that. Mary said
they knew that was true.

And last night, in a storm, we went to Big Abel Baptist

Red Hills

Church to listen to a colored quartet that was scheduled to appear from Greenville. Seven thirty came, then eight o'clock, and as the quartet had not arrived, an itinerant colored preacher came out from the church cloakroom and said we might as well sing ourselves until the singers appeared — maybe some of them were sick or maybe the T-model had broken down. One of the church leaders, a great enormous woman, stood up and lined a hymn about nobody's going to save you but yourself. High and reed-like and beautiful, her voice drifted above the other voices — a superb ecstatic note. Then Cecil, who works at the drug store, chanted a long extemporaneous prayer about if ever there were needing times these times were needing. We sang every verse of the hymn called "Telephoning to Glory." As the quartet still had not arrived, the itinerant preacher then said he would preach for a while and his text would be found somewhere in the fifth chapter of Daniel, and it would be about the hand-writing on the wall.

He told us not to be uneasy about how long he was going to preach, for about the time we thought he was getting started, he was going to quit. He was going to sit down in the high chair behind the pulpit; he told us if we wanted to keep up with him we would have to start in at the start. "Launch into the deep, Brother," said the

And Cotton

enormous woman who had raised the first tune. The lesson the preacher then drew for us was that too many people in their religion were like lightning bugs and crawfish — like lightning bugs for they went on and off, and like crawfish for wherever there was mud you would always find them. After some more poetic and beautiful expressions he suddenly raised his deep powerful bass voice in a song: " God don't want no backbiters in this band." A chorus of " Lord, Lord," came from the congregation — a chorus expressing approval of the superb ability of the preacher to sing. " God don't want no long-time liars in this band," continued the preacher. Without missing a beat, Rachel sang: " Hallelujah " in her high soaring soprano, and the congregation took up the next line: " God's going to raise his members higher in this band, in this band." At nine o'clock the quartet still had not arrived, so the preacher said: " Maybe we'd better get rid of the offering." He raised another song: " The Welcome Table," and the congregation raised two dollars and sixty-five cents and placed it on a table before the pulpit. The preacher inquired how much was there, and when he was told, announced we would have to do better than that — we would have to raise four dollars, we wouldn't want a strange preacher to come to Abel for nothing. Again he began singing, rubbing his bony long hands. " One more

dollar and fifty-five cents," he injected at the end of the
first chorus. After fifteen minutes he shouted the congregation would have to raise five dollars, not just four. For
a moment, he disappeared into the cloakroom, then re-
appeared with an overcoat over his arm and a white silk
scarf about his neck. Again rubbing his hands, he began:
" I want to be like Jesus in my heart." A deacon said:
" Thirty-five more cents." Twenty minutes later, halting
once more, the preacher asked: " How much is needed
now, Brother? " The answer was " Six cents." From the
back of the church Sister Stella rose and came forward
with a nickel and a cent. " Hallelujah! " shouted the
preacher, and everyone laughed. Then slipping into his
coat, the stranger announced to us what he had known
all the time and what we had known: the quartet would
not reach Abel that night; two of them were down with
influenza. Without losing a breath, the preacher thanked
the congregation for the good work that had been done
during the evening, he pronounced the benediction, and,
raising his long, thin palms, commanded: " All will remain
standing, and our white friends will pass out."

We live in a world of our own in our uplands, and if a
quartet does not appear for an engagement, some strange
preacher will. The excursion train is crowded and sometimes the engine breaks down, but we were not headed

And Cotton

for Chick Springs nor for Charleston anyhow — it was not the goal that really concerned us, the journey was the thing. Who ever reaches any goal? From what journey can we return? We know of the poverty about us, of the work and worry, but we know of a degree of freedom, of a stunted beauty. We have warm open days and sunshine in Carolina. Much is denied us. But what we have, we have. And an attitude is more powerful than any circumstance.

CHAPTER VII

THE THREE among the white people who taught my Southern generation most in the Upcountry hills were my Grandfather Bowen and my grandmother and my Great-Aunt Narcissa. At my grandparents' white house on Wolf Creek there was certainty about everything — about heaven and hell, about the South, about us and the purpose of our civilization. But at the old house on Twelve Mile, where my Great-Aunt Narcissa lived, there was little sureness about anything — only constant doubt and self-questioning and an uneasiness that increased for our future. According to my grandfather and grandmother, the American nation was caught in the nets of Northern capitalists, and the duty of us in the South was to wait until those nets had rotted with inevitable failure and decay. Our Great-Aunt Narcissa, however, was not at all assured that the grip of the industrialists would relax with the mere passing of time, and she was not positive in the conviction that even if this system were imperfect, we were wise in our time entirely to resist it. She asked how we knew we were not letting ourselves become like the carriage-makers and harness-dealers. It was more fundamental than that, was my grandfather's answer; the country was faced with two conceptions of living, with a Northern and a Southern ideal, and we in the South could not compromise, we could not give in. Our one value was our faith, our steadfastness, and if we budged we were lost, for we had no talent for the factory system; we had not the ability, even if we chose, to use money to make money.

None the less, our Great-Aunt Narcissa was not sure — she continued to consider the advisability of our trying to adjust ourselves to an actual situation. To my grandfather, all life was a tide, a roaring rip tide that ebbed and flowed. To my great-aunt it might not be a tide at all; it might be a steady forward-moving force, a river that ran over dams and in the end wore down even granite mountains.

I remember my grandfather and grandmother and my

great-aunt sitting one warm evening on the piazza at Wolf Creek, and of my great-aunt using buffaloes and passenger pigeons and mockingbirds to illustrate her thesis. "Buffaloes and wild pigeons were unable to adjust themselves to changing times; mockingbirds were able to make an adjustment, and mockingbirds are still with us — they sing just the same."

"Buffaloes and mockingbirds," announced my grandfather, quietly and positively, "have nothing to do with us. We are farmers. We intend to continue to farm."

"Perhaps," said my Great-Aunt Narcissa, "we should try to balance our farming with more industry."

"Where would we get the money for industries?" asked my grandfather.

"From the Northern capitalists," said my great-aunt.

This attitude outraged my grandfather and grandmother. Sometimes they said to us: "Your Great-Aunt Narce is like all the Claytons — she is actually proud of being peculiar."

It was true that our great-aunt had peculiarities. Year in and out she continued to wear the same flowing, trailing dresses, the same black satin bonnets, regardless of the whim of fashion, and her sister was the great-aunt who locked her bedroom door and another of her sisters

And Cotton

was the great-aunt who never ate at the table. Aunt Tempe and Uncle Alf, the double first cousins, belonged to her family, and one of her cousins built a wall, ten feet high, of chestnut slabs so that another of our cousins could not see into his bottom lands. Like many of her kinfolks, my Great-Aunt Narcissa was at times an eccentric, but there was almost nothing about her that was weak. She simply was not sure of the future, that was all; she was not certain. Except for this constant questioning and probing, she was as Upcountry and Southern as my grandfather and grandmother. She was a Democrat and a Baptist, she had never cared for John C. Calhoun, she loathed the name of General Sherman. She believed in small farms, in individual freedom.

"We must hold on," said my grandfather.

"But can we hold on and are we holding on?" my great-aunt would ask him.

"Some of us are. Some of us can."

"We are losing," my Aunt Narcissa would declare flatly.

"But those of us who don't lose will win. The country will swing to us again." My grandfather was confident.

My great-aunt would point to our waste of life, to our

squandered effort, to our lost opportunities, to our poverty, to the fields that were washing into the creeks. Was it right to stick to a system that had brought us so much trouble?

Sometimes my grandmother would wring her hands when my Great-Aunt Narcissa started one of these blasts. Sometimes my grandmother would leave the room. It was a sin, to my grandmother, to doubt. " Your Aunt Narce," she said once, " is like Thomas the Apostle — she is zealous and inquisitive, but if the disciples had said to her they had seen the Lord, she would have said to them: ' Except I shall see in his hands the print of the nails, and thrust my hand into his side, I will not believe.' " My grandmother had faith — a faith that never budged.

It was the facts that caused my great-aunt so much worry, such analyzing and estimating. For my grandparents, it was the soaring ideal. I can understand them all now, looking back, for the time they lived in was a hard one. Courage required as much daring of my grandfather as of my Great-Aunt Narcissa — as much recklessness.

All of them knew we were losing, that we were slipping, and how long any of us could withhold depended finally on time alone. As our assets in the struggle we had only ourselves and the land that we lived on and our climate, our long growing season, together with a formidable list of intangibles — an early-American conception of the perfect state, an old-fashioned religious faith, an ability to endure, a frontier indifference to discomfort, even to poverty. We had our love of family, our love of history, our resistance to change that was both for and against us. Once my Great-Aunt Narcissa said staidly: "We have eyes in the back of our heads, which are not used for protection, but to detect those who sneaked up on us in the past and did us dirt while we walked innocently and gallantly forward."

We were tightly knit and secretive, a closed corporation — a quality that often aided us, as we seldom allowed one another to fall down in public. We were rich in imagination, rich in history, with a sense of time, with a sense of leisure that often covered laziness and complete shiftlessness, without aim or effort. To a remarkable degree we still commanded our own time, but the price many of us had paid for it was economic defeat; we had our freedom because we had given in to defeat. Many colored people and tenants had touched rock bottom and did not care about anything any longer — they had given up the effort. Still, there was a place for everyone to sleep, something for everyone to eat, and we seldom suffered from cold. And somewhere for all of us there was some kind of home.

Balanced against these favorable conditions was a terrifying accumulation of adverse situations. As Southerners, we were among the poorest folks in the United States, but in South Carolina our hundred and ninety-seven thousand white families were waited upon by seventy thousand colored servants; we had nineteen thousand washwomen, thirty-two thousand cooks, which meant that too many of the women in our households sat on the piazzas and hymn-sang and rocked. Our birth rate was so much higher than the nation's and our death rate was so much lower that only a third of us could be counted among the productive-work age group. One third of us was obliged to support the other two thirds, where in the nation as a whole about a half supported the other half. Our ratio of population increase was much higher than the nation's, so that at a time when the United States was beginning to think about old-age pensions, we still wondered what we were going to do with so many children. Where would they get work? Where would they migrate to? What were we going to do to maintain even the existing standard of living? We were an old state with a youth problem.

Our soils were acid. We had an annual fertilizer bill in the South of a hundred and sixty million dollars; fertiliz-

And Cotton

ers alone consumed a large part of our farm income. And we had little spending power. We were not farming properly, we were not organized for productive effort. Our farmers did not raise chickens enough to keep a pot boiling once every Sunday, and they did not gather enough eggs for the farm families alone to eat a fried egg every morning for breakfast.

Our wagon was hitched to cotton's star, where it had been hitched for a hundred years and where it still is hitched. We have been growing cotton in Twelve Mile Valley since the time of the grandfather of our grandfather's father. Cotton is a state of mind with us, a philosophy, and we continue to plant it in spite of the fact that we have not made money on cotton more than once in about every ten years. We were prosperous once — in the early 1900's — and once we became temporarily rich — shortly after the first World War when cotton went to forty cents a pound. We went wild when cotton went to forty cents. We bought big cars and traveled to California on the train and bought twenty-five-dollar silk shirts and paid twenty dollars for shoes. We burned the wind with our sudden wealth, we enjoyed ourselves, and we have never had a regret — we would have lost the money in banks if we had not spent it, and we had rather throw money out the window than lose it in a bank.

Red Hills

Thirty years ago our Great-Aunt Narcissa began telling us the cotton kingdom was doomed — the world market was slipping irrevocably from us, we should begin substituting other crops. For at least fifteen years all of us have been fully aware that our reckoning day for cotton would inevitably come to hand, but even under these circumstances we have not turned away from cotton. We have gone right on plowing and planting. It is never easy for a people to give up a hundred-year-old tradition — our lives and our fathers' fathers' lives have been built around cotton. We have bought our clothes with a bale of cotton; we have built our houses with cotton money; we have sold a bale of cotton to pay our way through school. We have even campaigned in politics atop a cotton bale. And even our Great-Aunt Narcissa stated once in public that she did not care what anybody in Washington or anywhere else in the world said about cotton, it still was the greatest crop that heaven ever gave to any country.

The truth is we like to grow cotton. It is a beautiful crop to cultivate and gather. It has been fearfully hard on our hills and fields, but it has made life easy for us in our country, and up to this very day we have hoped against hope that something would turn up — that somewhere somehow the magic of science would find a new use for cotton fiber and we would be enabled to keep on

And Cotton

depending for our living on cotton. Even now my cousin Stephen John says he cannot really believe the cotton market is about to slip from us. He says ever since he can remember he has been hearing tales about the doom that was about to overtake us, but that we have managed to pull through. He remembers hearing years ago how West Texas was going to grow two bales to the acre without an ounce of fertilizer. But somehow the West Texas menace never materialized. Then there was the boll-weevil scare — every year it got closer and a little closer and everybody said we would have to go out of the cotton business for sure when the boll weevil hit us. But what happened — we learned to plant earlier, to rush and dust the crop, and the boll weevil did not knock us out; it just made us the more determined.

Stephen John feels about the cotton crop as Mary does about the mechanical cotton-picker. One morning Mary came in to inquire if it was true that a cotton-picker was on its way to South Carolina from Mississippi. She said Aunt Nan and Aunt Neat had told her such a story and that they had said when the picker reached Carolina it was going to put all of the colored people out of work.

" What did you say to that? " I asked.

" I told them," said Mary, " I have had so much trouble

159

in my life that I wasn't worrying about any cotton-picker until it was right here on us."

Cotton is an easy crop to grow. We can plant it in April, plow it and hoe it, work hard in the fields until August, and then lay the crop by and go off to camp meetings and all-day singings and fish fries. We need work but six months in a year in a cotton culture. Diversified agriculture calls for a twelve-month working season, and it would do us good to work twelve months — we admit that. Still, it would interfere with a lot of hunting and fishing and going to church. We have turned down dairying in our country, principally because a man is never free from a cow. Cotton gives you freedom. It does not perish, either, like melons or like an acre of lettuce. You can pile cotton bales in a shed and sit back and enjoy the sight of it for two years if you choose to. Once my Uncle Philip kept a crop of cotton for ten years in a barn. He did not sell it because he did not need the money, and he said he had rather have cotton in bales than cash in banks. It is a fine feeling to see your own cotton in your own barn — it gives you a sense of security that few know any more anywhere. Hard times and bankers cannot undermine a man so long as there is cotton in the shed. We have a song about that — about cotton in the shed, boys, sugar in the gourd.

And Cotton

Cotton, with us, is almost human. Cotton is like some member of the family that the folks have had a lot of trouble with, but in whom they still believe. My cousin Stephen John says in spite of all that cotton has cost us we would be poorer today if we had to exist without it. Mary says she had rather chop cotton than cook, and Jim says that of all the work he has ever done — cutting wood, mowing lawns, growing cotton, railroading, working around racehorses — cotton-growing is best. The white man in the South likes to grow cotton; the black man is a cotton man. Jim says even our mules like to work in a big field of cotton. Jim says when the Secretary of Agriculture ordered every third cotton row plowed up he had great difficulty with his mule — his mule knew he had no business walking on the boss's cotton. Sometimes I think a Southerner's idea of heaven is a fine cotton-growing country with the price of cotton pegged at ten cents a pound — I will amend that: heaven is a fine cotton-growing country with the price of cotton pegged at twenty cents a pound.

Speaking one time at the Courthouse, my Grandfather Bowen said he understood our feeling for cotton — cotton was the symbol of our existence, nevertheless, he said we would be obliged to turn to diversification, we must of necessity raise more feed, keep more cows, raise more chickens. We must live at home — it was our only hope of fighting off the machine civilization, our one chance of resisting the complicated insecurity of an industrial world. He realized diversification would interfere with fishing, but he asked how many fish were left to fish for; he said there were two colored men and one white man sitting on the banks of Twelve Mile for every fish in the river.

" We must work harder," said my earnest grandfather. " Forty per cent of our land is so acid that it will produce no crop from which we can realize an adequate standard of living; another forty per cent will produce only cotton, corn, and tobacco, leaving only twenty per cent suitable for diversified agriculture. But this problem, big as it is, offers us great hope, for all these soils can be limed — a relatively cheap process — and can be brought back into use. Our soils could support us all in abundance if we would make intelligent use of them."

South Carolina, said my grandfather, maintained for many years the highest corn yield per acre in the United States and at the same time ranked at the foot of the list in the general average yield. " That fact alone," he said, " shows our waste of opportunity." He said we had a high rate of infant mortality; we had hookworm; we had pellagra.

" We must work," he said, and he began to talk about

And Cotton

the 1890's. "Back in those days," he added, "the folks in South Carolina didn't expect to make money. They didn't care much what kind of clothes they wore, but they did expect to have plenty to eat. It didn't make much difference then what the price of cotton was; we sure had the rations. We lived at home in those days, and sometimes at camp-meeting time we would have thirty people at our house and it didn't cost us any money for victuals — we just cut down a ham in the smokehouse, and picked more beans from the garden, and rounded up enough chickens out of the yard. Today, if thirty people came to some of your houses and stayed for more than a meal or two, you would have to borrow money from the bank — you would try to borrow it, anyhow."

There was piercing laughter. Women in their best taffeta dresses fanned themselves with palmettos, red-faced outdoor men wiped little rivers of sweat from their foreheads.

"Cotton," said a tenant farmer, rising awkwardly from the audience, "used to be eight cents when we didn't know what it was to want an automobile, and now that we have paved roads and have to have automobiles and radios and electric lights, cotton is still eight cents."

"The reason cotton hasn't kept in line with other things," said my grandfather quietly, "is that we have to sell it on the world market — we have to grow it on a protected market but we have to sell it in an unprotected one."

"I understand that," said the tenant frowning, "I understand why cotton is still eight cents, but what puzzles me is the price of ham." He waved his long lean arms. "In the old days when cotton was eight cents, ham at the store was eight cents. Hogs in those days sold for eight and ten cents. Hogs sell now for seven cents, yet ham is anywhere from twenty-five to forty cents. It used to be eight-cent cotton and eight-cent meat — now, I be doggone if it isn't eight-cent cotton and forty meat." He raised his homely loud voice: "It's eight-cent cotton and forty-cent meat, and how in the world can the poor man eat?"

How? Indeed, how?

My Grandfather Bowen and my grandmother and my Great-Aunt Narcissa did their wrangling, their analyzing and estimating at the house at Wolf Creek and at the old house on Twelve Mile. In public all three of them mounted platforms. In the white Baptist chapels, at the Courthouse, at schoolhouses, they preached the devastating facts. In our state only a third of the farmers owned their own land. A third were renters, a third were croppers.

And Cotton

Thirty-two per cent of our entire population were members of tenant families — half a million people. There were five persons to the average tenant family, and the average cash income for those families for a year was about two hundred and fifty dollars. A fourth of all our tenants moved every year. One fourth of them packed everything they had in the world every autumn and moved on. The roads of our state were filled with old trucks and one-horse wagons in November and December. They were our own people and they had become migrants. The tenant system had to improve.

My grandparents and my great-aunt were sure of themselves in our valley; they were sure, too, of their audience. They knew by instinct what to say and how to say it, knew when to attack and when to retreat, when to lambaste and when to soothe. They would lunge forward — the white people in our state lived on eighty thousand farms, the black people on seventy-seven thousand farms; the white people made their living on five million acres of land, the black people on eight hundred thousand. As Southerners, my grandparents and my great-aunt knew how to strike at Southerners. "Who is there to be proud in South Carolina? Why should we be proud?" They asked those two questions and at that they stopped. They never moved beyond those two questions, they were constructive Southerners — they were not attacking for the sake of attacking, they wanted things to get better, to improve. "Who is proud? We all are. Why should we be proud? For many reasons." Then they would list our great Southern intangibles. We were poor, but in spite of poverty we had order in our life. We had a spiritual reason for being. We had a great well to draw from. We knew what we wanted from life. We were not easily discouraged. We were not giving up — neither our white people nor our black people. We would face our troubles. Troubles were nothing new to us. We were used to adversity.

"We are old," my grandfather would say, "but with so many young people about us, we also are young. We have both wisdom and energy. We will work our way out somehow. We must work our way out, and we will not only save ourselves — we will contribute to the readjustment of the rest of America as well. We at last are approaching a true American civilization. The North has been in the saddle since 1865, and the North has built up the magnificent physical structure of the United States — the physical structure we are so proud of. We Southerners believe the North is going to be obliged to alter its system to moderate the Yankeeness of the United States with some of the old principles of the South. We are going to

And Cotton

become part work-world of the North, part leisure-world of the South, and the America that we see coming up will have Northerners who can have a good time without a remorseful conscience, and Southerners who will stick a little closer to business."

Always my grandfather would end his sermons with one commanding double idea: we must work harder in the South than we had ever worked, we must wait for our time to come.

Once at a meeting at Praters Schoolhouse on Twelve Mile, a tenant farmer interrupted my grandfather. My grandfather was explaining how much higher the South's birth rate was than the rest of the nation's; he predicted the last final wave of American migration would come — not from Europe, but from the South to the North and West of the United States. Exultantly a tenant — coatless, in overalls and a worn old blue shirt — jumped up from a rear seat. " Brother Bowen," he cried, " damned if we won't whip the Yankees yet."

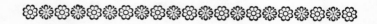

CHAPTER VIII

At Wolf Creek my grandfather and grandmother commanded our attitude, they dictated, and in a great degree they succeeded, for we understood the depth of their anguish and the warmth of their love. At the old house on Twelve Mile our Great-Aunt Narcissa made no attempt whatsoever to dictate, and she too succeeded. She continued to the end of her life to doubt our physical ability to hold out against the power of the North, our ability to last. So much would be decided by time alone, by circumstance. So instead of outlining thought for us, she suggested a type of action — whatever we had to do, we should know how to do it. We ought to prepare ourselves for any condition, to make ourselves ready, with

And Cotton

our minds free from brittleness. We should study, we should learn, we should try to know more than anyone else in the country. Our Great-Aunt Narcissa bought one dress a year, one pair of shoes; she spent a few odd dollars on wool for knitting, a few dollars on presents — everything else that she had she used to send us to schools.

Our Great-Aunt Narcissa was like a willow and a reed — tall, dignified, a lady with sweeping gestures, and like so many of my kinfolks she had corn-silk hair, and blue eyes, and high cheek-bones. Her face was ravaged like a rock, worn and wrinkled — a lovable face, for it made you think of the storms it had overcome. It had granite strength, granite security. You knew from that face that only time could conquer my Great-Aunt Narcissa. She had a quality, untouched after eighty years by struggle. She made me think of cathedrals — of their quiet and cool and peace. You felt there were depths within her.

My Grandmother Bowen, when she wished to be alone, would walk to the tops of mountains and stare into immeasurable space; my Great-Aunt Narcissa would slip under the dark rhododendron bushes and sit by the deep pools in the dimness of half-light and silence. I think my Great-Aunt Narcissa suspected that life came out of darkness, that the spirit welled from the depths.

She soared. She told us to live a life, to run risks, to

take chances. She said throw rocks while we were young, shatter glass. She read Browning to us: " A man's reach should exceed his grasp, or what's a heaven for? " Sometimes she talked with Margit, the last of her former slaves, about angels and premonitions, and once she told her there was more than music in the air — there were spirits, waiting for us to discover the signal of their being. She believed in things she had never seen, in sounds she had never heard, and she had faith in the resurrection, in the many mansions. But just the same, I think she was uneasy about dying, she had a fearfulness of death, of the loneliness of the actual shadow, and as she got older, this uneasiness seemed to increase. Sometimes in the flower garden she would ask Margit to sing to her the spiritual about death, about not minding dying but hating so to go, and about every son of man having to travel that final road alone. One time she confessed to me that the reason she always attended funerals was to help swell the crowd; she said she hoped when her funeral came that many would attend it, it was all that she wanted at her funeral — a very large crowd. Somehow she felt it would be a comfort if all of us stood by as she started on the journey. Once she asked my sister and me if we could pray for one single thing and have it granted, what one thing would we choose. My sister decided she would ask for happiness.

And Cotton

I said I would pray for fame. Our Aunt Narce said if she
had the chance she would seek the certainty of everlast-
ing rest. She lived longer than anyone else in her generation, and at times toward the end she seemed as lonesome
as the tomb.

She talked hardly at all about the Civil War. It was of
original America that she talked, of the West, of the times
before the Civil War, of the country before secession. Her
grandfather had fought in the Revolution, and she herself remembered the end of the Carolinian frontier — she
told us of the wild pigeons, of the wild deer, and she told
us tales of the British, whom she called the Redcoats. She
talked of people always leaving — of men telling of finding land in the West so rich that two hundred bushels of
corn could be grown on an acre without a sack of fertilizer
— strawberries grew as big as walnuts in the West, even
flowers were brighter in the West. She said she understood
why so many Western people often told such whoppers —
it was an inherited characteristic, they had acquired the
art from their fathers.

My Great-Aunt Narcissa deeply loved the West, she
had seen so many of our kinfolks pack up and start off
toward the mountains with all that they had in a two-
horse wagon. So many hopes had gone with them, and
such faith, such a desperate belief in the future. Many

Red Hills

had started in our Aunt Narce's lifetime, and few had ever come back. Pride had kept many of them ever from returning.

The West, to my great-aunt, was like all existence — it had been built upon the graves of hopes with tears and sweat. As she had known so many of the first Westerners, she often spoke of the open spaces to us in terms of wasted life, of lost effort — she remembered the weak ones, the ones who had not made the grade, she remembered the casualties in the battle. She asked us to remember all those who had given all that they had to the new country and who had failed; when we read in histories of the successes, to think of the failures. Daniel Boone, she said, had been a fortunate one. The Boones we should not forget, she said, were the three grandsons of Daniel Boone, whom Parkman knew on the Oregon Trail — the three tall young boys who died in obscurity in the Sierra Nevadas, opening a new trail to California. Our Great-Aunt Narcissa was like our Grandmother Bowen, who kept telling us about her dead brother Joel. Our great-aunt and our grandmother wept for the wounded and the slain. For the sacredness and costliness of the price.

One time in the attic at the old house our Great-Aunt Narcissa showed us a letter, dated from Texas, eighty years before:

172

And Cotton

"Dear Uncle Stevie — well, I suppose you have heared some wonderful tales about us all. I will tell the truth about it all. I suppose you have heared Pa had to come and live with us to get his living which is not so. Mr. Raney bought this place. It took all the money we could scrape together to make the last payment which was $1,000. We then had neither meat, bread nor money. We had been boarding, had that to pay. Pa and Ma had meat and bread but no home — what else could either of us do but join? You have heared Pa had run through and drunk up everything he had. Uncle Stevie, how could he do this when he had nothing — he never has had anything much since he left Mississippi. When he left Mississippi he had about $200 and Cousin Caldwell had the same amount and when we all got to Louisiana Pa didn't have a red cent. He borrowed $20 of Cousin Caldwell and when we landed in Texas, Cousin Caldwell had $53 in specie, $13.50 in greenbacks, Pa had $10, which he had borrowed, and he had two mules and the old mare. The mare died. He sold the mules for $150. He bought provisions with half of the money and the other half he paid the freight on Sam, Fred and Watts Caldwell's baggage and he never got one cent of it back. That is why I am going that far back, for now, the worst word that Sam, Fred and Watts can say about Pa and Ma, they say it.

I can't imagine why they say so much about him drinking and getting drunk so often when there is not one of them but will get drunk and loves whisky just as well as Pa.

"I have heared that Sam wrote back and said I was dissatisfied with Texas. I am well satisfied. Mother and all the rest that came in our crowd are satisfied — and even if they weren't they wouldn't let on. We all went to work when we got here and had plenty to divide with the others when they got here — Sam Caldwell lived in the house with Pa for a year and never put in one bite of provisions, then would curse at table because they did not live better.

"And as for the other boys — well, Fred Caldwell was owing $60 for his rations, he said he was going to stay in one place as long as he could get credit, then move again. It wasn't long before the whole of Texas was on to that fellow's tactics. Uncle Stevie, tell me what room has any of them to say such things?

"I will tell you another trick Sam Caldwell done on Mother. Mother, Cade and Emmer made them a separate cotton patch which made three parts of a bale. They all went to town to trade out their cotton. Ma took up all of hers but one dollar as there was no bed cord coffee nor black pepper. Emmer took up all hers but $2.15 Sam

And Cotton

went to the clerk, says he would take up that money of Ma's and Emmer's, when the goods come, Ma and Emmer sent for their things and the word came back Sam had taken up that money and was to settle with them. When Ma named it to him, he said it was not so, but guilty conscience needs no accusing.

" Uncle Stevie, I expect you believe all you heared but I think you will believe me. And if you could be here just a little while you would see that all the above was true. This and what you have heared before is both sides of it. So will say no more on this subject.

" This leaves us well. I will send you my little Tommy's picture so you can see how pretty he is — Ma and Pa send their well wishes to all the family and wish them to write. You must write soon and give us all the news there afloat. All the connection are all well so far as I know. With love, Mary Caldwell Raney."

Our Great-Aunt Narcissa said to us: " One of the real pioneers of Texas was your Cousin Mary."

Our great-aunt then showed us two letters, a hundred years old, written from Tennessee:

" Ma, maybe we'll get over the mountains next year. No hope for this year. Temple Caldwell is talking of going on to Alabama soon. What he is going to do is unknown, but if I was a man I'd try to be a man; there is plenty of

land among the kinfolks if he would take up farming for
a living. I can but wish him well. They put off the com-
munion and footwashing at Yellow Creek on account of
the bad behavior of Sarah Caldwell. I hate to tell you
but that girl is a wild one. And you ought to have seen
Cousin Temple walking barefooted, crying, with a flowing
duster on — coming down on his knees. Old Jim Kelly that
used to live below us on Keowee preached the sermon.

"Ma, I certainly would have enjoyed being with you
when you all found that bed of arbutus. I think of our
hunts for it — the walks we used to take on lovely Sab-
bath mornings when I was still there. How delicate arbutus is. I have never seen any of it since.

"Ma, wheat is a complete failure, oats is a failure, killed
by the rust. Times are very hard, but not so hard as they
are going to be this fall. Some people are going to suffer."

"Brother Carter, the day is very cold. I am sitting in
Mr. Carr's blacksmith shop and the fire is low. I am not
well but I am inured to sad changes and disappointments.
During the summer we had made preparations to move
to Alabama where Mr. Carr says there is more congenial
prospects than here — Mr. Carr says he don't like it in
Tennessee, says the country is all right but the folks are
rude and uneducated, they live like dogs. We were all
ready to go but the news came of Eliza Caldwell's sud-

And Cotton

den death and my own bad health prevented our doing so. Life is full of bitter days. When the news of Eliza's death came to us, I thought I couldn't stand it. Kindred affection will naturally cause us to weep for dear Eliza, but no one except Eliza's husband can at present feel her loss so deeply as I. Since her death I do not feel so satisfied to live in the West. I would gladly change my home in the West for any kind of a cabin in Carolina. Life is but a day at most, then why not spend it among one's own? I hope you will write soon as you get this nothing delights me more than a letter from home."

Our Great-Aunt Narcissa said our cousin Patience wrote those letters to the Stephen John who was the great-uncle of our grandmother. She said Cousin Patience and Mr. Carr wandered on into Alabama and there Cousin Patience died. Tennessee was fame for James Robertson, it was bitterness for Cousin Patience. Alabama was a cross to bear, a burden and a grave. The high Sierras were failure for the Boone grandsons. The yellow rose of Texas was sacrifice.

Our Great-Aunt Narcissa fed hominy to the birds in winter. She knew the names of all the wild flowers and she taught the names of them all to us — the small blue anemone that bloomed in ravines in February, the first of our blossoms and the purest blue, the flower of faith, of new hope; the bloodroot, the May apple, the wild yellow azalea, the corpse flower, the trailing arbutus, the purple gentian — the last of the blossoms of the autumn, struggling to perfection in the last minutes of existence. She loved the wildness of the wild flowers, she told us to consider the use they made of their chances — how the wild plum on the cotton terrace, growing wild, had beauty that no rose in any hothouse could match. The hard life was the best life — sympathy, understanding, strength resulted from struggle. This was the same exact attitude that our grandmother advocated: " Shrink not from facing sorrow. . . ."

Our great-aunt loved the fields, the hills, cotton plants, the clear star in our evening sky, the bastard saffron blossoms and moon vines, the crimson poke, and the south wind and the fierce Southern sun, shining straight down, a hundred degrees in the shade. She watched the white drift of the plum trees, the dogwood and the yellow jessamine and jewelweeds and the wild Indian turnips. She heard the hidden song of the hermit thrush. She loved the space of our country, its depth, and she would say to us: " It is ours." Like the thrush, like us all, she was born under the star.

Each day she read a chapter in the Bible. Of the ma-

And Cotton

terial world she was often in doubt, but when the spirit
was concerned, our Great-Aunt Narcissa had divine faith.
She believed the Bible word for word, verse by verse, page
by page. There were no contradictions for her in the great
Book, she accepted everything, and if there were passages
that she did not understand, then she did not attempt
to understand them; if it were intended that she know
the meaning of hidden passages, then the time would
come when she would know the meaning. Everything in
time would be made clear — you had to grow in goodness
in order to grasp meanings, you had to acquire glory.
Our great-aunt expected to be raised not only in the
spirit but in the flesh; she would wear celestial garments,
clothes that would never wear out, and in heaven she
would know the angels by their physical appearance and
they would know her. She believed. She would dwell in
the house of the Lord forever and with her would be all
of the dear ones she had loved.

She knitted socks, her one domestic virtue. She cared
nothing at all about the inside of a house so long as the
place was clean and comfortable. Cooking had no interest
for her, nor had sewing, and instead of canning fruit she
brewed it — she made wine of anything that would fer-
ment, blackberry wine, muscadine wine, scuppernong
wine, elderberry wine, dandelion wine, persimmon and

Red Hills

locust beer, a cordial of peaches. During the hard times of the Civil War she had sat for ten and twelve hours a day over a loom, weaving, but it was the duty alone of weaving that held her; she would prop books before the loom and read, she memorized *The Lady of the Lake* while weaving. She had taught herself the French language, and she could read its printed pages easily, but her pronunciation of French words was Carolinian English.

Our great-aunt's companions were Margit, the last living Clayton ex-slave, and Windy Bill, the gentle murderer who had served a term in the penitentiary. Margit and Bill were Senegambians, full-blooded black, and like my great-aunt they had been in Twelve Mile Valley since the beginning. They were of the children of the children of the children. Margit cooked; Bill fed the mules, cut stovewood, played on a banjo, drank lightning liquor, hunted possums, talked about the world and everything on the broad piazza. Margit was always getting in strokes for the Lord on the side — always urging our great-aunt to forgive more easily, always scolding Bill for living a bad life. Margit asked every child, white and black, who came to the old house: "Honey, what church do you go to?" If the child seemed confused, Margit would add:

And Cotton

"That's all right, honey, it don't make no difference. Still, I guess it does make some difference if you don't go to any church. Honey, do you go to the Baptist church?" If the child said yes, then Margit would beam. "That's fine, honey." If the child said: "I go to the Methodist church," Margit would reply sorrowfully: "Well, keep on, honey — the Methodist church is a good church in its way."

The three at the old house were restless. For days and weeks they would travel up and down the valley, visiting kinfolks and staying away from home. When our great-aunt would tire of the old house, she would hitch up the carriage and drive in any direction. Margit would ramble into town and cook in cafés. Windy Bill was a cuckoo — he had an understanding in a number of homes. Bill always left the old house in the autumn after he had sold the corn he had grown in his patches. The length of his trip would depend on how good his crop had been, for he never came home until his money was gone. He went to town and attended singings and dances and revival meetings. He seldom traveled more than five miles from the house, but always he came back with tales of tremendous activity and doings. Usually he had skirted and escaped the depths of trouble. In simple words he would always tell us what had happened. Usually the law would be involved — "I was at Bethany Grove Church, and the law arrived and arrested about half of the congregation. The law said we were drinking. One old brother, ninety years old, was eating fish and he laid down in the church-yard for a rest, and the law said to him: 'We'll give you a rest,' and they carried the old brother to jail."

Bill toted a razor. He never called a gun a gun — he called a gun a twenty-two, a thirty-eight, a special forty-four. He was at Cherrys Crossing the time Sampson, the gambling man, was killed by a thirty-eight. He said: "There was nothing in the cabin but a few smoking lamps and about fifty people, and Sampson came — he was a gambling man from the heart and he was just home from the chain gang. Sampson thanked the congregation for a hundred dollars and then the shooting started." Bill said: "I broke a window pane and eased across a cotton patch, and I don't know who did the shooting or who got the hundred dollars. I don't know nothing — nobody knows nothing."

It was at Bethany Grove Church that Bill himself was charged with killing one of the brethren. He told my great-aunt he drank some moonshine, and that when he came to, they told him a man was dead and that he had killed him. Bill said he did not believe he had killed the man, for if he had, then the man would have "hanted" him, and the man had not "hanted" him. Therefore he had not killed him. Someone else had done the killing. Bill convinced my great-aunt, but he could not convince the jury; witnesses testified they had seen Bill shoot. So down to Columbia went Bill — off to the penitentiary. As time went on, he became a trusty, he hunted possums in the swamps for the Governor's table, and during the entire term of one Governor he hoed roses around the State-house. Almost every day Bill would say to the Governor: "Boss, when are you going to let me go back to Miss Narcissa?" The Governor would answer: "Bill, if I let you go, who will hoe the roses?" Bill would say: "I reckon that's right, Governor."

The Governor who succeeded this Governor was a demagogue who began pardoning hundreds of men in the penitentiary. You made certain arrangements and the Governor granted a pardon. We objected to this procedure, but because of Bill we took one of the steps that have been characteristic of our conduct for a hundred years: we opposed this Governor, we opposed his abuse of the pardon power, but since hundreds of prisoners were being freed, we made arrangements and secured freedom for Bill.

Bill came back to the old house like a knight from a

crusade. Wonderful things went on at the penitentiary, he told us; wonderful gamblers were in there; wonderful guards stood on the stone walls — Bill said those guards had guns that would shoot from there to Richmond. He told us he was nothing but a plain cotton-field nigger when he went down to the penitentiary, but now he was as sharp as a Yankee. He went off to Pickens the first Saturday night of his return, and on the next afternoon my great-aunt and Margit, walking home from taking flowers to the cemetery, found him in a gully by the side of the road. He said: "I'm just resting, Miss Narcissa."

One of the happiest experiences of our lives, when we were growing up, was to visit Bill in his one-room house beyond the spring branch. The place was filled with the strong scent of home-raised tobacco, with the dusty smell of ashes on the hearth. There was a jug under the bed, a gun on the wall, a banjo in the corner, Sunday clothes on a peg. He was as fond of us as we were of him, and he would twang the banjo and sing to us by the hour — ballads, gambling songs, blues songs, hymns like " Rock of Ages, Cleft for Me."

Bill also was fond of hound dogs and mules. " Mules and colored folks," he said, " just suit one another." Horses were too temperamental for Bill. They required

And Cotton

too much care, were too high-strung to plow cotton on a broiling July day. Mule-traders often came by the old house to call on Bill, and sometimes he would buy and sell for my Great-Aunt Narcissa. Once he got rid of the worst mule we ever had and he got rid of it at a profit. Stella, this mule, would do anything except plow — the moment you hitched her to a plowstock, she would balk and nothing would move Stella, not even a small fire. Bill turned Stella into the pasture, fattened her, and sold her to an itinerant mule-dealer for a hundred and sixty-five dollars. " Bill," said my great-aunt, " that mule wasn't worth fifty dollars." Bill replied: " It's all in the game, Miss Narcissa."

Bill bragged; he told tall stories about the possums he caught, about his dogs, about his mules, about his corn being so tall he had sold the stalks for timber. Once when my cousin Billie asked Bill if he had made a good crop that year, Bill told him: " Mr. Billie, I stayed up all last night counting money."

When the first frosts came, nipping the sweet-potato leaves and sweetening the persimmons, Bill would light a lantern, call his lean hound dogs, and hunt possums. All night long we would hear his deep powerful voice echoing through the hills and hollows. He would yip like a rebel in the old Southern army and then he would call to the dogs: "Speak to 'em, boys." The hounds, picking up a trail, would move faster as they gained on the possum, their baying would swell into a steady chorus, and the woods for miles would sing the music. I always understood why Bill liked to hunt possums — somehow it lifted your spirit to thrash through deep woods at night, stumbling along by lantern light, directing a pack of dogs; it gave you a wild feeling of escaping, of being free, of standing alone against darkness and all the forces that bound and cramped you. I hunted possums whenever I had the chance, and sometimes I hunted when I was forbidden to — I would slip through a window and go hunting with Bill.

One autumn Bill went out six nights in a row. He slept most of the daytime and let everything but possum-hunting go. On the seventh morning my Great-Aunt Narcissa knocked on Bill's door and angrily forbade him to hunt another time until he had pulled his fodder. "The fodder is going to rack and ruin," said my great-aunt in exasperation, "and here you are running wild at night — chasing over the country when there is work to do. You ought to be ashamed of yourself. It's trifling to hunt possums when your fodder is still in the field." She shook her finger in Bill's face. " You're not going another time, do you hear, until the last bundle of fodder is piled in the barn?" Dejected, sorrowful, Bill sat in a low chair before the fire, saying: "Yes, ma'am," and "That's right," to everything my great-aunt said. "I won't go another time, Miss Narcissa — I'll get the fodder in."

That night we had hardly finished supper before once again the hounds started baying. "Speak to 'em," echoed Bill's deep voice through the hills. With that, my great-aunt got mad. Next morning she was up early, beating on Bill's door. "Miss Narcissa," said Bill, backing into a corner, "I didn't intend to go again, I didn't mean to." He swallowed hard. "I was sitting here, thinking, when I heard something running loose behind the spring branch — it was knocking down saplings like a bear. So I got the dogs and went to see what it was, and it was a possum. It was the biggest possum I ever laid my eyes on." Bill clasped his long hands. "Yes, ma'am, and finally I got it treed. I sawed off the limb it was hanging to, and the dogs grabbed it, and I chained it by a leg to a stump and then went over to the barn and got a mule and hauled that possum in. I dragged it. Miss Narcissa, that possum weighed more than ninety pounds."

"Where is it?" asked my great-aunt acidly.

Without batting an eyelid, Bill said: "Miss Narcissa, I

cleaned the thing and put it in the washpot to boil, but it was so fat it melted completely into grease.

Bill enchanted the brier patch for us. He told us all the stories that Uncle Remus told the Harisses in Georgia — the fables about the Tar Baby, about the hot ashes being dumped on the top of Brer Buzzard's head, about Brer Fox losing his tail in the freezing ice on the river. And with Windy Bill, just as with Uncle Remus, Brer Rabbit was the hero — he had to make his way by his wits in a world of trouble. " Brer Rabbit," said Bill, " had trouble with his low-down, sorry, trifling tramp of a wife. Brer Rabbit went to sunset prayer meeting to get himself freshened with the Lord, and when he got home, bless God, he found his wife had left him. She had slept with him in the same bed, had been the mother of his children, and she had left him."

" Yeah," interjected Margit, looking up from a pot she was stirring on the stove, " she left him because Brer Rabbit had been stepping around himself with Sister Nesbitt."

" Who is telling this story — you or me? " asked Bill furiously.

Margit stirred the pot.

" Well, Brer Rabbit's wife had left him. So he said, dog-

And Cotton

gone her, if that was the sort of good-for-nothing trash she was, then she could just leave and stay left — damn her, she could shuffle for herself. All women were trouble, Brer Rabbit said, and he made up his mind he was going to save his youngest boy from having to go through what he had gone through. He wasn't going to let him know there were women even in existence. With that, Brer Rabbit built a high brick wall and put his boy in there and kept him in there until he was twenty-one years old. Then, when the boy was twenty-one, Brer Rabbit cranked up the T-model and took his son over to Pickens to show him the sights. He showed him the Courthouse and the square with the county officials fanning themselves under the cool shade trees. He showed him the drug store, and the ten-cent store, and the filling station, and the jail. And everything was fine, the boy thought it was great. And then the boy saw something with silk stockings on and a red dress and an umbrella.

" 'Pa,' said the boy, ' for God's sake, what's that? '

" 'That there,' said Brer Rabbit, ' is the devil, and you leave the devil alone. The devil is trouble.'

" Brer Rabbit then grabbed the boy, shoved him in the T-model, cranked up, and headed straight for home and the high brick wall. By and by, after they had crossed Golden Creek and were close to Twelve Mile, Brer Rabbit said to the boy: 'Well, son, you've seen the sights. You've seen them all. Which one of them did you like the best?'

"'Pa,' said the boy, 'I liked that devil.'"

Windy Bill told us about John Henry, the double-jointed steel-driving man, who carried a ninety-pound hammer in his hand. Margit told us about God's telling Jonah to go down into Nineveh's land, and about Lazarus, poor Lazarus. Margit would pat her foot and sing: "Lazarus in heaven and Dives in hell." She told us she did not know what it was that Dives had done to Lazarus, she disremembered that story, but whatever it was, it was a sin and a shame.

Our Great-Aunt Narcissa told us about our Great-great-great-great-great-Aunt Narcissa, whom the Indians scalped. This Narcissa was a woman who would have liked to live in peace and quiet; she wanted a flower garden and a house, but she had to live on the frontier among Indians and wander from the cradle to the grave. Three times her people got the moving fever — Virginia had struck their fancy in Pennsylvania, North Carolina in Virginia, western North Carolina in eastern North Carolina. For sixty years they had wandered and at the end of that time all that Narcissa had to show for her life were graves of her loved ones scattered across six hundred miles of wilderness, a small yellow creek named with her name, somewhere in Virginia a grove of cedar trees of her planting, memories of tomahawks and scalping knives. There had been so little of love, of quiet or rest, so little of the safeness that a woman sought.

Then, when she was old, her grandson and his family decided again to move — this time to South Carolina. Narcissa's blood froze when she heard the menfolks making their plans. Old, tired, discouraged, she started to warn them that savages would harass them for the rest of their lives in South Carolina, that they would spend their lives in constant fear — the fall of every acorn, the hoot of every owl would sound a potential alarm. There would be wolves and wildcats. Panthers would scream. Then suddenly a great weariness swept over her, a realization that there would be no use, why raise a tired voice, who among them would listen to the experience of an old worn-out woman? How could she fight young men who when told of a fact would turn for answer to fancy, pick a tale from the sky? If she warned them of panthers, they would say to her: "Panthers? Oh, the savages admire panthers for their wonderful stealthy step and for their leaping; they make their sons sleep on pantherskins; they call the panther the cat of God." What kind of answer would that be for a woman who lived in terror of a cruel beast that screamed like a little child?

She knew her grandsons — the cold evening star, green in space and trailing into the western sky, a wild bird flying, these were enough to drive her grandsons from a garden and a cabin. They were born to explore, to travel, the great waters of the Mississippi flowed in their dreams, the wind blew over the Western deserts, not even the Pacific Ocean would stop her grandsons. Something drew them, like a magnet, farther and farther west.

Our great-aunt said that Narcissa accepted the inevitable. Since she could do nothing else, she obeyed. Her strength became as the strength of Israel, and home was where they would stop for the night — heaven was her real home, sweet Beulah Land far beyond the sun. She lived each day for that day, she rose like the wind, accepted all things as she accepted the daily weather. For what was an individual's life? — one more ant, another bug, a butterfly, a leaf on a tree; it was the tree that lived, not the leaves. She saw the wilderness as a great barren rock upon which a million settlers would have to lay down their lives like leaves, one upon another. The flower they hoped for — when finally it would bloom — would grow from the very dust of their bodies. So why resist lying

And Cotton

down? There was this comfort: they would make it easier for their children and their children's children. Still Narcissa was bitter. She was lost in the wild forest and there was nothing she could do about it.

So she packed the things she could not bear to leave — an *Arabian Nights,* a bottle of bear oil for snake-bite, volatile drops for the heart, peach stones, hollyhock seed, seeds of melons and roses, knitting-needles, a Bible. Finally she wrapped a shawl about a sugar bowl — this was a piece of yellow crockery with a gold band, a miraculous possession, for starting out with her, a bride from Pennsylvania, it had survived all the hazards that she experienced, it had come through murder and oxcarts and wagons and flatboats. It was a symbol to Narcissa.

Her packing done, she took up a goose-quill and began a letter home to Pennsylvania to tell of this newest development in the never ending journey. ". . . We have learned to endure hardship, to suffer affliction, and to brave the dangers of the wilderness with no more prospect of notice or reward than that promised by the Divine Master who Himself had not where to lay His head." There was no illusion left now for Narcissa, this was renunciation. From then on, she waited for her time.

So in the east the sun rose, clear and hot, and they turned their backs upon the east. The caravan had formed.

Red Hills

Uncovering his head in the early morning sunshine, Narcissa's grandson read the Twenty-third Psalm, about being led by God beside the green pastures, about walking without fear through the valley of the shadow. Then he prayed. "Have mercy upon us, guide us and protect us on the way, strengthen us to meet danger, to face death. Receive us finally, Father, into the safety of Thy breast."

Soon after there came a loud cracking sound. One of the boys had swung a long leather bullwhip, jerking the end. In another few moments they had started, they were moving still deeper into solitary forests. Wheeling about on a horse, Narcissa's grandson shouted: "Follow me, boys, we're on our way."

So they went on. It was a fine Southern day with the wind blowing and the hot sun of the South shining. They wound among deep swamps, over a marl roadbed, a soft calcareous clay that sometimes was quaky. For a long time tall cypresses rose around them, then pines, like green ice, green with long needles. Dense and deep was the gloom of this region, a dominion of the molds, hardly ever lighted by the direct light of the sun. There were tracks of swamp animals in the narrow trail that curved among dark-growing briers and elder bushes, tangled vines of foxgrapes. Later Narcissa's grandson led them on to higher ground into the plum blossoms. Sometimes in this region patches of blue sky crept into sight through the trees — bright patches of Southern blue with whorls of sensuous cloud. Riding through these scenes, down dark aisles amid luscious flowers and passionate Southern odors, even old Narcissa was aroused and the old excitement stirred within her — for like them all, she was on her way, moving again into the unknown; wheels were rolling. For a moment she knew again the old-time confidence. Perhaps Divine God would see her through once again — were not the hairs of her head numbered, was not her strength become as the strength of Israel? But this revival of the spirit was only faint and it soon vanished. Narcissa had a deep feeling about this trip, she had a premonition.

The child she was carrying in her arms stirred, it was fretful. Putting one of her wrinkled hands on its forehead, Narcissa noticed it was feverish. For a time the elderly woman sang to the child, and the baby slept. Looking at its tender innocence, Narcissa suddenly said aloud: "What chance have we got on a journey like this? A helpless old woman and a baby?"

For days and weeks, said Great-Aunt Narcissa, they moved on, starting at dawn, stopping at dusk. Sometimes by the glimmering campfire Narcissa would tell the children about Mary the Mother of God, and Joseph and the Three Wise Men, and she would tell them about Aladdin and the Forty Thieves, and about Pennsylvania, where people lived in houses and had barns for their horses and cabins — barns bigger than cabins. Sometimes, alone, she would think of the multitude who had died in the wilderness and had passed and left no sign — the lost whose dreams came to nothing, whose prayers were never heard. The wilderness and desolation and loneliness of the land, the loneliness of the wind in the pines. So many had died, were forgotten, their children would die. A panther screamed, and Narcissa.

They crossed long rolling hills, forded wide yellow rivers, gathered dewberries and early purple blackberries. They rested among chestnut groves. They saw the big-eared bat, cottontail rabbits, red squirrels, a swift-fleeing frightened chipmunk. And in the moonshine at midnight the mockingbird sang its mimic song. It rained, there was thunder, wolves howled. The travelers waited in soaked clothing for day to break. The water of a stream rose three feet in an hour and continued to rise, halting the oxcarts for the better part of a day, which fretted Narcissa's grandson, for nothing had ever taught him patience, not even high water.

Finally they came to their destination — to a valley filled

with wisps of mist, with drifting low clouds and showers of rain. They looked out over the valley from the top of a high hill, and Narcissa's grandson, with a sweeping gesture of his hands, said to them: " This is the valley I was telling you about; here we are." Narcissa's heart pounded against her ribs as she looked — at first half in fear of disappointment. A clear river flowed through a deep valley, patient and varied and as old as the world — a calm country, resting after a storm. It was as beautiful as her grandson had said it was, it looked as rich.

Our Great-Aunt Narcissa said that old Narcissa planted half of her hoarded stock of peach kernels and hollyhock seed, a quarter of the seeds of the roses. The other portions she kept dry and safe in a buckskin pouch. Narcissa no longer dared risk all of anything at one time; she had seen too many things happen to risk everything any longer. She worked, she took over the care of the younger children. " Mind your manners," she told them. " Never walk between anyone and the fire and always say 'ma'am' and 'sir' to older people and never speak when older people are speaking." She had them memorize the Twenty-third and the Hundred and Twenty-first Psalms; the Seventy-third Psalm, her favorite: " It is good for me to draw near to God; I have put my trust in the Lord God." She told the children to keep the Ten Commandments, to believe in God, to love their neighbors.

"Are the savages our neighbors?" one of her great-grandsons asked one day as they watched an iron pot boiling over an outdoor fire. "No," said Narcissa. "Savages have no souls."

Narcissa told the children always to do what they felt in their hearts was right, to do what was good, and to remember who they were when they grew up — they were to make something of themselves, to become somebody. "Settle down," she said, "become a credit to your kinfolks."

There were no schoolbooks in the wilderness, so Narcissa began to compose an arithmetic. "Arithmetic," she wrote, "is the art of computing by numbers." This work took up her spare time for many weeks, and at last when she had written as far as she could remember, the book was over a hundred pages long and besides addition, subtraction, multiplication, division, vulgar fractions, and decimals, this remarkable arithmetic contained many other things included in no other arithmetic in existence. For often in the midst of composing a page, Narcissa would become bored by the stern mental discipline of figures and she would rebel. Thus the pleased children in their arithmetic would suddenly discover: "A family of well regulated children is a charming sight," and "Good

And Cotton

breeding is often a surface without depth but politeness is the sunshine of the soul."

Our Great-Aunt Narcissa said that one afternoon old Narcissa decided to slip down to the spring to bring a bucket of milk to the house for supper. At the pool she bent over. Turning about, she was struck on the head. The next blow knocked her flat among some ferns. In another moment her side was pierced with darts, and then she was scalped. Warwhoops rose in the forest.

Some of the boys made a coffin for Narcissa from fragrant slabs of cedar, and through that night they sat up, burning a candle perfumed with pine and balsam scent. Burial took place in a deep grove of pines on the top of a hill beyond the cabin. It was a quiet meditative place, full of repose and rest, and brightened with yellow mullein and saw briers and wild eglantine roses. It was a free place for a free spirit. At the funeral service, Narcissa's grandson said: " She met life with calmness, resignation and the firmness of a Christian martyr." He said: " Disappointment did not change her, and no matter what happened, she always heard the birds singing and saw the beautiful wild flowers." They sang her favorite hymn, " By and by, when the morning comes." Then her grandson prayed. " Have mercy upon Thy servant, pardon her transgressions, shelter her soul in the shadow of Thy wing. Make known to her the path to eternal life." Then everyone broke down and wept.

Our Great-great-great-great-great-Aunt Narcissa was love itself to our Great-Aunt Narcissa. She was courage and faith. She was sacrifice. She was our holy mother — the great mother of everyone who is born in the United States.

Our Great-Aunt Narcissa planted boxwood, she worked with the bees in the beehouse, she planted a yellow garden, all yellow — the sun color of life, of love. Within a towering border of brooding cedar trees, hollies, and the formal boxwood she massed plants with golden blossoms — massed wild patches of blazing gold foxglove, moth mullein, wild wood sorrel, frostweed, partridge peas, the tiny yellow flax, sundrops, primroses, buttercups, yellow star grass, dog-tooth violets, and great gold beds of wild indigo and mustard. From March to November, our great-aunt kept this garden a constant scene of shifting yellow shades. It was a wild and beautiful sight.

Gradually she gave in to old age, took finally to her bed. Just before the end she slipped into a coma, and for hours talked to her brother who had been shot in 1856 in a brawl in New Orleans, to her brother who had died, a medical volunteer, during a yellow-fever epidemic in a

And Cotton

hospital in New York. She talked to her dead sisters, to boys who had been killed at Gettysburg and Cold Harbor. Margit said: " She's communing with the angels."

I never knew a person with such depths of understanding as my Great-Aunt Narcissa. She knew by instinct when those about her were in trouble. She herself must have touched the rocks of despair, the deep reefs of sorrow, for otherwise how could she have had such knowledge? For us her life was filled with glory and success, but I think she looked upon her life as a failure. No one knows what standard another has set, what hope has been held.

Our kinfolks never get together without some of us saying something about the goodness of our Great-Aunt Narcissa.

CHAPTER IX

I WAS born and raised in the cotton country among old Confederates and the last of the Confederate slaves. About me were my kinfolks and hundreds of colored folks and white sharecroppers and renters, and all of us were Baptists, and we plowed the fields and planted the crops, and we tried to live good lives and to be at peace with our spirit. We sought the eternal things, the values that should not change in any country at any time, the simple values that moved and exalted. We worked hard, we rested hard, we talked about living and dying, about the quality of a man's spirit that was more important than a man's life. We talked about backsliding and the meanness that was in us, and we thought it was wrong for us to dance and to

And Cotton

drink corn liquor. We talked very much about how we ought to live, day by day, for we believed that we had to make life worthy of death. We had to earn our right to die.

We were old-fashioned simple people. We were so simple that sometimes some of our kinfolks would rise up in church and shout. Our preacher approved shouting — it was an expression of the sudden soaring of the spirit, and the Baptist church depended for its life on spirit; the Baptist church denied the power of ritual in worship, and if our church lost its spirit, what would it have left of value? The Baptist church was a personal faith, Baptist prayers floated upward from the individual heart, and Baptists were responsible alone for their individual souls — Baptists belonged to a strong, lonesome religion, and the power of the church depended on the individual strength of our faith, on personal expression. " Shout if you feel like shouting," said our preacher. Some of the young boys and girls, back from the colleges, disagreed with our preacher. They held we should control ourselves and keep quiet. " The church is a free gathering-place," our preacher replied to them, again and again. " If any-one in this church wishes to shout, he is at liberty to do so." My cousin Clarissa always agreed with this view of our preacher's; she said shouting expressed the feeling of glory. My Aunt Bettie always disagreed; she said shouting was too common. One Sunday my cousin Clarissa jumped to her feet and yipped: " Glory! " and my Aunt Bettie tried to stop her. " Clarissa," said my Aunt Bettie in a low voice, " do sit down, you'll make your heart worse, you'll just strain your heart." My cousin Clarissa, raising her voice, hollered: " Oh, Bettie, let me praise Jesus." Embarrassed and blushing crimson, my Aunt Bettie sat back in her pew and fanned herself furiously with a palmetto fan. Louder and louder Cousin Clarissa shouted, " Oh, Bettie . . ." That incident that morning settled for all time the shouting issue among my kinfolks. Never again did any of the non-shouters attempt to stop the shouters.

Aunt Coot told us one morning that she tried to be graceful when she shouted — she stood up, took two steps to the left, then two steps to the right. And Margit was famous for her shouting. Margit was the biggest shouter in our county. She acquired such a reputation that jealousy of her was aroused and a challenger appeared, a resourceful cotton-field colored woman, who wore spectacles and two gold slip-on teeth — Sister Cannon. Sister Cannon began to shout louder and longer than Margit, and at a protracted meeting at New Olive Grove Church she suddenly announced that she had backslid and would have

And Cotton

to be rebaptized, she would have to be redeemed. This created a sensation, for Sister Cannon was well known for her pious life. Everyone asked how she had backslid, and for a week they talked more about Sister Cannon than they talked about Margit. But on the following Sunday morning Margit marched up to the mourners' bench and testified that she too had backslid and would have to go down again into the deep water. Then at her rebaptizing Margit came up from the spiritual burial shouting: "I seed Jesus." The entire congregation was impressed. The preacher sent her down a second time and again she came up shouting: "I seed Jesus." He sent her down a third time, and when Margit came up a third time, she said to the preacher: "You damn fool, you're trying to drown me."

There was nothing consciously profane about Margit nor about Sister Cannon. Both were good Christian women, and we understood them. We understood how easy it was to use the church to create a personal reputation, how especially tempting it was for a colored woman. Colored men became famous by cutting and shooting and doing time on the chain gang, colored women by the riotous quality of their shouting. Black and white, we were deeply religious somber people, but we had a quality of satire that could never be quenched, not even in the saving of our souls.

Red Hills

Sister Cannon and Margit were humble women; they tried to do what was right and they had faith — truly they believed. Once I went to Abel Church to a children's meeting, sponsored by Sister Cannon. The sun had hardly gone down when we assembled, but Sister Cannon said: "We better get started, I reckon, for some of the juveniles will get sleepy before long, and then too the balance of us got to get home and get our rest — we got cotton to pick tomorrow, and you got to get your rest if you going to pick two hundred pounds of cotton."

"Ain't it the God's truth?" said Margit.

Sister Cannon then raised a tune, very slow and in the perfect hymn cadence of the colored people. "We got to work, Lord; we got to worry in this world." Several of the juveniles read papers — proof of their ability to read. Finally one little girl got up and said: "I didn't bring no paper, I just come." Sister Cannon said: "That's all right, honey — you sing us a song." Timid, confused, the child began singing: "Don't you gamble." Patting her foot, Sister Cannon bellowed: "Join in, everybody — 'Don't you gamble.'" After that Sister Cannon said we would pause for the finance, and after that pause she prayed. Sister Cannon chanted in a kind of Gregorian greatness: "Lord, we thank You for our standing up and for our lying down; Lord, You have watch-cared over us and we

And Cotton

thank You. Lord, make us clean — make our hands clean
and our hearts clean, and make everything we touch turn
clean." In a burst of emotion Sister Cannon's spirit soared,
" God, we know You are God; You've always been God,
and when this world is swept away, You'll still be God."

We are at our best, I think, in church and at our political meetings; all that is great in us comes to the surface on those occasions. There we are as we would like
to be, as we would always be if we could get our hands
on things and force the world to be perfect. I think the
proudest I ever was of our kinfolks was at the meeting
we held at our Courthouse to send our delegates to the
state convention that was to send its delegates to Philadelphia to vote for Franklin Roosevelt's nomination for
the second time. We got there at nine o'clock one morning, some in overalls, some in town clothes, all with our
faces scrubbed and our hair brushed. There were two
hundred of us all told, representatives from every township in our valleys — from Hurricane Creek and Wolf
Creek and Twelve Mile and Eastatoe and Pumpkintown
and Liberty. We were landowners, tenants, cotton-mill
workers, two were doctors, three were lawyers, several
others kept stores at crossroads. There was the look about
us of ancient rural America, still alive and vigorous in its
living. We were original America, functioning as strong

as ever in our fastness in the South, and never in my life had I seen my kinfolks so serious. Some of them made me think of patriarchs right out of the Old Testament.

Cousin Stephen John was called on for a prayer, and he said we thanked the Lord that we were who we were, all of us blood relations, and that we had the privilege to live where we lived, on the land that had belonged to us since the time of old George II. He told the Lord we were grateful to Him that the greatness of America belonged to all of us by our right. There was a quaint religious atmosphere about our gathering. We had about us a combination of devoutness and gusto, and you could feel a reverence, a sensibility of public trust, a consciousness of duty. The chairman said: "Brethren, I will have to ask you not to smoke, as smoking is against the fire law, and I will be further obliged to you if you won't spit on the floor." We laughed, and then we sang " My Country 'Tis of Thee," in our slow old-fashioned manner of singing, the music swelling and receding and drifting away.

Next the chairman said we had to keep our politics clean; he praised the Democratic Party and President Roosevelt; then he said the keepers of all registration books in our county must let the voters sign their own names whenever possible, no matter how poor a hand they wrote. " Let 'em write anything, even if you got to

And Cotton

print the spelling after," he said. "We don't want the country to think we're ignorant just because nine hundred of the sixteen thousand on our present books are represented by their marks. We got to cut down that nine hundred — you hear."

We listened next to a keynote speech, to a response. The speakers quoted Jefferson, President Wilson, Roosevelt; they quoted Job and Judas and Jesus. After that, we chose our twenty delegates — five landowners, five tenants, five mill workers, five gentlemen from the towns. Cousin Charlie brought the convention to a close with a rip-roaring speech telling us that he was ninety years old, a veteran of the Confederate War, and a Democrat who with his own eyes had seen carpetbaggers and Republicans making speeches right here in our own country. With his own eyes he had seen Democrats placed under arrest in our county just for calling Republicans scalawags and liars. "Boys," said Cousin Charlie, his eyes sparkling with excitement, "let me tell you that eternal vigilance must always be the watchword for the Democratic Party. Boys," he shouted, "you got to keep your fences horse-high, bull-strong, and pig-tight."

We were land-loving, church-loving people. We looked down on towns — they were centers of weakness, offering

Red Hills

unto idols, forgetting the sunrise and losing sight of the stars; men in towns were close to decay. We liked the fields and the hills and the houses on the hills and the feeling we had about us of timelessness, the sense we had that we belonged. Days passed, weeks passed, and we plowed and chopped cotton; we forgot the passing of time. Sometimes we sang songs to the fields and hills, we sang to one another as we hoed the cotton rows. Bill would shout to us: "Who built the ark?" And we would shout back: "Noah built the ark." I remember Aunt Coot, battling and washing at the wash place, and singing: "Your clothes looks so lonesome, hanging on the line." Alone, we would talk to the sticks and stones.

One of our cousins even had a fight once with a fertilizer-spreader, with an inanimate machine. He was pouring fertilizer into cotton rows with this spreader, a brand-new expensive labor-saving device, and he could not get it to spread the proper amount. It dropped too much, it dropped too little. He worked for two hours on the adjustments; then in a sudden tempestuous frenzy of temper he picked up a rock and beat the thing into bits. Throwing the broken pieces over the pasture fence, he yelled: "You dirty low-down evil contraption, stay there," and going to the barn, he got out the old cow horn and from then on spread fertilizer as his father and

And Cotton

grandfather had spread it. This same cousin also had a row with a pig. This pig refused to eat when he came down to feed it. It pawed the ground and ran to the other side of the sty. "All right," said our cousin, "you either get some manners and eat when I feed you or you'll perish to death." He came to the sty the second day with a bucket full of buttermilk mash, and again the pig pawed and ran away. On the third day he said to the pig: "All right, damn you, you can just perish." On the fourth day, however, the pig ate ravenously as soon as my cousin put the bucket down, and from then on my cousin and this pig understood each other.

We slopped the pigs; we spread fertilizer, and mixed fertilizer; and about us were the cotton fields and the fine blue hills, and on the walls of our houses were shotguns. We drove into town to swap butter and eggs for coffee and sugar and black pepper; we swapped smoked hams for tobacco and cloth. We wasted opportunity, we wasted chance, but we held on to an attitude of living that some people had lost who did not waste opportunity and chance. We weighed and balanced many intangible things. We made up our minds about how we wanted things and where we wanted them. I remember once my Uncle Wade saying to us he had decided when he was twenty-one years of age that he didn't choose to live more than two days' drive from the Southern Railroad — he didn't intend to live any farther south than Greenwood nor any farther north than Pickens. And I remember a great-uncle who started off to Texas and then returned, saying he found out in Mississippi that old Mr. No Account was moving right along with him, and he decided if old No Account had to hang on to him, he had rather deal with the scoundrel in South Carolina than 'way out in Texas. We talked about great rains and great winds and great droughts — about all kinds of wonders. Once I remember Mary telling us she had seen an infidel. He was a Georgian, a fine-looking man, and he did not believe in God. Mary said to us Georgia was a wild place — preachers drank whisky in Georgia.

We discussed ultimate destinies — the asylum, the poorhouse, the graveyard, the jail. We considered chance and the power of faith over chance, and how strange and hidden was chance. We were caught by it like fish in nets and like birds snared in traps. And the race in our valley no more went to the swift than it had in Ecclesiastes, nor did the battle go to the strong, nor did riches come to men of understanding. When our time would arrive, it would arrive, and we would go out like Cousin Temperance and the chimney would hit us, and the lightning would strike as it had struck Cousin Forrest, and the mad dog would bite as it had nipped Sister Cannon. How would we die? How had we rather die? From cancer? From hardening of the heart? From burning within? We would choose to go suddenly, we said, but with a little notice, with a little time for the preparation. But here again all would be chance. Would we die in the poorhouse? Always we had that fear in the back of our heads. We were haunted by the chance of our becoming a public charge, by the abject possibility of appealing at last to charity. Chance would bring even the poorhouse to some of us — it would bring everything in time. It brought an Indian to Mary. Mary told us that one day she was hoeing corn in the bottoms, and singing an old familiar hymn, and on hoeing her way to the end of the row — there stood a red man. He said to Mary that God had " delighted her song in his heart," and she replied she was glad if that was so. The Indian asked Mary her name and she told him, and she asked him his name and he said it was George. Then he asked Mary where her father lived and she told him: " On the hill." The Indian went to see Mary's father and told him he had a great singing in his heart for Mary, and he asked if he could write to her about it. Mary's father said: " Don't you write that girl — she don't know nothing about writing." Mary said that for a long time the Indian stayed around, lurking at the end of corn rows and hiding in the thickets. He ran back and forth through the woods on a little path like a pig, and he carried a red satchel. One day he said hello to Mary and her brother, and while Mary talked to the Indian, her brother searched the satchel and found cat bones, snake bones, doodle bugs, red flannel, and many other kinds of conjure things. Mary said she told the Indian she was not afraid. She told us that all of her life she had pretended to conjurers that she was not afraid of them; she said if you treated conjurers rough from the start, they would leave you alone — it was weak people that conjurers gripped, people who would not face their sorrow.

"What happened to the Indian, Mary?" I asked.

Mary grinned. "That Indian was a bird," she said coyly.

"What happened to him?"

Mary ducked her head.

"What happened to him?"

"Well," said Mary, "one day he ran as fast as he could down his pig path, and he never came back any more."

All of us lived close to pig paths, close to the darkness of the forests, deep in the mold and mud, but at the same time we knew the cleanness and freshness of the sun. We were so near to nature that once when I asked Mary what had happened while I had been away, she said the yard had been full of jaybirds, a pack of barking dogs had passed by, and the locust tree had cast some noble shade.

"What else happened, Mary?" I probed.

"Sister Cannon been dog-bit," Mary said.

"What else?"

"Brother Nelson died."

"What else?"

"That sweet-smelling bush done bloomed."

"What else?"

"Reverend Durham been so sick that nobody was let in to see him except Sister Durham and the treasurer of the church."

"What else?"

"Brother Dawson is in jail."

"What else?"

"The law has caught Brother Benson."

"What else?"

"Brother Roper is singing again at Abel."

"Who is Brother Roper?"

"Brother Roper is a stranger."

"Why is he singing again at Abel — what's it all about?"

"Well," said Mary, "Brother Roper rambled into this country about six months ago, and he came into Abel Church one Sunday night and sat down on the back row, and when Sister Cannon raised a tune, Brother Roper began to sing. He sang so fine and bassed so low, that when the service was over, we all went back and tipped him of our own accord — Brother Roper could everlastingly sing. Then he met up with Carrie Lee and they got married, and Carrie Lee got so jealous of Brother Roper's singing that she told him he couldn't go any more to Abel. She said either he gave up singing or he gave up her. Well, last night right in the middle of a hymn, bless God, if we didn't hear the voice of Brother Roper — bassing on the back row. We all patted our feet, and Sister Cannon said: ' Uh-oh.' "

Always there has been finality about our country. Always the bush blooms, a man dies, a man is caught by the law, the singer comes back to the choir. And the sun shines and the lightning strikes the forked pine, and for every catfish in the river there are three of us fishing on the bank. We sit on the piazza and rock and we talk in the kitchen, and the days and the years go by and we get old. Rocking, fishing, talking — all in the midst of leisure. We take our time in our country.

This morning Jim sat on the woodbox by the kitchen window and Mary sat in a chair in front of the stove and I ate breakfast at a small table by the sink.

Jim dipped a slice of toast in his coffee cup.

And Cotton

"If I had a radio," said Mary, sipping cold coffee from a saucer, "I wouldn't step a foot out of my house at night; I'd just make me a nice warm place 'way down in the middle of the bed, and I'd turn the thing on and lie there and listen."

"What is your bed hour, Mary?" inquired Jim mischievously.

"You want to know my bed hour?" said Mary, grinning and sipping coffee. "One thirty, two, sometimes three o'clock in the night."

"Sleeping out," said Jim, cackling.

"I don't ramble across any railway tracks," said Mary.

"What you going to say about rambling across railway tracks?" replied Jim belligerently.

"I ain't going to say nothing," said Mary, laughing.

Speaking then to me, Jim said: "Boss, she knows I got her treed." Jim slapped his thigh. "They don't give me any back talk, boss. I speak to them one time, and that's all. I'm that kind of a man."

Roaring, Jim got up and put on his cap and shuffled out.

"Who lives across the tracks, Mary?" I asked.

"Maggie lives across there somewhere," Mary replied.

"Maggie!" said I surprised. "Why, Maggie is seventy years old."

"So is Jim," said Mary.

Red Hills

I lived like a wild bird when I was growing up in our valley. All about me were my kinfolks. Old and very old and young, and still there was solitude, and in spite of all the barns and houses and cultivated fields I always had the sensation of space. I was surrounded by all sorts of re-strictions — by the rules of the church, by all the personal rules of my kinfolks, by the rules of the white and colored races, but I was not aware of restriction. I thought I was free. Even time, I thought, was my own, but I realize now that it, too, was cadenced, it moved in cycles, over and over again, in the Southern rhythm. Everything with us had the beautiful motion of simple routine. I rose at day-light and started fires, and I remember how powerful it made me feel to be up before anyone else, to have in my own hands the opening control of the day. I discovered early the realness of the pleasure of getting up at day-light; it gives you a feeling of living as all life ought to live; you are surged onward and outward, beyond your-self, and you know a sense of smoothness within that is like the wind blowing and the sun shining. There is quiet and rest about everything and you feel very close to the mystery of existence.

I milked the cow and I went to the rabbit traps as the sun was rising. Five days each week I went to school, and at sundown I split kindling and brought in wood for the woodboxes, and at twilight I milked the cow. On Saturdays I cut wood and worked in the garden and roamed the woods and hunted and did nothing. I went to Sunday school on Sunday morning, to the cemetery on Sunday afternoon, and I never thought of time at all until I was about ready to go to college. I led a happy life. Time is always timeless whenever a person is happy.

I went to Charleston once when I was a small boy to see the ocean, and once I went to North Carolina and pitched pebbles into the French Broad River, but except for those excursions I stayed at home, almost within the valley. Always I knew I would go far away when the time should come, so I never bothered about going anywhere before I started to college. I was not concerned, nor were my kinfolks, about travel for a child. The travel that I knew was the roaming of fancy. My parents did not care whether I saw an opera or understood a statue; all that could be considered in time, in the future, for operas and statues belonged to urban culture, and my kinfolks said any person with any kind of background could acquire a city civilization, but that few city people could ever learn the culture of a rural country. Urban culture was wax, a polish, and was superimposed, it was gloss. They wanted to instruct me in the rural beauties, to ground me in the Southern fields, to give me an anchor that no storm could

ever loose, to give me an attitude, a philosophy, a purpose. There must be an original flavor that would stay
with me always, a particular savor. I was to know one
special life and to know all that could be known about it.
I was to understand cotton farming and how to live with
tenant farmers and colored people on a cotton farm. My
kinfolks did not believe in a broad education for a small
child. They believed in narrowness for a child. My kinfolks were not afraid of narrowness, nor were they skittish
about being called fanatics. They wanted me to have a
point of view, to have my mind made up from the start
on a number of things. I was to be tolerant but I was not
to budge beyond a certain point, and if ever I was threatened at that point, I was to stand where I was and fight.
My kinfolks thought more about character than about culture. They said culture could be acquired but character
had to be formed. Character had to be hammered into
shape like hot iron on an anvil. It had to be molded in
the most exact and unrelenting form.

So they gave me books to read and work to do and they
gave me time of my own, but always they were guiding
and directing and advising and pouring their own wisdom
into my growing mind. Hundreds of precious hours were
devoted to my education by my parents and aunts and
uncles and by my grandparents and my Great-Aunt Nar-

And Cotton

cissa and by Margit and Mary and Bill. They left culture to chance — I was free to develop in that realm as I chose. They left nothing to chance about character. With that they did what they could. So they read to me from the Bible, took me through the woods, worked with me in the fields, and over and over tried to make me understand that the value I must search for was x. My kinfolks did not care a hoot that a bridge was a thousand feet long or that a tower was a hundred and two stories high. They wanted to know why the bridge was there, what purpose it served, what sort of strength the tower possessed, what beauty it held. My kinfolks were never interested in 2 plus 2; their principal interest was centered in a plus b. Over and over again they told me I had to amount to something, I had to be somebody, I had to hold on, to wait, I was to live with dignity, with honor, I was to do what was right. My kinfolks wanted me to stand like one of the mountains, like the granite of the Blue Ridge. The sculpture, the decoration, they would leave to me. What they wanted to do was to set me in the mold — to make me a Carolinian, a Democrat and a Baptist. Once they had accomplished that — well, hell and high water could try as they liked.

So I lived the cotton life. Round the clock it went, round the calendar, year after year. Our beautiful old

Red Hills

hills were heavy clay, red and rocky, and we could never plow them when they were wet. We could never prepare the land for the cotton crop until the heavy rains of the winter were over, usually not until March. Sometimes in winter we would hear that strangers said a crow could not make a living flying through our fields, the cotton patches looked so old and poor; but we understood our land, we knew its virtues and its stored wealth; our hills could grow a bale of cotton to an acre, there was strength in the clay. Even the most eroded clay lands could be brought back into fertility if they were handled properly for a few seasons, if they were fertilized and sown in pea vines and in winter grain. In March we planted cotton and in April we planted corn. In May we hoed and chopped and thinned, and in June we hoed and ran around the cotton with a plow, and we also cut and thrashed our oats and wheat. We planted pea vines and sorghum cane, and we plowed under the stubble in the grain fields and planted corn. We liked to finish all that by the Fourth of July. Through the long hot sultry July days we plowed and hoed some more, and when August came we laid the crops by. We rested and went fishing and attended family reunions and went to camp meetings and to all-day singings, and enjoyed ourselves to the fullest. It gave us a fine feeling to look out over our

And Cotton

well-tilled fields and to see the heat radiating upward in dazzling waves, to see the cotton blooming and the corn tasseling out. August was cotton-growing weather, and the hotter the better — cotton liked the blazing heat, chilled now and then by a short sudden August shower. The fields blossomed like islands in the South Seas, white and red splotches on a glorious green and crimson — the white and red hibiscus-like cotton flowers on the green cotton plants that spread away in long curving rows across the silky vermilion of the fields. Nothing gave us more satisfaction than to watch cotton growing in August in the fields that we ourselves had plowed and planted. Jim said he was just as satisfied in a fine cotton patch as the angels were in glory. During September we sowed the winter turnips and pulled the corn fodder and gathered in the corn. We dug sweet potatoes and picked cotton through October, and in November we went to town.

I liked to plow cotton, to stand between the swerving handles of the plow, to hold the handles lightly, to guide the shares in the smooth furrow, and to walk barefooted in the fresh earth. No wonder there is so much singing about cotton-plowing; it is a simple, complete way of work. It is hard and the sweat pours, but there is an open freedom about it, and the waterboy brings you a cool drink, and you drink and rest — it is an exquisite sensation — and at night when you come in tired, you sleep the wonderful sleep of the really weary. It is a fine sensation really to be thirsty and to drink cold water, really to be tired and to crawl into a bed and rest. The reward is worth the effort, especially if cotton is bringing ten cents a pound. Of course it is discouraging, year after year, to plant and plow and pick and to get only five cents for the crop, but even then we somehow never give up. We always expect something to come along and boost the price of cotton. Cotton is cash to us, it is faith, it is hope. We can make more money picking cow peas in the autumn than we can make picking cotton, but somehow cow-pea money has never meant to us what cotton money means. We can sell grain for cash, but we have never trusted grain as money. We do not understand grain as we understand cotton. So all summer long we plow in the cotton fields and sing and tell the mule what we intend to do when we have the cash in hand from our cotton.

Our cotton country swarms with non-producing hangers-on who scheme the year around to get their fingers on our cotton dollars. They come around throughout the spring and summer and trade on our hope; they sell us things on time, credit us against the cotton crop that we will gather in the autumn. They sell us radios and phonographs and Sunday suits, and they sell the colored people funeral insurance and enlarged photographs of themselves and their kinfolks; they even sell them fifteen-dollar Bibles. Once in the late autumn Aunt Coot dashed into the house with a Bible in her hand and breathlessly told me the Bible man was coming for his money and she would be obliged to pick cotton a few more days before she could pay him. She said maybe he would let her keep the book, maybe he would extend her time if the book was written in — would I write in it the names of her children?

" All right, Aunt Coot," said I. " How do you want me to start? "

" The first one," she said, " is John the Divine Christopher Columbus."

I had known Aunt Coot all of my life, I knew all of her children well, but never had I heard of anyone in her family with the name John the Divine Christopher Columbus.

"Aunt Coot," said I, " who in the world is that? "

" That's Son," she answered.

" All right, who comes after Son? " " Emmalina Kathaline Jollycosey Julianne."

" Which one is that? "

" That's Doll Baby."

I listed them all — the first batch, the second batch,

Red Hills

Brother John's children, Brother Joe's — Lord Wellington
Lord Nelson, Queen Victoria, Matthew Mark Luke John,
Bathshebabe States Rights, Narcissa Clarissa Temper-
ance, Miss Mary B., Miss Hattie Boone.

And Aunt Coot kept the book.

There was great commotion in the hills when at last
the sweeping fields turned white. There would be frost in
the air, and whole families would appear with crocker
sacks slung over one shoulder — old and young would
take to the cotton patch. They would bend to the stalks,
picking with both hands, and they would sing old
rhythmic hymns — " In grand mansions above," " Lord I
want to be like Jesus," " Must Jesus bear the cross alone,
and all the world go free? " They would start at the first
light, before the dew had dried, for dew on the cotton
would add to the weight, and all of them were interested
in weight, as they were paid at sundown by the pound.
Everything was fair in cotton-picking — even rocks in the
sack — and you had to watch every bagful of cotton.
" There's nothing like a good field stone," Mary once said,
" to bring your poundage to two hundred." One time
Mary was paid for a stone in her cotton bag; the weigher
did not detect it, and that night Mary had that rock on
her mind. She worried about it and she worried — what if
the rock should slip unnoticed into the cotton gin, would

And Cotton

it not ruin the gin? Next morning, she said to my cousin Stephen John that she had dreamed there was a rock in her cotton, she did not know how it got there, but she believed one was there — someone had better go through her cotton bag, for she had dreamed about a stone. Mary had true goodness in her heart, and I have always known why Mary could be so happy with so little to show for her work. Always she has done what our grandparents said all of us should do: she has lived with dignity, she has lived with plainness and honor.

After we had picked the cotton and had sold the bales, we paid for fertilizer, we settled with the stores, we paid for the Bibles and clocks and radios and cars. Then we bought a pair of shoes, a few clothes, we bought a bottle of government liquor, and after that little or nothing was left. All that we had to look forward to was hunting and fishing and the next year's cotton crop.

During laying-by time in August, on the second Monday in the month, we always held a reunion of all the kinfolks, usually at one of the houses over on Chauga Creek. About three hundred would attend, and we would arrive in carriages, in wagons pulled by mules, and on horseback and afoot; we would drive up in automobiles, and once one of our cousins landed in the bottoms in an airplane. During the morning we would sit in the shade of the trees and our cousin Unity and our Great-Aunt Narcissa and our cousin Ella would begin at the beginning of time, long before the Revolution, and trace the kinfolks from then until the moment of that reunion. They would tell us who had married whom, who had gone where, and what had happened. At noon someone would ring the yard bell and the three hundred of us would sit down on benches before long board tables — three hundred of us would eat an old-time dinner. About a hundred chickens would be fried and served on platters, and there would be fried steak, venison, fried fresh pork, whole boiled hams, sugared and spiced, and there would be roasted duck, baked turkey, cold veal, stuffed eggs, and beans, potatoes, roasting ear corn, cheese straws, lemon tarts, and bowls of highly seasoned chowchow pickles and peach preserves made from the wild clingstone peaches that grew on the cotton terraces, and there would be clingstone peach pickles, and blackberry jelly and apple jelly and pound cake, chocolate layer cake, coconut layer cake, marble cake, banana layer cake, caramel layer cake, sponge cake, angel-food cake, apple pie, peach pie, huckleberry pie, ambrosia, boiled frozen custard, fresh grapes, cold watermelons, cantaloupes, muskmelons, pomegranates. For drink there would be blackberry cordial, cider, hard cider, blackberry wine, sweet and deep purple in color, and there would be a dry scuppernong wine and muscadine wine, a strong elderberry wine and dandelion wine, clover-blossom wine, and pitchers filled with sweet milk, buttermilk, and water from the spring branch. Of course, we considered it outrageous and disgraceful for any of our kinfolks to drink corn liquor, so we did not serve white lightning at the dinner table. Those who drank that did so behind the barn.

Once I remember seeing my Great-Uncle John coming up the garden path smiling and talking to everyone and all the time mopping his fiercely flushed face. At the gate he started to walk toward the far edge of the yard, but at that moment my Great-Aunt Kate yelled to him from the front porch.

" John," she cried, " where did you get that liquor? "

" Why, Kate! " exclaimed my great-uncle, astonished.

" You heard me," continued my great-aunt. " Where did you get it? "

" I hardly touched it," said my great-uncle. " Just took a drop."

" You come on up here and sit down," said my great-aunt. Obediently my great-uncle went up on to the piazza, and from then on until time to go home he sat there in a chair. He sat there in silence — he did not say a word.

Red Hills

When we had eaten dinner at the reunions, somebody would talk about us and olden times, and then we would pack up and start early for our houses. All of our lives we had to start early from places, for we had stock at home to attend to. We had to milk and feed, and my kinfolks were the kind of people who believed that cows should be milked and mules fed at exactly the same hour, day after day. We might inconvenience ourselves, but not our livestock. It was low-down and trifling to inconvenience livestock.

CHAPTER X

ONE day when I was growing up, Harve, the son of a tenant, came to the house, a rifle in hand, to suggest that we go into the thick woods west of the river to hunt for gray squirrels. This suited me, so we called Popcorn, one of the colored boys, and the three of us started out across the bare March hills, pretending we were a band of Cherokee Indians. We had only two bullets among us, but that did not bother us as we did not care much whether we shot squirrels or even saw a squirrel. It was the woods that we wanted to wander in — the wild and mysterious forest.

" I'm Chief Black Bear," said Harve, his eyes glistening.

" I'm Chief Wild Panther," I said.

" I'm Chief Wolf," said Popcorn, but Harve and I objected. "Can't everybody be a chief, Popcorn," said Harve. "Somebody's got to be a brave for the chief to be chief of — you've got to be a brave."

We made Popcorn be a brave and bring up the rear. Our marauding party halted for a few minutes in a deep red gully to see whether the last rains had washed out any quartz crystals and whether we could discover gold, but finding none, we moved down to the moss- and fern-bound bank of a small stream to inspect a hole that a skunk lived in. We looked at the wild Indian turnips that just then were beginning to spring up in a patch of marsh. Farther down this stream we stopped to carve our names in the hard gray bark of a beech tree, and then we found some tracks in wet sand that we followed. They were raccoon tracks, but we said they were wildcat's; we hoped at any minute to run face to face into a wildcat.

Suddenly Harve decided the little stream which we were following ran round the wrong side of a granite boulder, so we brought dead logs and daubed them with red mud and we forced the water to change its course, to run in a different direction — we stood and watched the stream follow the course we had willed it to follow, and this gave us a sense of satisfaction. This was our first feeling of power.

We found the loose woven sticks of a dove's nest on the

swaying end of a pine limb, and as we came near, the nesting dove flew away through the trees, pretending its wing was broken, trying by ruse to draw our attention from the nest. We listened to the hollow drumming of a red-headed woodpecker, drilling a home in the old dead trunk of a willow tree. Crossing a small swamp, we stepped lightly across a mud flat and made our way through a grove of alders that were breaking into bud, through blooming red maples, and we frightened a drove of snowbirds that already had been frightened by a hawk. Beyond in the open we saw green wheat-fields and we heard wrens singing. It was spring, another spring in Carolina, and on all sides we could see the signs. The wild plum was sweet-smelling and white in the wild hedgerow, a fragile and wistful beauty, and blue forget-me-nots studded the green pasture with the blue newness of hope.

The world was fine and warm, and we lay down on a high ledge above the river and watched a lizard sleeping. Far below us ran the red river, glistening in the afternoon light; a rag of white cloud hung across the sun, revealing a burst of light-rays that drew water from half of Carolina; over the valley hung a fine blue smoke, filled with the smell of old leaves burning, and there was the smell of the earth, of the country warming.

"When I grow up," said Harve, folding his strong arms

under his chin, "I'm going to see the world before I settle down. I'm going to roam around and travel." Harve said to us: "I want to see the Mississippi River and look at Texas and hear a coyote howl and watch buffaloes on the move and see the Missouri and the great plains and the Rocky Mountains and be in a dust storm." Harve shifted himself. "When I find the right country," he said, "I'm going to settle down and live right, and I'm going to make a hundred thousand dollars."

I listened as I always listened to Harve's restless, roaming talk. I said that I too was going away. I would see the Pacific Ocean before I came back home. I would go completely round the world.

"I'm going to Sandusky, Ohio," Popcorn said; "I'm going to get a job in an automobile factory and make eighteen dollars a week."

Suddenly Popcorn raised the rifle to his shoulder, aimed, fired. And a squirrel toppled from the limb of a hickory tree.

Many times like this I idled the days away with Harve and Popcorn. We hunted, we fished, we went swimming in Twelve Mile, we built a flat-bottom boat. One winter we ordered a half dozen steel traps and dreamed of getting rich, but all that we ever caught besides a few muskrats were some skunks and Clint Taylor's best possum dog, old Blaze. Clint was so angry when he found old Blaze trapped in the little swamp among the Indian turnips that he tore the trap apart with his hands. He was so mad that we did not tell him for ten years that we had set the trap.

Harve had a hard life. His people were lazy and loafing and were accused of all kinds of crimes; they drifted from farm to farm, never staying long anywhere. They were undisciplined and self-indulgent and they drank hard liquor. Often they had almost nothing to eat. Harve's father, who was one of my best childhood friends, mended chairs and fished and fiddled and was suspected of things we did not ordinarily mention. Harve's mother was not beyond suspicion. One of his sisters was Miss Mattie, the girl who threatened to kill Aunt Nan and Aunt Neat. I never was able to understand how Harve grew as he grew — strong and tall and broad. Sometimes when I think of Harve I wonder if the germ theory of disease is a correct one, sometimes I wonder if a balanced diet is important. Harve was raised on cornbread, hominy, collards, and fatback, and he grew bigger and better than any of us who were fed lettuce and pine honey and tar and iron in the spring.

Harve was full of spirit, anxious to know things, to experience, to feel. He belonged to the stock that we all belonged to in the hills, to a heredity that no environment could beat down. He had the leanness, the angular cast, the ruddy high-cheeked face, the blue eyes, the sandy thin hair that characterized so many men and women in the uplands, and he was restless — always he wanted to be moving, to be doing something, to live a life of action; yet he could lie on the rocks and dream. He also was reckless, and sometimes he got into trouble. Once a great family accused Harve and his brother of stealing from their barn; they charged the two boys in court with stealing, and a judge sentenced them to attend the Baptist Sunday school every Sunday morning for six months.

Harve left Twelve Mile Valley when he grew up. He saw what he wanted to see, and then he became a steelworker in a mill in Indiana; he became one of the best men in his trade. For ten years he stayed away from the hills, and then he came back. It must have been a journey he had wanted to make for a long time, it was a kind of triumph. He arrived in a long purple automobile, trimmed with shining nickel, and he drove up to a filling station that was operated by a boy who belonged to the great family that had accused him of stealing. Harve told the boy to fill up the tank; then he reached into his pocket, pulled out a large wad of money, and handing the boy a twenty-dollar bill, Harve said: "I'm sorry, Bud, but that's the smallest change I have."

Popcorn went to New York instead of Sandusky, Ohio. Popcorn runs an elevator now in one of the big skyscrapers in midtown Manhattan, and he is a member of the Abyssinian Baptist Church in Harlem and has joined the Republican Party.

Like all of my kinfolks, I spent much time alone. I walked far in the forests, deep into the woods, and sometimes I would feel presences near that I could not see, and I would know that eyes were on me. Sometimes this sensation would frighten me, and even though I had a shotgun in my hands, I would run. I would feel there were forces about me that a gun could never touch. I would watch the stillness of the great Southern summer days, watch the light slowly circling the passing hours, forming a swinging pattern of dark shadows. I learned from picking blackberries that the person who at the end of the morning had the most berries in his bucket was not the person who had rushed from place to place looking for the finest and the biggest and the best berries; the person with the filled bucket had stayed in one place and had picked steadily, taking the small with the large. I learned that the shade of the tree by the river was never

so deep or so cool as it seemed when I was plowing corn
in the hot sun and surveyed its depths and coolness from
the corn row and the open heat. Shade and rest were an
illusion. Gnats and sweat bees swarmed in shade, and the
air there was stifling — you smothered in the depths of
the shade. I learned too that stillness often was rewarded
and that many things came to you by chance. By sitting
still on a bank and looking up into an oak, I once discovered a hummingbird's nest — a nest I could never
have found if I had said to myself I would find a hummingbird's nest. I learned there were many things that
could never be revealed unless you sat still and looked
and listened. I learned great lessons alone in the forests,
but I did not often profit from this knowledge. I, and the
people I belonged to, had to learn by the hardest way.
We had to burn our fingers to dread a fire. I almost never
trusted the prudence of the mind, I followed the impulse
of the heart. The mind, I have always thought, is cold
and safe and it will lead you from milepost to milepost
across a tremendous plain. The heart will plunge you into
chasms and lead you to peaks, but I have always enjoyed
chasms and peaks, and I had rather learn from the spirit
than from the brain. I know now that I shall never fill my
bucket with berries and I shall never discover many nests
of the minutest birds, but I think that eventually I may

And Cotton

develop an understanding of distances, of sweep — some
day I hope to know the meaning of trouble and suffering,
to discover mercy in the soul. I know now that I am
Southern in all of my outlook. I am a child of the South.
Why should anyone follow mileposts? Who would never
die?

In the early days in Twelve Mile Valley I would watch
the hawks, darting with such precision and power, and I
would listen to the catbirds and to the song sparrows —
for them all there was compensation. I would stare into
the sunsets, which in our Southern country were filled
with the wildest beauty. Sometimes they would be yellow, solid yellow, and again they would be gold and crimson and glowing. But these were not the sunsets that ap-
pealed to me most — not the yellow, not the great red
and indigo sunsets of the Southern summer. I liked the
winter sky — the clean gray, the clearness. Sometimes on
chill winter evenings the gold disk of the sun would sink
into a pure sky of light, into pure light, into a great space
of colorless color-perfection. This was the light I sought.
I and all of my kinfolks watched the sunsets, we watched
the moon rise, always we discussed the open weather, we
believed in signs. Sometimes I would be held breathless
by wild flying mallards, moving between immensities, between unknowns, beating so sure a course across the sur-

Red Hills

face of the present. My Great-Aunt Narcissa said what she admired about wild ducks was the unquestioning of their flying, their acceptance of their fate. I said that what I liked was their speed, the beauty of their power — they had energy, they were strong. What we really admired, I think now, was the unity the duck had achieved with all existence. Its flying was like the freezing of water, like the forming of steam. Somewhere there was a law, and water froze and steam formed and a duck flew. We sought that law too for ourselves, and if we could put our hands on it, we would live as the wild mallard flew — with absolute grace and perfection.

I learned contemplation when I was growing up. In the solitude of the long Southern afternoons I found how to retire within and retreat and how to hear in the great orchestra of the wind the high note. I learned to lie fallow, like the fields in winter, and to live beyond the world and some of its loneliness. That is a quieting habit to acquire; it helps to overcome restlessness. Like most Southerners, I learned early to wait.

To amuse ourselves when we were growing up, Harve and Popcorn and I would build secret cities; far out in the cotton patches and in thickets we plastered mud on stumps and laid out streets and set up towers and palaces and forts — all from sticks and red clay and tin cans and

And Cotton

bottles. In the biggest of our cities we built a temple to the sun, and here at sundown we would burn offerings of cotton soaked in kerosene. As the dark smoke rose, we would beat on a sheet of metal and chant a wild hymn. We surrounded these cities with rock walls and built fleets of ships out of barrel staves for their protection. Then suddenly we would turn on these creations of our loneliness and patience. Like Jeremiah threatening Jerusalem, we would threaten our cities with evil out of the north, and standing away in a rage, we would shower them with rocks. We would bombard all the palaces and towers and sink all the ships. Then we would begin over again and build bigger and better cities. Periodically we would build up, periodically we would destroy.

I would sit for hours in the garret of the old house, rummaging through the old chests and reading the fading letters. I would read about the battles and about the crops of a hundred years and the gossip. There were the letters from our Great-Uncle Carter — hurried notes, hastily scribbled from many places between New Orleans and St. Louis, from Natchez, where he said he was resting, from Memphis. I knew why he had been in all of those places — Windy Bill had told me. He was a gambler and he worked the steamboats up and down the Mississippi. There were old newspapers that another of our great-uncles had edited, and in them I often read about the editor's indispositions. " The editor has been very unwell with the bloody flux, so much so that he has been unable to prepare any editorial at all. We hope the editor will be well enough to get out the next issue, when he will have many things to discuss." That great-uncle, Bill said, had died from drinking liquor.

There were the Tennessee letters and the Texas letters. " Dear Folks, Just to let you know we are pulling up stake, leaving for Texas. We have just heard from Cousin Caldwell and his folks out there and they say they were wonderful pleased with the Texas country." " Well, here we are and well pleased, I reckon, but I thought when I first arrived that if all Texas was mine I would not have it." " Tell the girls that when we went to Austin, we spent a night at a mansion house with some folks by the name of Johnson. Their folks came to Texas when Mister Johnson was a boy — had a brother killed by the Indians. He is one of the aristocracy, if there is any here, has a splendid house, magnificently furnished — to be short, is rich, has thousands of acres of this fertile Texas land — AND NOT A CHILD. Now, don't you know I wish he would adopt me or his fat old wife would kick the bucket. This is a wild country but the wildest of all are the young men."

And Cotton

There were letters about the gold rush. "Dear Pa, I have not heared from any of you in so long a time; I hear from Habersham who is thousands of miles away twice to your once; he or Uncle Silas has written every two weeks but we have not heared yet whether they have reached California. They set out safe from Panama. Aunt Sarah is very uneasy, she has grieved so much she has become unhealthy. She said she never was so weak before and I don't know any other cause without it is living exposed to the cold winter. She said after Uncle Silas left she could not get warm all night. I do not see any use of her staying in Texas as she will have no stock when she gets her hogs fat and kills them but one lone cow and calf, one sheep, and one sow — and I don't think she will have any pigs soon. But she stays on. Well, we are waiting for news, and while I'm waiting, I will start this letter and keep on adding until we hear. . . .

"I went to the Methodist Church last Sunday. Three persons were to be baptized, but one of them was not prepared. The first one went to the creek and had the water dipped up in a pitcher and poured on. The second went in the water and knelt and had it poured. The minister said straightaway come up and out of the water. The third one was to be immerst had she been ready. I went to Two Tree that night to hear Rev. Reid preach. He did not attend — I do not know any cause without it is the report that has got out about his becoming lonesome at a late hour when he should have been at his own house sleeping — he got lonesome, they say, and went visiting at a California widow's house. This has caused more laughing than anything I have heared since I been here, but I can't write it — will have to send word about it by the first person going to Carolina.

" I have concluded I will not close this letter until the California mail comes, even if I have to hold it a month — my littlest boy is not well. He has the summer complaint that is common among children. I think some of the grown persons were troubled with it last Sunday. They kept going out while the preacher was talking. Habersham wrote the boys to study their books, but the boys are confused, they can't study the book nor nothing else much. Aunt Sarah says she hopes she will not have to go back home for a support. I told her that she has a plenty and is said to be the most industrious woman in Texas. She canned two bushels of peaches in one day and had the back door trots besides, very bad. I tried to get her to quit work but she said she will not until the men come in from California."

These letters were old and the news they told was old. The trunks were old and the garret was old and the Con-

federates who talked on the piazza at night were old. All
about me, on every side, was age, and history was con-
tinuous, and somehow men were not allowed to finish the
walls they had started, nor did they complete their houses.
Time and chance happened to them — in America as in
Ecclesiastes. They were called to Texas, to California —
and the first were last, and the last first, and many were
called but few chosen. I was Southern, I was old.

Like other Southerners I have known from the start
that the way is long, and that we live and leave what record we can of our hopes, of the cry in our hearts. We plow
the water, and it is the spirit alone that is ever free, and
it is only memory that has no time. How often do we
picture the way ahead and dream of it and plan? But the
actual road is never the dreamed one, and the sights that
we start out to see are not the scenes that we remember.
It is not the cathedral that lives. It is something else, the
sudden and the unexpected. Not the great famed thing,
but a mist, an expression on a face, a whisper. Often it is
the fragile things of a moment that never die, that one
remembers on and on through a life. The lines of a mountain lie in the mind, a sunset never fades, a peach blossom
never shatters. The light of a star shines on, and there is
the dim glimmer of distant lightning, and the good that
one has done and the evil. It is regret that never dies.

Red Hills

Like other Southerners, I have known from the start
that there would be no new Texas for us, no California.
I have always known that the procession we march in has
already arrived in the promised land. It is here for us, not
there. In the South, I have known that from our time on,
we would be obliged to find what it is we look for within
ourselves. It is not to be found in change of scene, nor in
pulling up stakes. It is ourselves now that we must settle,
it is the state that we must take hold of, we must enrich
old fields and stop erosion. It is in the state that we can
find the riches, the perfect security, and the peace. We
cannot turn our backs — we cannot pick up and leave any
longer. We are old and we must do what all who are old
must do; there is the responsibility to assume and the
duty. No one can be young always. Who would wish to
be? Texas is Carolina now, and California is Texas, and
we can fly to them all in a night.

I went to the grist mill with my grandfather, rode on
the cotton wagons with Windy Bill; I went to Tabor
Church with Mr. Beasley, the tenant; I hunted with Harve
and Popcorn, and I lay in the shade under the water oaks
and listened to Harve's father. Harve's father picked tunes
on banjos and fiddles, and he taught us to catch fish in
fish-traps, which was against the law, and he showed us

And Cotton

how to weave chair bottoms. He told us about a woman up the road who had children without a husband, and about some other children who had no father, and about a woman who was stingy; he said this stingy woman was so mean that once the neighbors had caught her chasing a mouse that had stolen a seed of cotton. He told us about a man he suspected of murder; he believed this man had shot and robbed a Tennessee horse-dealer. He told about a woman who put a shotgun across her knees and hauled liquor.

Almost all of the stories that Harve's father told us were evil, but they did us no harm as we were not interested in evil — we were interested in hunting and fishing and in weaving chair bottoms and in learning to daub the bottoms of flatboats with tar. I did not connect people in our valley with actual evil until years later, and by that time it did not matter. Harve's father did us no harm. He was a friend with time on his hands, he had time to give to children.

During those years I spent hours and hours with Jim and Mary, for like my parents and grandparents and like my Great-Aunt Narcissa and Windy Bill and like Harve's father, Jim and Mary raised me. They were casual and easy-going, and they had charity for all and compassion, and they drifted with the current, and met each day as time brought them to it. They did not believe in any of the Puritan abstinences that my kinfolks preached; they believed in repentance, and in the willingness of the heart. The flesh, for them, was beyond resistance — it was as the Book said it was, it was weak. Time and again they fell by the way, but always they got up again, told the Lord sincerely and simply they were sorry, and continued on. Both of them were members of the Baptist church, both had been totally immersed.

One morning Jim stomped into the kitchen, very angry.

"God said in the Bible," he said, "that He was the Father and the Son and the Holy Ghost." Furiously Jim added: "I'm not going to let any damned no-account drunkard tell me God didn't say that."

"Jim, quit that cussing," said Mary scandalized.

Ignoring Mary, Jim continued: "I have read the Scripture." Lowering his voice, he added with disgust: "The trouble with all of that House of Prayer crowd is they skip a verse."

"Who said God didn't say it, Jim?" I asked.

"Brother Ike," muttered Jim. Brother Ike was a deacon at the House of Prayer.

Still fuming, Jim sat down on the woodbox and flung his old hat over his crossed knees. After he had cooled off, Jim then began to tell us what had happened. In the woods he had met Brother Ike, and Jim as a Baptist had told him it was a sin and a shame for the House of Prayer to charge two dollars for baptizings.

"The two dollars," said Brother Ike, "is for a special baptizing. If you go down to Columbia and pay the two dollars, you get baptized in the River Jordan."

"It ain't the River Jordan at Columbia," Jim said, "It's the Congaree River."

"It don't matter if it's the Congaree or the Santee," Brother Ike said; "if you got faith and the water has been made holy, it's the River Jordan."

That made Jim mad, but he controlled himself. Then Brother Ike further tantalized him by saying he had belonged to the Baptist church and to the Methodist church, but had never found the Holy Ghost until he had joined the House of Prayer.

"The Holy Ghost, man," replied Jim, "has been here ever since I was born, and I'm twice as old as you. Brother Ike, if you haven't found the Holy Ghost, it isn't the Baptist church's fault, it's your fault. You got to find the Holy Ghost in your own heart. God is the Holy Ghost."

"That ain't true," said Brother Ike. "The Holy Ghost has got to be brought to you by a prophet."

"You're a liar," Jim said.

Red Hills

"You're a God-damned liar," said Brother Ike.

So Jim knocked Brother Ike into a ditch and ran.

At practically any time and at any place Jim was ready to argue about doctrine. He loved to preach.

One time we had a high wind during the night, and the next morning we were all talking about it. Mary said she had spent the night at Lucille's house, trying to persuade Lucille, with fourteen children, not to marry the preacher, with seven. "I heared the first bluff," Mary said, "for if there's anything that wakes me it is a wind. I shook Lucille. 'Lucille,' I said, 'it's a wind storm, get up.' With that, we got up and dressed and sat up the rest of the blessed night. We sat it through. I always sit when there's a high wind, for I made up my mind many years ago if a wind was going to take me off it was going to take me on my feet. I'm going to be up and waiting with all of my clothes on."

"Sister Mary," said Jim sanctimoniously, "it ain't going to do you a God's bit of good just to be up — you got to be up in faith."

"You are talking sense now, Jim," said Mary. "The world is full of fellows that's got pretense."

"I ain't talking about the other fellows," said Jim; "I'm talking about Mary."

And Cotton

Both bowed their heads then and laughed. They roared with laughter.

When Jim had finished eating, he came over to the table where I was eating. " Boss," he said, " could I speak to you in private for a minute? "

" How much do you want, Jim? " I asked.

" A dollar, boss, until Saturday."

That morning Mary too asked if she could borrow a dollar until Saturday.

" What do you want a dollar for, Mary? "

" For a purpose," she answered.

" What purpose?

" That wind disturbed me, so I thought I would go over to Pendleton and buy me a smile."

Mary and Jim, simple and friendly and kind, lived full and complete and exciting lives within a radius of three miles. They had experienced high winds and the devastation of five-cent cotton crops and the sudden madness of the forty-cent boom; they had gone through poverty and the approach of death and had been where there was shooting and shouting, and they had been happy and sad and had grown wise from experience — from actual knowledge. They were religious and they believed that the purpose of living was happiness, and that everyone here must get ready for the hereafter. They wanted to do good, and they believed in working for a living, and, like us all, they were conservative, holding that the slow way was the sure way; they stood for progress.

Mary was born in a cotton-field house, the child of a former slave. She worked in the field, but she was restless and she roamed about for a while, cooking.

"One time I worked for a rich policeman in Georgia," she told me. "I was doing fine over there, making good money. I had good things to eat and on Saturday night they treated me from demijohns. But I didn't like Georgia — that's a wild place. Even preachers drink whisky in Georgia. So one Sunday when Brother Isaac and Sister Sug came on the train to see me and we went to church and sang sweet music, I decided I couldn't stand it any longer, far from home. So I came on back to South Carolina."

For ten years after that, Mary cooked for the Newman family.

"I worked for them ten years," she said, "and then I quit. They weren't mad and I wasn't mad, but one day I went to the house and all of a sudden I said: 'Miss Grace, I'm going.' Miss Grace said: 'What's the matter, Mary, are you sick?' I said: 'No'm.' 'Well,' she said, 'what's the matter?' I said: 'I'm just going.' Miss Grace

And Cotton

called four times: 'Mary, are you gone?' I didn't answer.
I had done got tired. I had already raised all the children
at that house, they were out and gone, and I was tired,
so I went over by Cherry's Crossing and stayed a week,
resting. Then Mrs. Smith from Calhoun sent for me to
help run her hotel — paid me a dollar a day. There was a
man there who liked my biscuits. He sent me a silk dress
from Washington. Well, June came, and the boarders left,
and I went into the field, and one day here came Mrs. Foy
and I went with her, and I stayed there awhile, and then
Banker Anderson tried to get me, but by that time I had
decided to come here to you all."

A lady from the North one time asked Mary how long
she had been with us. " Mum," Mary told her, " I been
here God knows how long — just patiencing along."

Late one afternoon, years ago, my younger sister Hattie Boone and Mary had a falling out, and Hattie Boone in
a flurry of anger told Mary she was fired. Mary put on
her hat and walked out the front door. Next morning, at
breakfast time, she was back in the kitchen, boiling hominy and coffee and frying ham and kneading biscuits.
" Miss Hattie Boone," she said, " I've been here longer
than you have." And that closed the incident.

" Miss Hattie Boone," Mary said, " we ain't got any
rice. I forgot to tell you we ain't got any rice. And can I

get a nickel's worth of meal, please? I want some corn-bread."

"Have we got lard, Mary?" asked Hattie Boone.

"No, ma'am, we ain't got any lard."

"Have we got sugar?"

"No, ma'am, we ain't got any sugar."

"Mary, what have we got?"

Mary said: "We got flour."

Once when I came home from school, Mary told me she was having some trouble with the church.

"What sort of trouble?" I inquired.

Sitting before the stove, sipping from a coffee saucer, Mary said it was about a boarder staying in her cabin.

"Who is the boarder?"

"It's Salem."

"Salem?" said I, startled, for I knew Mary's cabin had only one room.

"Yes, sir, Salem — but he's only a boy."

"How old is he, Mary?"

"He's thirty-three."

"Well," I inquired, "what does the church say?"

"They say either I marry that boarder or kick him out, or they are going to kick me out of the church."

"What are you going to do?"

And Cotton

"I don't know yet," said Mary, sipping quietly. "I haven't decided in my mind."

Soon after that, I returned to school, and when next I got back home, I asked Mary how she was getting along with the church.

"Just fine," she replied.

"What happened about the boarder?"

"Well, Mr. Ben," she said, "I decided I had already sowed my wild oats, so I just married the boy."

Mary enjoys beautiful views, she likes to sit under the cool shade of trees, she gets much pleasure watching birds. She delights to sing. She is not absent one day a year from her work. She can fry chicken and boil rice and make as good biscuits as any woman in South Carolina. She is always willing and anxious to help anyone in trouble. And, like my grandmother, she likes to make plans about what she intends to do when she gets to heaven. Once she told me that when she arrived up there, she was going to ask the Lord to let her look for one hour at New York City. She said she would like to see what that place was like, for just one hour.

I remember a morning when Mary came to the house with one of her arms in a sling.

"Mary, what has happened?"

Red Hills

"I been car-hit," she said.

"Bad?"

"Not too bad."

"Where did it happen?"

"Over at Pendleton. I'd been standing outside the liquor store, looking at the government liquor, and then I stepped out into the road, and I looked up but I didn't look down. And a white gentleman hit me in a big V–8."

Mary began to laugh. "Lord," she said, "he was the scaredest white gentleman I ever saw in my life. He slapped on the brakes and stopped the car, and he ran over to me and said: 'Auntie, are you hurt?' I said to him: 'Don't you bother, Captain, it wasn't your fault — I was looking up the road instead of looking down the road.' He said: 'That's right, Auntie.'"

"Did you get his number, Mary?" inquired Jim.

"I wasn't going to take down any white gentleman's number," Mary said; "I wasn't going to get in any tangle with white folks. I just took the broke hand and went on. Because wasn't I looking up the road?"

We telephoned the doctor.

Jim came to work with us long later than Mary. Jim did not come until his days on the railroad were over. He was already old when he first began to cut wood steadily

And Cotton

and to cut the grass and rake leaves. One morning soon after he first began working, Jim dashed into the kitchen, and right behind him came a deputy sheriff.

"Mr. Ben," said Jim, "I got to have five dollars — it's five dollars for me or thirty days."

Jim said he had taken a crocker sack down to the coal chute at the railway station and had intended to pick up a few chunks of coal. "Just a few little chunks," he explained breathlessly. "I didn't aim to pick up anything but pieces that had fallen off the trucks — just the little pieces 'way across the roadway out in the edge of the cotton patch."

"He was right on top the chute," said the deputy sheriff.

Jim grinned sickishly. "I got to have five dollars, Mr. Ben," he said.

I gave him the money, and the deputy sheriff filled out some sort of receipt and left. Sitting down on the woodbox, Jim laughed with relief. "Boss," he said, "I thank you. Lord God, I thank you."

From that morning on, Jim always called me "boss."

Our relationship with Mary and Jim, and theirs with us, were intimate and personal, and at the same time strict — on both sides they were strict, old-fashioned, and Southern. The standards of behavior for both sides were established and we knew it, and we knew why it was so, we knew what had happened to make it so. Memory with all of us, white and black, was long. All of us remembered.

Both races wanted to live dignified lives, to live with some individual meaning. The facts in the South were the facts, and they had caused us all trouble and suffering. None of us was satisfied, but we did the best we could, and we had faith in the future, and slowly the race question improved. In spite of lynchings and riots it got better, and steadily it will continue to get better.

The trouble, of course, started with slavery; and it got worse rapidly after the Civil War. In 1865 we came home from Appomattox, lost from a lost war. In South Carolina in 1861 there were forty thousand white men old enough to vote, and between 1861 and 1865 our state lost forty thousand white men — killed or permanently disabled. Our dead and disabled were forty thousand out of a total white population of one hundred and forty six thousand. No wonder our grandparents could not bear to think that so many of our kinfolks had died for nothing more than failure; no wonder they determined to give the dead some sort of immortality, determined to pass on to later generations some memory of so many sons. William Gilmore Simms in his *History of South Carolina* wrote that property in our state was valued at four hundred million dollars in 1861, and at fifty million dollars in 1865. During the four years of the Civil War, Charleston was continuously in a state of siege, and large areas of the city were left in ruins from constant shelling. Sherman burned Columbia, our capital. The southwest section of our state, around Beaufort on the seacoast, was held by Union armies from 1862 onward, and all over South Carolina Sherman's men burnt bridges and houses and flooded rice fields and destroyed granaries. We were beaten and crushed and bowed in the dust, but that was only the start of our disaster.

The Federal government in Washington established the Freedmen's Bureau to protect the Negro, and our state legislature at its first session after the surrender passed a series of acts to protect the white man against the black. Our legislature also passed measures to give the freed slaves the right to acquire property, to make contracts, and to receive protection under the law in his person and property. But as there were many more black people than white in South Carolina, it then drew up the laws to protect the white minority against the black majority. There was indignation in the North, especially in New York City, and these Carolina laws became known as the Black Code.

Red Hills

We intended to accept the results of the war, but we never had the slightest intention of being dominated by the former slaves — not even Appomattox could saddle that upon us. We would give the black man equal protection under the law but not the right to vote, and in keeping with this view we refused to ratify the fourteenth amendment to the Constitution. With that, the North forced the Negro vote on us with the bayonet. They abolished our legislature, they put the army over us, they put Negro troops over us, they treated us as a crushed province and ruled us with an absolute military autocracy. And then came the scum of the earth — the Northern carpetbaggers. Low-down Yankees whom no respectable Northerner would speak to came to our conquered province. They came like buzzards, and brought all kinds of foreigners with them, and for a decade they ruled our state. They were judges, and legislators, and they came to pillage for themselves, not to help the respectable Negroes of our state. It is this period of the Reconstruction that left us so bitter about the Civil War, and it is because of carpetbaggers that we still become angry whenever anyone in New York City tries to tell us in South Carolina what we ought to do. We have had one Northern government — we have had Northern ideas tried on us, and we decided we had rather die than live under such a government. There were terrible cases of assault and murder, and it was at this time that the talk about Southern womanhood started. This started the memory that our demagogue politicians have harped on for the last eighty years. Old Cotton Ed Smith even tried to win votes on the issue of Southern womanhood as late as 1938. Campaigning at Abbeville for the United States Senate in that year, he saw four young girls in white dresses sitting on a fence, and immediately he began pointing at them and telling the voters that there sat the flower of Southern womanhood that he forever would protect. I never saw four more embarrassed Southern girls in my life; they had come to the meeting merely to hear the Senator harangue, and there they had to be Southern womanhood for half of a solid hour.

During Reconstruction we had a carpetbag government and a radical black government; the worst elements in both the white and the black races took South Carolina in charge. In 1868 General Sickles, the dictator, issued an order calling for a general registration of all voters, black and white, and the general then ordered an election to vote for or against the holding of a Carolina convention to get us reconstructed. So many white men were barred from voting in this election that in Beaufort County the military let only sixty-five cast a ballot. Two thousand five hundred Negroes voted in that county. Of course, the convention won, and never in any American state has such a convention assembled. Forty-four of the delegates were not even natives of the state. They debated for days about their pay, and finally they adopted a constitution for South Carolina. Congress in Washington approved this constitution; so did we become reconstructed.

Restored now to the Union as a state, a new Carolina legislature was convened with seventy-eight Negro members and forty-six carpetbaggers and scalawags. In one session these legislators increased the debt of the impoverished state from five million dollars to fourteen million dollars, and at the second session they increased it to twenty-two million dollars. Expenses for the first session were six hundred and eighty thousand dollars. They bought chandeliers for two thousand five hundred dollars apiece, paid one thousand five hundred dollars for window curtains, ninety dollars for Gothic chairs. They sold state bonds and put the cash in their pockets. Everywhere there was bribery, perjury, graft, and corruption.

In 1876 we decided that life was not worth living under the circumstances — the North could send another vast army against us if it liked, it could shoot us, but we would not tolerate any longer the government the North had forced on us. So we got together and rebelled. We organ-

And Cotton

ized the Red Shirts. We took over. We intimidated, we hanged and shot, we voted tombstones in the election of 1876, and we won. Wade Hampton became our Governor.

All of my kinfolks joined the Red Shirts. A small boy, my father rode in the Red Shirt parade at Anderson in 1876, sitting in the same saddle with my Great-Uncle Alf, and ever since that time, we have been very positive about the subject of the white and the colored races. The North liberated the colored people, suddenly with a proclamation, but it did nothing to help decent colored people make an honest living. All of that was left by the North to the conquered South. The North was not interested in the Negro, it was interested in freeing the Negro. The South was interested in the colored people, in a solution of freedom, for the South was the colored man's home just as it was the white man's home. The South belonged to all of us, white and black, and we intended to live, side by side, in the South until the end of time. Suddenness was not the way. There was too much poverty and too much ignorance for suddenness. We would move step by step, generation by generation — from position to position.

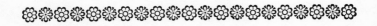

CHAPTER XI

THE CIVIL WAR gave the slaves their freedom, but the Southern white folks lost the war, so for thirty years after the surrender we all had to work like slaves in our country — the white and the black. All that we had left after Appomattox, besides ourselves, was the land with its sunshine. Also we had cotton, and we knew how to graze cows and fatten pigs, and we happened to like hominy for breakfast, and turnip greens and cornbread for dinner. Being poor was not so hard for us as it would have been for many people. Being poor has never caused the South so much grief as it has caused some regions, and even in those rare times when we have had considerable

264

money we have believed in living as though we were poor. We have wanted a certain amount of money very much, but we have never wanted more than so much. It has been satisfaction that we have sought rather than a lot of dollars; we have always wanted to live satisfied lives, and to discover some spiritual meaning in existence.

We had practically no money at all for thirty years, so we stayed at home, and worked in the fields, and sat on the piazzas and talked, and we fished and trapped rabbits and went to all-day singings and to old Confederate reunions at the Courthouse. We were told to limit our wants, to enjoy what we had, to do without, and although we did have a hard time, we did not suffer greatly. Our folks were soldiers, and by nature they were stoics, and they would have made us eat all the food we took on our plates if we had been as rich even as Crœsus. We were simple; always the home was the center of our life.

It was cotton that saved us during those first thirty years after Appomattox. We had a monopoly, all that time, on a product that the whole world would buy. It was our cash crop, so we grew it and let the North run its own course with its new system of factories in its big new cities. Cotton gave us the chance to rest and recover, and at the same time the opportunity to hold on to our original beliefs and to raise a new generation of men to take the place of all those lost in the Civil War battles. Not a single one of my kinfolks, however, was able to attend college during those thirty years. After 1860 we did not produce a college graduate until 1896. There was never enough cash for college.

We lived in our plain big houses about as the tenants lived in their plain three-room cabins, and as the colored people lived in their houses. All of us wore homespun clothes and hobnail shoes. Nor was there much social difference between us and our white tenants in those days. Tenants came to the front doors of our houses and we called them " mister " if they were not kin to us, and drove with them to the same church, and we attended the same one-room country school. All of us came from the same stock, from the same beginning, and we knew one another and we knew one another's grandfathers and great-grandfathers; we had nothing to explain to one another, no pretenses nor appearances to keep up. We were Democrats, we were Baptists. All of us had the same sort of pride, and we were all spontaneous, religious, philosophical, romantic, emotional, and occasionally murdersome — tough as nails, and set in our ways. We liked to visit, to plant cotton, to sit and stare at the stars. All of us knew what we wanted. We set the same measure for a life.

And Cotton

Tenancy was natural for us at that time. We lived in a country that had almost no money, that had no chance of raising cash to pay for wages, so we made an arrangement that did not involve money. We owned more land than we could tend, so we provided families who had no land at all with a house and livestock and with plows and fertilizer, and they and we shared the crop. The tenants were either white families who had lost or sold their original property or black families that until lately had been slaves. It was the best arrangement we could make at the time, and it worked reasonably well for everyone from 1870 until about 1910. All of us on our cotton farms were secure through those years — the colored tenants; the white tenants; the landowners, so long as they kept their fields clear of mortgages from the banks. We lived in a sort of luxurious poverty. Without a dime, we lived at home and in plenty. We had butter and milk and eggs and chickens, frying-size the year round, and we had hams in the smokehouse, and fatback and lard and collard greens in the garden, and turnips to boil through the winter, and there were sweet potatoes in our cellars, and dried peaches and dried apples. We had ambrosia and cake.

Until 1914 we bought very little from stores other than cloth and shoes and black pepper and salt and sugar and rice, and even for these commodities we did not often pay cash — we swapped eggs and ham for shoes and sugar. We had houses to live in, rough clothes to wear, abundant victuals to eat, and no matter what happened to the price of cotton, we never worried about starving or about sleeping in a ditch. We had everything except money. We had all the things that money could not buy. We even owned our own time.

We grew our own tobacco in patches behind the barn, and in our orchards and gardens there was something of almost everything that grew — honey and strawberries and the finest peaches in existence. We even had tenants sometimes who brewed their own corn in the thickets. We even had kinfolks who distilled moonshine, but of course we knew nothing about that, for our kinfolks were our kinfolks, and besides they belonged to Mount Tabor and New Hope; they were members of the congregation.

Those were hard years, but they were not unhappy ones for us. Throughout all that time all that was required of us besides hard work was self-denial, and our folks had been raised for two hundred years to work and to do without. It was not the years between 1870 and 1910 that tested us in the South. Our trying time came between 1910 and 1930. Those were the years that bled us and

And Cotton

nearly dried the well of our faith. That was the period
that so worried my Grandfather Bowen and my Great-
Aunt Narcissa. Like the other Southerners of their generation, they were fighting men and women, believing always in standing and in having things out whenever their
ideal was threatened, but the chaotic industrial triumph
that followed the paving of the roads bewildered them.
The boom was worse for them than the Civil War, for in
the Civil War they had been able to take up positions
with artillery and to shoot, but during this latter era they
were unable ever to pin the enemy down. They could not
get within shooting distance of engineers and presidents
of corporations.

Big business men did not fight at such places as Gettysburg and Chickamauga — they hired lawyers and re-
treated through court after court with the letter of the
law as their protection. My grandfather believed in the
freedom of the spirit. The engineers believed in a standard of living. My grandfather scarcely believed in a
standard of living at all — it was a secondary considera-
tion. A nation sought wisdom and strength before a
chicken in every pot. A nation must walk before God in
integrity and uprightness. Otherwise God would cut it
out from the land He had given it and would cast it from
His sight, and the nation would become a proverb and

a byword. My grandfather believed in a standard of faith.

In 1919 my Great-Aunt Narcissa asked my grandfather: "How much longer can we hold out?"

"Twenty years," my grandfather answered.

In 1919 my grandfather died, and then my Great-Aunt Narcissa died, and my Uncle Tom and my Uncle Philip took over on Wolf Creek and at Twelve Mile. Under them we planted new orchards and began to prune regularly and to spray. We turned to the Cleveland Big Boll, an improved variety of cotton; we began to plant cotton earlier and to hurry it toward maturity ahead of the boll weevil; we began to rotate — to alternate a crop of cotton with a corn crop and with a crop of winter wheat. Some of us began to use multiple harrows, and my Uncle Wade began to experiment with a tractor on our hilly rocky fields. We began to concentrate our culture, to increase yields. We bought automobiles, and almost all of my grandfather's grandchildren were sent off to colleges. We took trips to Texas to see the kinfolks; we went to Florida in the summertime when the rates were cheap; we visited the battlefields of the Civil War. But we held on to the land, we did not mortgage a foot of it for any reason, and whenever we were not able to buy with cash, we did without. We still put more faith in a bale of cot-

And Cotton

ton than in an account in a bank; and we continued to oppose tariffs and always we voted against presidential candidates who stood for money, and the force in government that we called Wall Street. To us, money was not enough. A government had to stand beyond money, for money could not face disaster. In bad times money was timid; it could see only its own nose, and it would sacrifice the future for today's dividend. Money took the short-time view, and we did not believe in a government being influenced by anything short-time; for a government, we believed in the philosophy of the long time. Accordingly, we voted against Harding, against Coolidge, and against Hoover. With a shudder, we voted for Al Smith. He was the nominee of the Democratic Party.

In our valley our Uncle Tom made speeches about the Hawley-Smoot Tariff — it would ruin us. All over the world, governments were retaliating against this tariff. Governments, at any cost, were attempting to free themselves of America and its system of tariffs. In India, in Turkestan, in the Egyptian Sudan, in the Kenya Colony, in Brazil, in Queensland, in Peru, farmers were growing more cotton and still more cotton. Our world cotton market was slipping from us. Whether we liked it or not, we could not depend solely on cotton much longer. We would have to diversify our agriculture, to grow our own grain, raise our own hay, keep dairy cows. Whether we liked it or not, we would have to work twelve months a year instead of six. We would have to work more and fish less.

At a big Southern meeting in New Orleans my cousin Bo preached a sermon on "Live at Home." The time would come, he said, when the corporation system would run its course, for the corporation depended on acceleration, on pyramids, on the top spinning faster and faster. The corporation was the solid rock that a state should build on; the land was the only solid rock. Our Southern population was increasing more rapidly than the nation's population, our birth rate was higher, our death rate was lower, our excess population was moving North and West, but the time would come when those fields of labor would be filled; the South would have to support its own population. Machines were displacing labor on farms; machines were now making machines; they were displacing labor in factories. To maintain even our present standard of living, we would have to balance agriculture with industry, and on the farms we would have to raise everything that we needed — we would be obliged to live at home.

After our grandfather and our great-aunt died, we held on for thirteen years. Then came the catastrophe that saved us — the bursting of the industrial bubble. At

And Cotton

last the failure that the old Confederates, for seventy years, had hoped for took place. Corporations and banks collapsed. There was a panic in Wall Street, and for the first time since 1860 the North began to question itself, to revalue its civilization. Once again the North turned to other voices, to other advice. A President with an ancient American background was elected, and once more the capital of the United States moved back to Washington from its long exile in New York.

So seventy years after Appomattox the cycle ended. And in the South we refound our chance, for the America that President Roosevelt represented was older than Mr. J. P. Morgan's. It held that the people were more important than all of a nation's wealth.

I wish now that my grandfather could have lived until 1932. We had held on, we had followed his advice, we had kept every foot of the land, we had waited. I do not believe that my grandfather would have been alarmed by the terror of the depression, for he was used to terror and suffering; nor do I believe that the compromise that was patched up under the New Deal would have worried him either. He always told us that history was progress in its finality, and compromise, whether we admitted it or not, was history. What our grandfather believed in foremost was a state that put the people's security before its riches. A nation to him was greater than corporations. To him, the state of the union was not to be gauged by quoting the price of wheat on the Chicago Exchange nor by quoting the price of cotton. A nation was bigger than business.

I remember when big business first moved into our uplands, when corn fields and cotton patches in the edges of towns were cleared and rows of cabins were built about red brick barn-like structures, designed like other red brick barn-like structures in Pawtucket and New Bedford. Lying in a feather bed in winter, I sometimes would wake up and hear the whistles blowing — long before day — and I still remember how uneasy I would feel. We ourselves got up before daylight, but there was something alarming in being ordered to rise by a factory whistle. It was the command that frightened, the imperative in the note. It was a sound that we had never heard before in our valley.

On Saturday afternoons, I would see the cotton-mill people at the store. Their faces were pale in those days for they worked in the winter from before daylight until after dark, seventy hours a week. I thought it was terrible to spend six days of every week in a mill. I had never spent all of a day in any house in my life. The mill people at the store made me feel that they had been captured, that they were imprisoned, that they had given up being free.

For a long time they felt that way themselves, for they were cotton farmers, born to the wild wind and to the Southern fields and to warm dry sun. I remember the problem they had to face when they decided to make the trade — to swap the furrow and the open for the cash of a daily wage.

I remember the day Mr. Tom Rampey came to the Old House at Twelve Mile to talk over this matter with my Great-Aunt Narcissa and my Uncle Phil. Mr. Tom was a rangy man, tall and stooped, with gangling arms and legs, strong but very thin. He was deliberate and methodical, and he sat with one foot on the floor of the front piazza and the other foot on the ground.

" Ought I to go, Miss Narcissa? " he asked, his tanned face furrowed with fret and worry.

" I can't tell you, Tom," said my great-aunt, rocking slowly. " It is something you must decide. You must make up your own mind." Quietly, my great-aunt rocked. " What do you want to do, Tom? "

" Well," he said slowly, " I do and then again I don't."

Mr. Tom had rented thirty acres of cotton land from the Old House for twenty years. Almost all of his adult life he had lived with us, sharing a crop. "I'm a landless man," he said, "As long as I stay with you, I have a house and I'll have something to eat, but what chance have I got to get ahead? What chance have I got ever to own any land of my own?"

My great-aunt and my uncle did not answer. They knew that Mr. Tom was not asking that question for information. He was really talking to himself, he was examining his own mind in their presence.

He was secure at the Old House, but he was a tenant, a renter. "I could have money at the mill," he continued. "I ought to be able to save enough in no time to buy a few acres of my own — it oughtn't to take me long to save enough for that." Again he hesitated. "How do I know how long the mill job will last?" he inquired. "I don't know the folks who own the mill. They don't know me. I don't like to work for folks I don't know. I don't like to live in a house either that belongs to a stranger."

Mr. Tom leaned back against one of the slim white posts that held up the roof of the piazza. He shifted himself and twisted. "What would you do, Phil?" he inquired.

"What do you want to do, Tom?" asked my Uncle Philip.

"I want to improve my condition," said Mr. Tom. "I

And Cotton

want to educate my children. I want them to have things
better than I have had them."

All through a solemn autumn afternoon Mr. Tom and
my great-aunt and my uncle sat on the piazza, weighing
and debating. Then suddenly Mr. Tom announced: " I'm
ambitious and I'm strong. I'm going to do it."

A few days later the Rampeys piled their things into
a two-horse wagon and drove off. They moved into a
house on the side of a steep hill at Cateechee Mill — into
a house on a winding dusty road. The whistle blew for
them at half past four o'clock, and at six their work
started. Six to six was their shift. It was a hard life for a
family accustomed to the open, but Saturday was payday
— every Saturday. Sometimes on Sunday Mr. Tom would
come back to see my Great-Aunt Narcissa at the Old
House. He would eat dinner and my great-aunt would
tell him he could move back if he cared to, and always
this seemed to comfort him.

Finally one Sunday at Praters Baptist Church the
preacher announced that Brother Tom Rampey and family desired to remove their letters of membership from
Praters to Cateechee Mill Baptist Church. When the
preacher asked the congregation what was their wish
in this matter, my Uncle Philip moved that the request

be granted. One of the Boldings seconded the motion. Thus did the Rampeys cut their last tie. They bought a new coal stove with their cash money. They bought an icebox, a car, a radio. Mr. Tom's oldest boy eventually was graduated from college.

The Nalleys were the next to leave the Old House for the Little Mill in Liberty. The Beasleys moved from Wolf Creek to Pickens Mill No. 1. The Ropers moved to Woodside Mill in Greenville. The Richards family went to Honea Path, the Adamses to Pelzer.

Those were draining years on the cotton farms — the 1920's. Nearly all of the strongest tenant families left the cotton fields. Only the old and the young and the determined stayed on — only such families as the Pilgrims who had been with us for seventy years, only Mary and Jim. Popcorn left for New York, Harve for the steel mills of Ohio. Mr. Tom's oldest boy went to work with the Westinghouse Electric Company in Pittsburgh. Winnie Mae and Dazarene and Lulu left on the day coach for Harlem, and my Aunt Bettie began to regard her kitchen as a training school for servants for Park Avenue; she said that as soon as she taught a colored girl the difference between a tablecloth and a sheet the girl left her for Philadelphia and New York. They left for higher wages, for the things that money could buy. Willingly they gave

And Cotton

up the security of a cotton farm for ten and twenty dollars a week. They were the young and the strong and they did not fear the future. What they wanted was money, and where they wanted to live was in town.

In New York, I understood who bought the fatback bacon in the Harlem grocery stores and who bought the hominy grits and the collards. I understood the singing and the preaching and the praying and I knew who attended the fried-chicken suppers and the watermelon cuttings. One time at one of the Baptist churches on Seventh Avenue I heard a sermon on Daniel in the lions' den; I heard a preacher say that when Daniel finally got ready to leave, the head lion said: " Daniel, we sure hate to see you go." That night I heard a woman testify she had sinned at eleven o'clock on Thursday night at —— — West 145th Street with John Smith. " Lord," the woman said, " I'm sorry." The congregation sang: " Lord, she's sorry."

And one time, in South Carolina during the middle of the depression, I went to a fishing place on Twelve Mile River, and there I found the bank almost lined with white men from the cotton mills — all of them fishing because they were out of work. They looked at me suspiciously, even angrily, and one of them asked me point-blank: " Mister, what's your name? "

Red Hills

"My name is Robertson," I said.

Again point-blank I was asked: "Are you a game warden?"

I said: "No."

Still suspicious, my questioner wanted to know if I was a Robertson what Robertson was I. When I told them, they became friendly at once. "I used to live at your Uncle Phil's before I went to the mill," one of them said. Another said: "I knew your Great-Aunt Narcissa and your Uncle Wight." Still another said: "I knew your Grandfather Bowen, and your mother — I knew your mother when she was only a girl."

I understood these men who had left the cotton farms for the cotton mills. In the cotton fields they had conducted their dealings with the landowner as one independent man with another. Their relationship was individual and personal, and at the mill in town they still were inclined to deal with the overseer as they had with the owner of the cotton field. It still had not fully dawned on these men that the overseer in their mill was not the mill, that he was only an agent. It still was difficult for them to realize that they were not working for any individual as an individual — that they were working for a corporation, complicated and technical and highly organized and involved. These men were individuals, they

And Cotton

were cotton farmers who had moved into town. I understood why they were afraid of joining labor unions. They
were afraid of all industrial organizations; especially they
were afraid of organizations that sent delegates to them
from New York. These men were Southern, and they remembered those Northerners who had come to the South
as missionaries to do good after Appomattox. They remembered the carpetbaggers.

At the Old House and on Wolf Creek, when the depression of 1932 hit us, we retrenched and retired and re-
treated as we had done on many other occasions. Again
we stayed at home and we did without. We lived on fried
chicken and beef and turnip greens and sweet potatoes
and string beans and cornbread and sweet milk. We
planted enough in the gardens for us to eat and enough
in the fields for the stock to eat, and we waited for the
hard time to pass.

One morning the Farmers and Merchants Bank did not
open for business, and my Aunt Nora said she had never
had any faith in that bank anyhow. My Aunt Bettie said
it was only money that we had lost and that this ought to
make us have sense enough never again to put dependence in money.

Bill met the banker not long after this in the road and

said to him: "Boss, didn't you see that minus sign coming up? "

Embarrassed, the banker replied: "What could I have done if I had seen it, Bill? "

"If it had been me, boss," said Bill, "I sure would have nol-prossed."

I remember how elated we were when we heard that two men down at Walterboro, in the lower part of the state, had broken into a closed bank, had held up the cashier with shotguns, had taken as much money as they had on deposit, and then on going out and burying the cash had turned themselves over to the sheriff. When a Carolina jury refused to indict those two citizens, my cousin Stephen John sent the jurors a telegram congratulating them on their sense.

The Peoples State Bank failed. The First National failed, and I remember climbing the hill to my Aunt Fanny's house with the news. I remember finding my Aunt Fanny sitting on the front piazza and rocking and fanning herself with the leaf of a palmetto. "Aunt Fanny," I said, "do you know what has happened? " Leaning forward in the rocker, she inquired quizzically: "That last bank has failed? " I said: "You've guessed — it failed this morning to open." My Aunt Fanny kept right on fanning.

That evening my Aunt Fanny and I drove to see my

And Cotton

Aunt Bettie and my Uncle Wade, and we found them sitting on their porch and resting. They already had heard the news, but they were not unusually depressed. My Uncle Wade already had drawn out as much cash as he felt he could and still be polite; the cashier was a friend of his, and he had not wished to have his friend think he had no faith in his bank. My Uncle Wade had sent four hundred dollars to my cousin Alfred, who was studying at Heidelberg, and had told him to come home on the first ship. He had sent my cousin Bernice two hundred dollars. That made six hundred. He had paid the oil company ten dollars for a fifty-gallon drum of gasoline. That made six hundred and ten.

" How much did that leave you, Uncle Wade? " I asked.

He shrugged his shoulders. He pretended he did not know.

My Aunt Fanny began to talk about cotton — it had dropped to six cents a pound.

My Uncle Wade began to talk about the year that cotton had gone to forty cents. " I got all the folks on the place together," he said, " and we divided the crop, bale for bale, and I said they could do what they liked with their share, but I was going to sell enough to pay for the fertilizer, and then hold on to the rest — cotton at that time had gone to about thirty-six cents. I had seventeen

bales left and I put them in the cotton house, but I began
to get nervous — that cotton began to try to jump right
out of that house; it began to rear up every time I went
out there to look at it; I had to put a padlock on the door
to keep it in. Then one day, a man at the Little Mill called
up and said he would give me thirty-eight cents for ten
of those bales and forty cents for the other seven. I said to
him I'd not take thirty-eight cents for any of it — I would
take forty cents. Well, he said he would have to think
about it, and the next day he called again and said all
right, he would give me forty cents for all of it, and
I told him he sure could have it all, and to get it out of
my cotton house before dark. He got it out that afternoon,
and about a week later the price went to forty-two cents,
and then it began to drop. Boys, I was lucky," said my
Uncle Wade. " I got thirty-six hundred dollars for those
seventeen bales, and I like to broke myself — I went right
out and paid nineteen hundred dollars for a Studebaker
car."

He laughed and shifted himself in a deep porch chair.
" Your Uncle Philip," he said to me, " wouldn't take forty
cents for his crop — he wouldn't even take forty-two, and
in the end he sold a lot of that cotton crop for fifteen
cents a pound." My uncle leaned back. " Philip didn't care
much, though," he added. " He didn't need the money,

and he said the other day he wished now he hadn't sold it even for fifteen cents — he wished he had kept it in the barn, for five-cent cotton is worth more in a barn than forty-cent money in a busted bank."

"It's time for us to go to prayer meeting," said my Aunt Bettie, so the four of us got up and walked through the main street of Liberty to the Baptist Church, a church which our kinfolks had founded in 1776. On the way my Uncle Wade began to tease my Aunt Bettie. He said: "Bettie's been putting on airs again. The other day old Mrs. Roper came by the house, and she and Bettie sat in the parlor, and Mrs. Roper said: 'Who painted that picture over the mantel?' and Bettie said: 'It's one of my paintings.' Mrs. Roper said: 'Why, Miss Bettie, I didn't know you painted,' and Bettie tossed her head like a mare and said: 'Oh, yes, when I was a girl.'"

"I used to paint from models," interrupted my Aunt Bettie. "I could copy things, but I never could paint from nature — I couldn't look out at the hills and get the look of them; I'd lose proportion."

"Hills?" snorted my Uncle Wade, roaring. "You mean mountains. You know very well you were raised in the mountains — you came right out of the mountains."

"I never could paint the hills," said my aunt firmly.

My uncle guffawed. "Mrs. Roper asked Bettie if she

still painted, and she said coyly: ' No, I got married.' " My
Uncle Wade interpolated: " That was the crowning climax of Bettie's life."

" I had to start cooking," said my Aunt Bettie, " and
there was no time for painting." My Aunt Bettie said Mrs.
Roper asked her if my Uncle Wade had ever done any
painting. " I told her," said my aunt, " if Wade ever
painted anything it was a wagon body."

All of us laughed.

We came through the depression. We and the people
about us came through with the blessings of the poor. The
home still was the center of our life, the church the center
of our faith. Also we still held to our original Confederate
theory that the land and not the factory was the rock to
build the state on. The land was our home and it was not
to be exploited. In Carolina over half of our people continued to live on farms; eighty per cent lived either on
farms or in small towns. We were rural and poor, we were
ravaged by poverty, but our character was like the granite of the mountains. We were tough, and the lesson the
depression taught us was that the country we lived in
was tough. The plain citizen of our country was greater
and better at heart than anyone had imagined.

So in the midst of the depression we began really again
to hope. We could hardly believe our eyes when we heard

that President Roosevelt had appointed a Carolinian to
his Cabinet. Of course, it was only Uncle Dan Roper, but
just the same he was a Carolinian, and there had not been
a South Carolinian in a President's Cabinet since the time
of John C. Calhoun, when of course we in Carolina had
run cabinets. Again we were startled when we read in the
papers that Professor James Harvey Rogers, a native of
Society Hill, South Carolina, had been called to the White
House for a conference; a member of the Calhoun family
had said that no one born at Society Hill had sense
enough to advise the President of the United States. With
this statement, some of us began to realize that we had
fallen into the habit of belittling ourselves, of making fun
of ourselves. It was a habit of defense that we had acquired during the seventy years that we had been down
and out. Finally the President appointed a Carolinian to
the United States Supreme Court. At last, for us, things
truly were picking up.

My Uncle Tom continued to make speeches in our uplands. He formed an association for rural electrification,
a co-operative marketing association. My cousin Bo made
a survey of tenants in our county and discovered that not
one of them had ever sent a son or daughter through college. We were horrified by this information, and immediately we tried to deny it. We went over in our minds

the names of every tenant we could think of, trying to find one who had educated his children. We could not think of one. We were appalled by this discovery, for we knew what it implied. The tenants were becoming a caste, a class was being formed in our midst. Tenants had begun to be born into tenancy, to marry into tenancy, and to die in tenancy. These were our own people, and in our own country; this had become their fate. In only eight counties in Carolina, said our cousin Bo, did the percentage of landownership equal the nation's.

We must do something about it, said my Uncle Tom, and under his leadership we and our tenants began to take advantage of the new Federal farm schemes. We began to rotate more, to diversify more, to rely less on cotton. My Uncle Tom began to encourage tenants to strike out on their own. My cousin Bo, like my Uncle Tom, took to the stump, telling everyone who would listen that our Southern problems were not beyond our ability to solve. Too many of our farmers, he said, over and over again, were not living at home as they once had, but they could do so with a little leadership and direction. Our soils were too acid for a diversified agriculture, but they could be corrected cheaply with lime. Our tenant farmers moved incessantly throughout their lives; many of them were losing hope and ambition, but they could be stabilized

And Cotton

and encouraged with an intelligent leasing system that would make it worth their while to take better care of a crop. Farm contracts should be in writing, so that tenants could be protected from landlords who would rob them. Our section had a strong textile industry, but we needed additional industries — smaller ones and more scattered ones. We had water power for industry. We had the people, willing to work. A big part of our population was young, but this was a great resource if we diversified. Like my Grandfather Bowen, my cousin Bo held that we ought to live on small farms and work in small factories. He believed in deurbanization, in decentralization.

The depression inspired my cousin Bo. One night, when things were at their worst, he came to our house. "The country," he said, standing before the fire, "has found out what the old Confederates have known all along — that dollars and cities and factories aren't enough for a nation. The country has found that out, and it is going to turn away from the purely material. The pendulum is going to swing again to the spirit." Elated, excited, he said: "People are going to become friendlier and more simple. The home is going to mean more. Folks are going to visit more and to take more pleasure in neighborliness and conversation. The people, more and more, are going to think about things such as national health and about education for the masses. They are going to value life more and more by intangibles, by the things that can't be bought with cash. Northerners are going to work less without feeling remorseful, and somehow as Cousin Tom Bowen predicted, maybe even Southerners will stick a little closer to business."

My cousin Bo said: " The country is swinging from the Hamiltonians back to the Jeffersonians. A plus b is again becoming more important than 2 plus 2. The trend is toward the old ideal of Virginia and Carolina — it is toward the old South, for it has been the South that has preserved the spirit of the original Federal Union. We are going to flower in this country," my cousin Bo said. " As sure as you are living and a foot high, we in the United States are going to accept our world responsibility and our world obligations, and we are going to enter an era of glory."

In the South we still listen at night to the katydids and the crickets. We sit in the darkness and stare at the stars. We believe in simple things — in praying, in playing the fiddle for amusement, in saving some time for yourself, in taking charge of the circumstances around you, in living beyond prosperity or beyond failure. In our uplands there are hundreds of hymn-singers who still think a pleasant way to spend a Sunday is to sing all day in a church. When the crops are laid by in August, we like to attend the same sort of all-day singing that our fathers attended.

We still sing from music books printed with shaped notes instead of round notes — with shaped diamonds, circles, squares, and triangles as William & Smith devised them at Philadelphia in 1798. We use the nomenclature of the sol-fa system — the fa, and the sol, and the la. Our singing meetings are organized according to a pattern that our forefathers learned in early politics: each of our townships has a singing convention, and each county has a convention formed of the township conventions, and there is a state convention formed of the county conventions. We have a tremendous local machinery for teaching and disseminating this music; we have singing professors and itinerant singing schools, and we have our own printing presses that turn out thousands of hymnals that even great American libraries have never heard of. We have held singing conventions every August since 1800, and we remember the feud the seven-toners had with the four-toners. The seven-toners favored the modern octave against the ancient four-tone scale. The seven-toners won, but the influence of the four-toners can still be detected in our songs — often it gives our hymns a minor-pitched tonal effect that is almost the sound of the blue-note that

our colored people use in their music. Any person in our
uplands understands the kinship of the ancient Protestant
white hymn with the black jazz music of the South. We
sing hymns to banjo accompaniments and to twanging
guitars.

Any singer who wants to sing a solo can do so at our
singing conventions, and any trio or quartet can have a
trial on the platform. All that any singer has to do is to
ask the professor who presides if he may sing, and the professor must say yes. The convention is a democratic as-
sembly. As a result, much of the singing is dreadful, but
always the audience is patient. And not all of the music is
dreadful by any means — the congregational singing is
magnificent.

At our state singing convention in the great Textile Hall
in Greenville, there sometimes are ten thousand singing
delegates. We take fried chicken in boxes, and hard-boiled
eggs, and apple pies, and we spend an entire Sunday singing. At one of these state conventions recently I heard
Governor Olin Johnston of South Carolina tell the delegates he was born on a cotton farm, the son of a poor tenant farmer, and he knew what singing meant to Carolinians. He said if anybody got into trouble and landed
in jail while in Greenville, just to let him know. The Governor then led the ten thousand in the hymn: " When our

And Cotton

work here is done and our last crown is won." Slowly the
song moved from note to note, from strain to strain. It
swept upward from the heart in a grand triumphant burst
of melody. It was superb singing.

It overcame Mary with its glory. Mary shouted; she
cried: " Hallelujah! "

In the South we are patriotic. We believe in the original
hope of the original American state. We believe in Jefferson's ideas — in the creation of men as equals, in the doctrine that Bacon outlined to Queen Elizabeth: The purpose of a government is to keep wealth from accumulat-
ing in the hands of a few. We believe in men more than
in machines. We believe in the spirit. We realize that the
spirit alone is not enough, but on the other hand neither
is the machine enough. We do not believe in any return
to medieval ruralism. What we believe in is going on toward an American state that will be ruled by the Northern mind and guided by the Southern heart.

In the South we have believed always in fighting. We
are hill people, threatened eternally by the men from the
plains. Thus, we knew by instinct when the British re-
treated from Dunkirk that the American state as well as
the British was in danger. We are old in the South; we
have lost a war and do not ever wish our country to lose

another; we are inclined always to think in world terms — for a hundred years we have had to sell the world a crop of cotton. We knew by intuition when France fell that American liberty instantly had become threatened. Throughout the South we did what we could — we preached, we prayed, we began to organize a home guard, and our boys in great numbers began to join the army, the air corps, and the navy. Our record is on the record.

On December 7 the sun shone bright in our valley. The wind blew, clear and cold from the far northwest, and leaves rustled and fell. When the news came, my Aunt Nora, who was in bed ill, said to my cousin Enid: "Get my clothes — I must get up; there are things that we must do." My Aunt Bettie said: "We will give everything."

We cried privately, and then we went out and got into our cars and went to visit the kinfolks. Suddenly all the past seemed to sweep forward into the present, and we seemed again to take our place in the vast eternity of time. We were in trouble and our country was in trouble, and as always whenever there was trouble, we found that automatically we had come together. No longer were we merely ourselves. We were who we were because all of those who had lived before us had been what they had

And Cotton

been. My cousin Billy said he was ready to go. So did my cousin George. So did J. B., Mary's nephew. We went alone to the cotton fields. There before us stood the hills. Our people had turned to them when the men had left for Kings Mountain; they had turned to them when our delegate had gone to vote against the Constitution; they had turned again when the news had come from Appomattox. The hills were eternal. Always they gave us strength.

Within a few days after the 7th, word came that one of the Rampey boys had been killed at Pearl Harbor. A boy of whom we were very fond was captured at Guam. A friend from down the road was fighting on Cebu. Tom and Soph and Manny and Henry were at Manila with General MacArthur. A letter came from Otis — a letter from Fort William McKinley, P. I., dated December 1. "Many things around me have changed," Otis wrote, "but I have not changed. In my heart, everything is the same."

Soon afterward my cousin Hovey drove by the house to ask us if we had read about Lieutenant William Porter, whom the newspapers had called the second Sergeant York — he had shot fifty Japanese on the Lingayen Peninsula in northern Luzon. "Do you know who that is?"

Hovey said with pride and excitement in his voice. "That's Cousin Unity's brother's boy — he's one of our Texas kinfolks."

He also was the nephew in the fifth generation of Daniel Boone.

The following morning I ate breakfast as usual in the kitchen, and as usual Mary sat on the woodbox by the stove and sipped coffee from a saucer. I switched on a radio for the latest news, and it was bad news that we heard — all of it was bad. We were retreating southeast of Manila; we were retreating northwest of Manila; in the Atlantic Ocean the Germans had sunk a tanker.

Silently we listened. Motionless, Mary held the saucer. Tears began to roll down her face. "Mister," she said, "we got to work. Lord God, we got to work, and we got to get down on our knees and bow our heads and pray."